THE
BEZOS
BLUEPRINT

THE
BEZOS
BLUEPRINT

COMMUNICATION SECRETS OF
THE WORLD'S GREATEST SALESMAN

CARMINE GALLO

ST. MARTIN'S PRESS
NEW YORK

First published in the United States by St. Martin's Press, an imprint
of St. Martin's Publishing Group

www.stmartins.com

Design by Meryl Sussman Levavi

Library of Congress Cataloging-in-Publication Data

Names: Gallo, Carmine, author.
Title: The Bezos blueprint: communication secrets of the world's greatest
    salesman / Carmine Gallo.
Description: First edition. | New York: St. Martin's Press, [2022] |
    Includes bibliographical references and index.
Identifiers: LCCN 2022028658 | ISBN 9781250278333 (hardcover) |
    ISBN 9781250278340 (ebook)
Subjects: LCSH: Business communication. | Communication in management. |
    Leadership. | Bezos, Jeffrey.
Classification: LCC HF5718 .G3524 2022 | DDC 658.4/5—dc23/
    eng/20220722
LC record available at https://lccn.loc.gov/2022028658

Our books may be purchased in bulk for promotional, educational, or business
use. Please contact your local bookseller or the Macmillan Corporate and
Premium Sales Department at 1-800-221-7945, extension 5442, or by email
at MacmillanSpecialMarkets@macmillan.com.

First Edition: 2022

1   3   5   7   9   10   8   6   4   2

For dreamers everywhere

ACKNOWLEDGMENTS

When you pursue bold dreams, it helps to have a champion by your side. Vanessa Gallo is my champion. We met in 1996 and married two years later. Vanessa's unwavering support gave me the confidence and courage to pursue my passion. Vanessa and I run a business that transforms CEOs and leaders into extraordinary communicators, and we enjoy teaching executive education classes together at Harvard University. My two daughters, Josephine and Lela, could not have asked for a better role model.

I also wish to thank the team at St. Martin's Press for championing my work. Sally Richardson, St. Martin's Publishing Group chair, has celebrated her fiftieth year at the company. I'm thrilled to be part of Sally's orbit. Tim Bartlett, my editor at St. Martin's Press, is a friend, sounding board, and supporter who always elevates the quality of my writing. My gratitude also goes to St. Martin's sales, marketing, and publicity teams, as well as the good folks at Macmillan Audio who turn my writing into the spoken word.

I'm deeply grateful for a long-standing relationship with my literary agent, Roger Williams. Thank you, Roger, for your invaluable insight, feedback, and history lessons.

Tom Neilssen and Les Tuerk, my keynote speaking agents at Bright-Sight Speakers, are promoters, teachers, friends, and truly inspiring people. Thank you for your guidance.

I'm blessed to be surrounded by a wonderfully loving family: my mom,

Giuseppina, my brother, Tino, and sister-in-law, Donna, and my two nephews, Francesco and Nick. I love you all.

I'd also like to add a special thanks to the readers who champion my books. Your amazing ideas drive the world forward.

Wishing you success,
Carmine

THE BEZOS BLUEPRINT

Communication Secrets of the World's Greatest Salesman

Part III: Deliver the Plan

INTRODUCTION

It's *Always* Day One

In the summer of 2004, Amazon CEO Jeff Bezos made a surprising decision that shocked his leadership team. He banned PowerPoint. Instead of slides and bullet points, Amazon's executive team would have to pitch ideas in the form of memos and narratives. The world's most advanced e-commerce company had replaced a modern presentation tool with an ancient communication device invented more than five thousand years earlier: the written word. The new system forced everyone to share ideas using simple words, short sentences, and clear explanations. The blueprint that Bezos introduced set the foundation that would fuel Amazon's astonishing growth for the next two decades.

Jeff Bezos is a dreamer who turned a bold idea into the world's most influential company. Along the way, he created strategies to radically reimagine the way leaders deliver presentations, share ideas, and align their teams around a common vision. A student of leadership and communication, Bezos learned to motivate people to achieve what few thought was possible. Now the tools he used are available to you.

This book is not about Bezos the billionaire or Amazon the e-commerce juggernaut. Those subjects are covered in other books and in endless debates about the role of wealth or the impact of Amazon's influence in the economy. No, this book is about something more fundamental that applies to each and every reader. *The Bezos Blueprint* focuses on an overlooked and underappreciated part of the Amazon growth story, a topic that's foundational to the success of your life and career: communication.

Until now, no author has focused squarely on the writing and story-telling skills that set Bezos apart. No book has analyzed the forty-eight thousand words Bezos wrote over twenty-four years of shareholder letters. And no author has interviewed as many former Amazon executives and CEOs who have adopted the Bezos communication model to build their own companies.

One legendary Silicon Valley venture capitalist told me that business school students should be required to learn about Bezos's writing and communication strategies. He even said he'd teach the class himself—if he were "twenty years younger."

Bezos pioneered communication tools to elevate the way Amazonians write, collaborate, innovate, pitch, and present. By doing so, he created a scalable model that could grow from a small team working in a Seattle garage to one of the world's largest employers. In short, Bezos drew a blueprint.

I teach communication skills to executives in an advanced leadership program at the Harvard University Graduate School of Design. They are leaders in the "built environment": designers and developers who have created magnificent structures, buildings, and even cities around the world. Their vision is to build smarter, healthier, greener, and, overall, better places to live. Communication-skills training is an essential part of the curriculum, because if they can't sell their idea to investors, stakeholders, and community members, there's little chance that anything will be built.

But no matter how grand the vision, nothing happens without a blueprint.

A blueprint translates a designer's vision into a detailed model that others can follow to bring the idea alive. It acts as a plan to make sure everyone in the construction process is on the same page. In addition, blueprints are scalable, so the designer does not have to be present for engineers, contractors, and workers to turn the vision into reality.

Although Jeff Bezos stepped down as Amazon's CEO in 2021 to pursue his passion for philanthropy and space exploration, the communication blueprint he created continues to serve as a model for employees and leaders in every part of the company. Current Amazon executives use the same language and expound on the same principles that Bezos consistently repeated in speeches, interviews, and presentations over his twenty-seven-year tenure.

The communication strategies that Bezos pioneered at Amazon stretch far beyond the company's giant footprint. Amazon is known as "America's CEO Factory," spawning a legion of entrepreneurs who have founded their own start-ups, many of which touch your life every day. They are part of what *The Wall Street Journal* calls the "diaspora of Amazon alumni spreading the business gospel of Jeff Bezos across the corporate world." These former executives, many of whom you'll meet in this book, are adopting aspects of the Amazon culture that fit their leadership style and discarding the parts of the culture that do not work for them.

The blueprint left an indelible impression on Adam Selipsky. After working at Amazon for eleven years, Selipsky left the company in 2016 to be the CEO of Seattle software giant Tableau. "One of the things I flagrantly ripped off from Amazon was the narrative,"[1] he admitted. Bezos's ideas like replacing PowerPoint with written narratives or crafting a press release before building a product (strategies you'll learn in upcoming chapters), served as a model for Selipsky well after his career at Amazon—and when he came back.

Selipsky returned to Amazon in 2021 to run Amazon Web Services, Amazon's cloud-computing division that powers the backbone for more than one million customers such as Netflix, Airbnb, and Zoom. In his first televised interviews as the chief executive of AWS, it was hard to tell Selipsky apart from the Amazon founder, even though Selipsky had never worked directly for Bezos (he worked for Andy Jassy, who replaced Bezos as Amazon CEO).

"It's still Day One for AWS and for our customers,"[2] Selipsky said, referring to a metaphor that Bezos instilled as a guiding management philosophy in his first shareholder letter. "The long-term business strategy is to focus maniacally—not on competitors, but on customers," Selipsky continued. "We need to wake up every day understanding exactly what customers need us to build next, and work backwards from there." Selipsky was communicating a message that, as you'll learn later, was pure Bezos.

Amazon alumni are not the only evangelists for the Bezos blueprint. The strategies revealed in this book have been implemented by CEOs and senior leaders at Best Buy, Whole Foods, J.P.Morgan, Hulu, and scores of other brands that are household names. Some leaders like former PepsiCo CEO Indra Nooyi have jumped at the opportunity to learn more about Amazon from the inside. Nooyi joined Amazon's board after she left PepsiCo to get "a front-row seat to the thinking of one of the most innovative, customer-centric companies I've ever encountered." By reading this book, you, too, will have a front-row seat to a dreamer whose idea transformed the world in which we live and who turned communication into a competive advantage.

SELL DREAMS, NOT PRODUCTS

The company that started as an online bookseller has grown into an internet retailer that sells an astonishing 350 million products globally. But Bezos is not "the world's greatest salesman" because Amazon sells everything to everybody. He's the world's greatest salesman because he sells dreams, not products. And that has made all the difference.

One year before Amazon had sold a single book, Bezos had to sell something more important than a product; he had to sell his vision. In 1994 and early 1995, Bezos held sixty meetings with family, friends, and potential funders. He asked each person to invest $50,000 in his revolutionary idea. Amazon was a tough sell at the time because few people had any experience with e-commerce. The most common question they had for Bezos was, "What's the internet?"

The meetings did not all end successfully. Bezos failed to convince most of the people he pitched, but he did persuade twenty-two people to invest in his start-up. A pitch that lands one of three investors represents a remarkable success rate for any start-up. It's even more striking for an e-commerce company in the mid-'90s. Amazon's earliest investors were not placing a bet on the company; they were betting on the person behind the idea. They were sold on Bezos and his vision.

Tom Alberg wrote one of those checks. By the time he stepped down from Amazon's board after twenty-three years, Alberg's initial investment was worth more than $30 million. Alberg said he was impressed with Bezos in those early meetings, especially his skill at putting numbers in perspective that proved to be irresistible to long-term investors (I'll cover data storytelling in chapter 15). Over time, Alberg also grew to admire Bezos's ability to build teams who live his principles every day.

Later, in June 1996, Bezos received another $8 million from John Doerr's venture capital firm, Kleiner Perkins. It was the only VC capital that Amazon raised before going public a year later, an investment that would return more than $1 billion. "What I saw was an amazing founder and an amazing opportunity,"[3] Doerr recalls about his first meeting with Bezos.

"He had a technical background and a dream that he could get big fast and change the way the world works."

When Doerr flew to Seattle to visit the company in a "seedy part" of the city, he was surprised to find desks made out of wooden doors purchased at Home Depot. As you'll see in chapter 14, the doors were a visible metaphor that constantly reminded employees to follow one of Amazon's core principles: frugality. After Andy Jassy replaced Bezos as CEO, Doerr predicted that the company would not lose sight of its values because Bezos had ingrained his principles throughout the organization.

That's the power of a blueprint—it's a model that scales as your idea or company grows.

You can have a great idea, but the secret to success in any endeavor is convincing someone else to take action on your idea. You don't need a sales title to consider yourself a salesperson. Selling is everything, and you do it more often than you think. Studies by Dan Pink and other researchers show that business professionals spend 40 percent of their time on the job doing something akin to selling: persuading, influencing, motivating, coaxing, and convincing. That means your impact over twenty-four minutes of every hour of every day requires sharpening a skill that you can learn from the masters of persuasion.

According to Ann Hiatt, who worked three feet from Jeff Bezos for several years, "The greatest gift in my life has been sitting next to the smartest CEOs in the world and learning step-by-step how they think, act, motivate, and make decisions."[4] Hiatt says the most important habit she learned from her former boss is to prioritize learning. She says Bezos walked into the office each morning with three newspapers tucked under his arm. Once he was finished reading them, he moved on to articles and briefing documents. Hiatt got the message and snagged the papers off Bezos's desk to read during her lunch break.

The moment you think you know it all is the moment you stop growing. Bezos grew as a leader over time—and made remarkable improvements as a writer and speaker. You can make dramatic changes, too, but only if you see yourself as a learn-it-all and not a know-it-all.

The writing, storytelling, and presentation tactics you're about to learn will unleash your potential, setting the foundation for your success as a student, entrepreneur, executive, leader, or business professional in any field. Once you have a solid foundation in writing and communication, you'll find that these skills work like Amazon's famous "flywheel," creating an unstoppable cycle of success.

The communication strategies that Jeff Bezos pioneered at Amazon impact our lives each and every day. Even if you're not one of Amazon's three hundred million active global customers, you likely interact with companies powered by Amazon or inspired by Amazon. No single entrepreneur has had as much influence on your daily life as Jeff Bezos, and few business leaders have given as much careful consideration to communicating his vision as Bezos has—from Day One.

WANTED: TOP-NOTCH COMMUNICATION SKILLS

On August 23, 1994, Bezos placed his first job listing. Although he had yet to decide on a catchy name for his e-commerce company, Bezos did have a clear vision of the skills required to make the "well-capitalized Seattle start-up" a success. Since Bezos was looking for a Unix developer, job candidates had to know the programming language C++. Bezos added that familiarity with web servers and HTML would be helpful but "not necessary." But Bezos considered only one skill *essential* for every position: "Top-notch communication skills."[5]

Bezos was ahead of his time. A quarter century after Bezos posted the first job ad for Amazon.com, a LinkedIn survey of four thousand hiring professionals concluded that "communication skills" are, indeed, essential for success in any field. Hiring managers reported that, out of 120 skills, communication was in high demand and low supply. In most cases, technical know-how isn't enough to rise to the top even in highly complex fields, such as machine learning, artificial intelligence, and cloud computing. According to LinkedIn CEO Jeff Weiner, "Human beings are underrated."[6] Speaking and writing—human skills—are fundamental to success in any field. According to surveys of hiring managers, writing and communication are the most sought-after skills across nearly every industry and even technical fields. In one report from Indeed.com, one of the world's largest job websites, the trend toward remote work has only elevated the importance of foundational skills. Communication skills—both written and verbal—topped the list of eleven skills that employers desire most. Teamwork and leadership skills came in second and third, both of which are enhanced by learning to speak and write effectively.

The shift to remote work as a result of the COVID-19 pandemic and the wave of employees quitting their jobs to become their own boss has only elevated the importance of communication skills. A McKinsey survey of eighteen thousand people in fifteen countries identified the skills required to "future-proof" your career.[7] The 2021 report was one of the most comprehensive studies to take into account changes in a post-COVID workplace along with advances in artificial intelligence, automation, and digital technologies. While "digital fluency" is a skill set that tomorrow's employers see as highly desirable in job candidates, most of the top skills required to future-proof a career fall under communication in all its forms: storytelling, public speaking, synthesizing and clarifying messages, translating information for different audiences and contexts, crafting an inspiring vision, developing relationships, and inspiring trust. McKinsey calls these "foundational skills," and you'll learn much more about developing each one throughout this book.

WHY STUDY BEZOS?

Bezos didn't need anyone to tell him that communication skills were foundational. Very early in Amazon's history, he connected effective communication to uncommon innovation. While he understood the power of data to improve the customer experience, Bezos recognized that innovation would propel Amazon's growth. And innovation required intelligent human beings with excellent interpersonal and communication skills.

Award-winning author Walter Isaacson says he's often asked who, of today's contemporary leaders, he would put in the same category with his historical subjects: Leonardo da Vinci, Albert Einstein, Steve Jobs.

Isaacson's answer? Jeff Bezos.

"They were all very smart, but that's not what made them special,"[8] Isaacson said. "Smart people are a dime a dozen and often don't amount to much. What counts is being creative and imaginative. That's what makes someone a true innovator."

Bezos shares traits with Isaacson's other subjects: a passionate curiosity, a fervent imagination, and a childlike sense of wonder. According to Isaacson, Bezos also has a "personal passion" for writing, narrative, and storytelling. Bezos connects a deep interest in communication and a love of the humanities to his enthusiasm for technology and instinct for business. "That trifecta—humanities, technology, business—is what has made him one of our era's most successful and influential innovators."[9]

I agree with Isaacson because I'm often asked a similar question: *Who's the world's best business communicator?*

In my book *The Presentation Secrets of Steve Jobs,* I called the Apple cofounder the world's best corporate storyteller. In *Talk Like TED,* I featured TED Talks as a platform to celebrate the world's best public speakers. But when I'm asked to name the world's best business communicator, one name stands out above all others: Jeff Bezos.

48,062 Words

Bezos is a masterful communicator, according to former Amazon executives I've interviewed. These leaders—many of whom have started their own successful companies—often cite the annual Amazon shareholder letters as models of business writing and communication. Some have suggested that the Bezos letters should be taught at business schools because the lessons they offer apply to leaders in any field.

Bezos personally wrote twenty-four letters from 1997 to 2020. The letters contain 48,062 words. I analyzed and scrutinized every one. I dissected and inspected every sentence. I grokked and grasped every paragraph. Few business leaders use metaphor as skillfully as Bezos. He built *flywheels* to power Amazon's growth. He planted *seeds* that grew into massive business enterprises. He created *two-pizza teams,* explained why failure and invention are *inseparable twins,* and hired *missionaries* over *mercenaries.* And those metaphors are just the tip of the iceberg.

Jeff Bezos isn't Ernest Hemingway, but his mission is not to write the next great American novel. Both writers, however, share something in common: Although their topics are complex, their writing is simple and accessible to most readers. Simplicity matters. According to a study in the *Harvard Business Review,* "Simplicity increases what scientists call the brain's processing fluency. Short sentences, familiar words, and clean syntax ensure that the reader doesn't have to exert too much brainpower to understand your meaning."[10]

One of the most remarkable lessons you'll learn from the shareholder letters is that writing is a skill anyone can learn and sharpen over time. As

Amazon grew larger with each year, Bezos grew as a writer with each letter. Most of the letters that rank lowest in quality and clarity came in the first few years after Amazon's IPO, while the highest-quality writing appears throughout Amazon's second decade of being a public company. The last letter that Bezos wrote, in 2020, ranks higher in nearly every objective measure of quality than his first letter in 1997. Did I mention that writing is a skill you can sharpen over time?

Day One isn't a strategy; it's a mindset. In his first shareholder letter in 1997, Bezos wrote that today is "Day 1" for the internet and Amazon .com. For the next two decades, he used the catchphrase as a metaphor for creating and sustaining a culture of innovation no matter how large a company becomes. Amazon started with a big idea and a small team. As Amazon grew into a massive enterprise of more than 1.5 million employees, Bezos made sure it kept the heart and spirit of a start-up. Always learning. Always improving.

The Day One mindset isn't about the skills you failed to learn yesterday; it's about learning new skills to avoid failing in the future. Day One will set you up to succeed for what promises to be the most transformative decade in human history.

This book is divided into three parts. In part 1, you'll set the foundation, learning to write with the "clarity of angels singing." You'll learn how to harness the power of persuasion by understanding the persuasive power of the written word. You'll find out why strong writing skills are more essential than ever. You'll discover that the road to the top is paved with the fewest words. You'll find out why Bezos and other innovative leaders use simple words to explain complex things. And you'll find out how a deliberately chosen metaphor fueled Amazon's innovation and helped it survive the dot-com crash. You will also learn:

- Why persuasive writing and engaging presentations start with the big idea.
- How the active voice energizes your message.
- Why 1066 was a pivotal year in the history of the English language and what it means for today's business leaders.
- Why leaders who simplify ideas aren't dumbing down their content; they're outsmarting the competition.

- How to use metaphors and analogies to educate your audience and explain your ideas.
- What great presentations have in common with song hooks that get stuck in your head.

In part 2, we'll examine the elements of building a story structure to move your readers and listeners to action. Once you know exactly why Bezos banned Powerpoint, what inspired him to do it, and what he replaced it with, you'll be empowered to think differently about crafting your own story. And rest easy—you can still use PowerPoint. The difference is you will no longer rely on presentation slides to tell your story. Instead, you'll use presentations to *complement* the story you tell.

You'll also hear from former Amazon executives who worked closely with Bezos to introduce new and effective communication tactics that Amazonians follow to this day. You'll see how one of those changes—written narratives—fueled Amazon's growth and sparked many products and services that directly impact your life. In addition, you'll learn:

- How a simple, time-tested storytelling structure holds the secret to creating indelible presentations and irresistible pitches.
- How to adopt Amazon's "working backwards" strategy to pitch bold ideas.
- Why you need to identify an origin story and learn to tell it.
- Why Bezos and other creative leaders read far more books than their followers, and how their reading habits make them extraordinary public speakers.

Part 3 is about sharing your plans and delivering the message. You'll learn how Bezos played the role of repeater in chief to build a team of inspired missionaries. You'll discover the tactic that Bezos and other new persuaders use to make data and statistics memorable, understandable, and actionable. I'll explain why great communicators are made, not born. In addition, you'll find out:

- How you can develop your communication delivery by focusing on three variables.
- How to articulate a short, bold vision that aligns and inspires teams.

- How a simple brain hack will unleash creative ideas.
- Why three is the most persuasive number in communication.

In this part, you will also find communication tools and templates like the Gallo Method that I've introduced to CEOs and leaders at the world's most admired brands—including senior executives at AWS, Amazon's giant cloud division that allows businesses to rent computing, storage, and networking capabilities. The method will teach you to build a visual display of your story on one page, a message that you can share in fifteen minutes or as little as fifteen seconds.

WIN OVER HEARTS AND MINDS

When I was writing this book, I had a unique opportunity to speak to the U.S. Army Special Forces (the Green Berets) at the John F. Kennedy Special Warfare Center and School at Fort Bragg, North Carolina. The Green Berets are globally recognized as an elite fighting force: brave, smart, and superbly trained. Their motto is to "free the oppressed" by prioritizing humans over hardware. That means the Green Berets are well armed, but as warrior-diplomats, persuasion is their weapon of choice. Their mission is to win over hearts and minds.

These unique warriors are always looking for new and innovative ways of thinking. I learned that soldiers with an entrepreneur's mindset are ideal candidates for the Special Forces. A successful mission requires small teams of creative thinkers and problem solvers who can quickly gain the trust of people who live in different countries, quickly adapt to different cultures, and speak in different languages.

The tactics you'll learn in this book resonate with elite military professionals because written and oral communication skills are essential to leadership. Team leaders must excel at skills such as delivering clear and concise presentations, applying the rule of three, writing in the active voice, telling engaging stories, and identifying the one thing the commander needs to know.

Communication and leadership skills are more critical today than at any time in human history for three reasons. First, your manager, customers, peers, and everyone else you need to influence are bombarded daily by an explosion of data and information. They need strong communicators to cut through the noise, set priorities, translate complexity into actionable advice, and to clarify and condense important content.

Second, as I mentioned earlier, the COVID-19 pandemic accelerated the trend toward remote work and virtual meetings. The pandemic triggered "the Great Resignation," when the U.S. economy saw an unprecedented number of people quitting their jobs. As I was writing this book, a Microsoft study found that 41 percent of workers were considering quitting or changing professions. Changing your job or starting a company requires exceptional communication skills to stand out or attract partners. Remote collaboration is more effective when written communication and virtual presentations are clear, concise, and specific.

Third, while you might enjoy the flexibility of remote work, it increases the competition for coveted jobs. Job seekers are no longer competing with candidates who live near the company. Hiring managers can choose talent from anywhere in the world. Those who can speak, write, and present effectively will stand out and get ahead.

Here's the good news. Although the tools we use to communicate have changed, the human brain has not. Once you understand how your listeners and readers consume information in person or in a remote setting, your ability to engage them will soar—and so will your career.

If Day One is a metaphor for having a beginner's mind, always looking for opportunities to learn and grow, what does Day Two look like? According to Bezos, Day Two is "stasis. Followed by irrelevance. Followed by excruciating, painful decline. Followed by death."[11]

Few people can afford to be complacent when it comes to improving their skills. We all want to avoid that slow, painful decline that Bezos imagines. "And *that* is why it's *always* Day One," Bezos adds with emphasis. Learn the tactics in this book and you won't decline. You'll rise.

One of Amazon's Leadership Principles is to *Think Big*. Thinking small is a self-fulfilling prophecy, says Bezos. Day One leaders dream big and have mastered communication skills to inspire others. By picking up this book, you've committed to joining those leaders. By adopting the strategies in this book, you'll unlock your ideas and unleash your potential.

With every chapter, you will grow in confidence. With every chapter, you will acquire the necessary skills to step into a bigger, bolder, stronger future. Today is Day One on the road to building that future. But as Bezos reminds us:

It's *always* Day One.

Part I

SET THE FOUNDATION

1

SIMPLE IS THE NEW SUPERPOWER

Anytime you make something simpler and lower friction,
you get more of it.

—Jeff Bezos, 2007 letter to Amazon shareholders

Jeff Bezos majored in theoretical physics at Princeton. He felt confident
about his ability to handle the major's demanding coursework. After all,
he'd been the valedictorian of his high school class. For two years, he
cruised along, receiving A-pluses in most of his classes.

At that point, Bezos was proud of the fact that, out of one hundred
students who had entered the program, only thirty remained. The number
was about to shrink again, only this time, Bezos would be among those
leaving. A roadblock appeared in his junior year, one that would change
the direction of his life and the future of the internet.

Bezos and his roommate, Joe, were enrolled in a quantum mechanics
class. They were stumped as they tried to solve a partial differential equation, or PDE. A PDE, by definition, is "an equation which imposes relations
between the various partial derivatives of a multivariable function." Bezos
was good at math, but the problem left him perplexed.

After three hours of getting nowhere, Bezos and Joe had a better idea.

"Let's ask Yasantha, the smartest guy at Princeton,"[1] Bezos suggested.

They walked to Yasantha's room and asked him to take a stab at it. Yasantha thought about it for a short time and calmly said, "Cosine."

"What do you mean?" Bezos asked.

"That's the answer. Let me show you."

Yasantha wrote three pages of detailed algebra to demonstrate how he
had arrived at the answer.

"Did you just do that in your head?" Bezos asked incredulously.

"No. That would be impossible," said Yasantha. "Three years ago, I solved a very similar problem, and I was able to map this problem onto that problem, and then it was immediately obvious that the answer was cosine."

It would be a turning point in Bezos's life. "That was the very moment when I realized I was never going to be a great theoretical physicist," Bezos recalls. "I saw the writing on the wall, and I changed my major very quickly to electrical engineering and computer science."

Years later, Yasantha was thrilled to learn that the richest person in the world had called him the smartest guy at Princeton. Yasantha posted a tweet that read: "You would not have Amazon if it weren't for me, since Jeff Bezos would have gone on to do physics, and the world would be a different place." Bezos wasn't the only one in that Princeton dorm room to change history. If you have an iPhone or Samsung phone, you're using a chip or technology that Yasantha helped build. Footnotes are replete with stories.

The decision to switch majors worked out well for Bezos. In 1986, he graduated with the highest academic honors in computer science and electrical engineering. Nearly a quarter century later, Bezos was invited to deliver the commencement address at his alma mater. The students graduating in the Princeton class of 2010 were among the brightest in the country. Four years earlier, Princeton had received a record number of applications, granting admission to just 10 percent of the students who applied.

On May 30, 2010, Bezos, a supersmart billionaire, gave a commencement speech to supersmart Ivy League graduates, speaking to them in words fit for a seventh grader. Bezos delivered a profound message in simple language, making the speech an instant hit. National Public Radio called it "one of the best commencement speeches, ever."

In the rest of this chapter, you'll learn *how* Bezos and other successful leaders simplify complex information, *why* they consider the ability to simplify a competitive advantage, and *what* steps you can take now to make simple your superpower.

YOU'RE NOT DUMBING DOWN THE CONTENT,
YOU'RE OUTSMARTING THE COMPETITION

Bezos told the 2010 Princeton class, "What I want to talk to you about today is the difference between gifts and choices. Cleverness is a gift; kindness is a choice. Gifts are easy—they're given after all. Choices can be hard. In the end, we are our choices."[2]

Six years after his speech at Princeton, Bezos revisited the theme of taking pride in your choices, not your gifts. "This is something that's super-important for young people to understand, and for parents to preach to young people. It's really easy for a talented young person to take pride in their gifts: 'I'm really athletic,' or 'I'm really smart,' or 'I'm really good at math.' That's fine. You should celebrate your gifts. You should be happy. But you can't be proud of them. What you *can* be proud of is your choices."[3]

Did you work hard? That's a choice.

Did you study hard? That's a choice.

Did you practice? That's a choice.

"The people who excel combine gifts and hard work, and the hard work part is a choice," Bezos said.

Bezos's commencement speech consisted of 1,353 words, 88 sentences, and registered a "readability score" of grade 7. Readability is a measure of writing quality. The score tells you how hard it is for the average reader to understand a piece of text. In this case, the score concludes that Bezos's Princeton commencement speech is likely to be understood by a reader who has at least a seventh-grade education (age twelve).

The readability score was originally created in the 1940s by Dr. Rudolf Flesch, a scholar and evangelist for simple, uncomplicated prose. Flesch isolated the elements that make a passage hard or easy to read. His test was based on the average length of sentences and words, among other variables. "Reading ease" is measured on a scale of 1 to 100. The higher the score, the easier it is for readers to understand your writing. For example, a score of 30 is "very difficult" to read. A score of 70 is "easy," and a score of 90 or above is "very easy." Newspapers and publishers who adopted the system after its introduction in the late 1940s saw their readership rise by 60 percent.

J. Peter Kincaid, a scientist and educator, worked with Flesch in the 1970s to make the formula even easier to interpret. Together, they converted readability scores into grade levels. The Flesch-Kincaid test examines the number of words in a sentence, the number of syllables per word, and the number of sentences written in the active versus passive voice, an important writing concept we'll examine in chapter 3.

If you're writing for a broad audience of adults, what grade level should you strive to achieve? The answer might surprise you: eighth grade.

Content written at the eighth-grade level can be read and understood by 80 percent of Americans. For context, academic papers, incomprehensible to the vast majority of readers, are written for grades sixteen to eighteen. The *Harry Potter* series of books are readable for students in grades six through eight. Amazon employees are instructed to aim for a Flesch-Kincaid grade level of 8 or lower.

And Bezos's speech to Princeton graduates? Seventh grade. The world's richest man inspired the country's smartest college graduates with words a twelve-year-old could understand.

Here's the key. A seventh-grade readability score does not mean that Bezos sounds like a seventh grader, because the score does not reflect the complexity or sophistication of a person's speech. It simply tells us how much mental energy the listener or reader expends to absorb and understand the information. The easier it is to follow a speech or presentation, the more likely it is that your audience will remember your message and take action on it. When you express complex ideas simply, you're not "dumbing down" the content; you're outsmarting the competition.

Bezos wrote annual letters to Amazon shareholders from 1997 to 2020, twenty-four letters in all. Here's how the letters score in readability:

- 48,062 words
- 2,481 sentences
- 18.8 words per sentence
- 11 Flesch-Kincaid grade level
- 6 percent passive sentences, 94 percent active sentences (in active sentences, the subject performs the action; active sentences get to the point faster, are shorter, and, in most cases, are easier to follow than passive sentences)

It's an impressive feat for someone as smart as Bezos to write 48,000 words in language the average high school student can read and understand, especially when you consider that he covers arcane financial topics such as free cash flow, generally accepted accounting principles (GAAP), and pro forma income. He also writes about highly technical topics like data mining, artificial intelligence, and machine learning years before those terms entered the business lexicon.

Writing, like any skill, can be sharpened. Bezos honed his writing over time. Take a look at table 1, comparing the first Amazon shareholder letter that Bezos wrote in 1997 to his last letter as CEO. As Amazon grew larger, shareholder letters grew in length as well. But as Bezos wrote more frequently, he became a better writer. The length of his sentences shrank by an average of four words, and the years of education required to read the letters fell by two grades.

Table 1: Readability Comparison Between Bezos's 1997 and 2020 Shareholder Letters

Readability Factor	1997	2020
Words	1,600	4,033
Sentence Length	20	16
Flesch-Kincaid Grade Level	10	8

A popular passage from the 2020 letter is simple and easy to read, even for sixth graders:

> If you want to be successful in business (in life, actually), you have to create more than you consume. Your goal should be to create value for everyone you interact with. Any business that doesn't create value for those it touches, even if it appears successful on the surface, isn't long for this world. It's on the way out.[4]

COACHING DRILL

During Bezos's tenure as Amazon CEO, he helped to create sixteen Leadership Principles Amazonians use every day to discuss new projects, pitch ideas, or determine the best approach to solve a particular problem. Above all, the principles reinforce the company's ethos that keeps customers at the center of every decision.

The way the principles are written is one of the primary reasons they are thoroughly integrated and understood by people throughout every level of the organization. The entire document consists of just seven hundred words written in eighth-grade language. Each principle is simple and clear and includes a few short sentences that translate the principle into desirable behaviors.

For example, the first and most important guiding principle is:

CUSTOMER OBSESSION

According to Amazon, customer obsession means that "Leaders start with the customer and work backwards. They work vigorously to earn and keep customer trust. Although leaders pay attention to competitors, they obsess over customers."

Key principles that are also relevant to this book include: Ownership, Invent and Simplify, Learn and Be Curious, Think Big, Earn Trust, and Insist on the Highest Standards. You can see the principles clearly displayed on the Amazon website because the company wants every job candidate to know them, every new hire to learn them, and every leader to internalize and share them.[5]

You can see the principles clearly displayed on the Amazon website because the company wants every job candidate to know them, every new hire to learn them, and every leader to internalize and share them.

Author Brad Stone, who chronicled Amazon's rise in *The Everything Store*, wrote that the clear articulation of these principles is a calculated leadership strategy. While employees in many organizations muddle through their jobs because their company's goals are confusing or complicated, the Amazon principles are simple, clear, and consistent.

The principles or values that make up your company culture are intended to be acted upon. But it's impossible to act on a principle no one can remember or understand. Make your principles simple to read, remember, and follow.

Trimming the length of sentences and replacing long words with short ones reduces the amount of mental energy required to absorb your idea. Why does that matter? Because our brains are not made to think. Our brains are made to conserve energy.

"Energy efficiency was the key to survival," writes Lisa Feldman Barrett in her award-winning book *Seven and a Half Lessons About the Brain.*

"Your brain's most important job is to control your body's energy needs. In short, your brain's most important job is not thinking."[6]

It's a sign of genius to express sophisticated arguments and complex ideas in simple words and sentences. Who says? A genius by the name of Daniel Kahneman, a Nobel Prize–winning psychologist and economist.

"If you care about being thought credible and intelligent, do not use complex language where simpler language will do," writes Kahneman in his groundbreaking book *Thinking, Fast and Slow*. Persuasive speakers, says Kahneman, do everything they can to reduce "cognitive strain." Anything that requires mental effort adds to the load that people carry in their heads while reading or listening. Every unfamiliar word, every unknown acronym, every convoluted sentence, every new idea—all add to the load. If you keep adding weights to the load, your reader or listener will drop everything and give up. Kahneman says that "cognitive ease" offers a more pleasing experience, and when people are pleased, they're more likely to support your idea.[7]

Simplicity—creating cognitive ease—is a theme that runs throughout this book. You'll learn why the human brain is wired to remember stories more easily than random facts. I'll take a deep dive into two rhetorical techniques that Bezos uses as mental shortcuts to explain complex theories: metaphors and analogies. And you'll learn why leaders on the fast track use the fewest number of words to reach the top.

Simplicity is all about knowing and selecting: knowing your audience and selecting the information your audience needs to know.

KNOW YOUR AUDIENCE

Jay Elliot vividly recalls the moment he met Steve Jobs. Jay, a thirty-nine-year-old executive at IBM, was sitting in the lounge of a Mexican restaurant in Los Gatos, a posh suburb in the heart of Silicon Valley. Jay was reading a newspaper article while he waited for a friend. In walked a young man sporting a beard and wearing a T-shirt and ragged jeans. He sat next to Jay and noticed that the newspaper article was about IBM.

"Do you know anything about computers?"[8] he asked Jay.

"Yes, I do. I'm an executive at IBM."

"One day, I'm going to bury IBM," the stranger responded.

Who is this guy? Jay wondered.

"Hi. I'm Steve Jobs."

As they spoke, Jay was mesmerized by Steve's vision of a simple, easy-to-use personal computer for the masses.

"What will it take to get you to come to work for me?" Steve asked.

"I'm happy with what I'm doing. I don't know you, and I haven't heard of Apple," Jay answered.

"What will it take?"

"I like Porsches. Buy me a Porsche, and I'll come to work for you," Jay quipped.

Two weeks later, a Porsche arrived in Jay's driveway.

I guess I'm working for Steve Jobs, Jay thought.

Elliot became a mentor to Jobs as Apple designed the first Macintosh. "Never trust anyone over thirty," Jobs often joked. "Except for Jay."

Jobs wanted to build a personal computer that was so easy to use out of the box it could ship with no instructional manual. "That was the number one goal," Elliot recalls. But the mouse—a device to control the computer—was so foreign to people, the Mac team realized that an instruction manual had to accompany the product.

During a meeting with Elliot, Jobs, and some marketing folks, someone in the room suggested that the manual should be simple enough for a twelfth grader to read it, understand it, and learn to work the computer from the text alone.

"Fine," Jobs said grudgingly. "Jay, go to a high school and find a twelfth grader to write the manual."

Jobs wasn't joking. Elliot visited high schools in nearby Cupertino and held contests to find a good writer. They found a student writer and brought him to a secret facility where the twelfth grader could sit with the Macintosh, play with it, and figure it out. The Macintosh was the first personal computer simple enough for the average person to use, accompanied by a thin manual written for anyone with a high-school-level education. It contained simple sentences, such as:

"You're about to learn a new way to use a computer."

"This chapter teaches you what you need to know to use your Macintosh—how to create documents (the name

for anything you create on Macintosh), make changes to them, and put them away."

"The finder is like a central hallway in the Macintosh house."

"Part of Steve's genius was that he looked for the right people to help keep everything simple—from design to content," says Elliot.

Great communicators don't start with what *they* know; they start with what the *audience* knows.

Shortly after working with executives at Amazon Web Services, I met with executives at another cloud company, an AWS partner. The fast-growing Silicon Valley start-up sold a product to IT and security professionals to help them analyze a tsunami of data much faster than ever. It cut the time required to investigate potentially catastrophic security breaches. That's the simple explanation.

Silicon Valley venture capital firm Greylock Partners, whose early investments include Facebook, Dropbox, Pandora, Instagram, and Airbnb, was the cloud company's leading investor.

Greylock had a lot at stake in fielding a successful IPO. Its 23 percent ownership propelled the start-up to a value of over $1 billion.

"The company's doing great. Why do you need me?" I asked one of Greylock's partners.

"Computer security specialists understand our value, but now our job is to translate it to a wider audience of investors, analysts, and shareholders." While the company's executives were comfortable speaking to other experts in their jargon and language, everyone else struggled to understand the product's implications. The original presentations suffered from wordy slides, unfamiliar acronyms, and too many details buried in too many weeds. There were no stories or concrete examples to bring the story alive. In short, the presentation was "uninspiring."

Investors needed to know—in simple language—what problem the product solves, why it matters that the company is "cloud-native," and what makes the company different from the scores of security platforms in the cloud universe.

The company had a good story. We just had to cut the fat and get to the meat before cognitive overload set in. Since the company had a simple-to-use cloud application (simple for experts), we focused on the fact that

IT professionals in large organizations used the platform to troubleshoot problems in less than fifteen minutes.

The road show was a massive success. Investors clamored for a piece of the action. The start-up went public in 2020 and became one of the top-performing IPOs of the year. Today, the company is worth more than $2 billion.

WARREN BUFFETT'S SIMPLE TRICK FOR CLEAR WRITING

Bezos isn't the only leader whose shareholder letters are considered a must-read by the business community. Billionaire investor Warren Buffett has been writing annual letters to Berkshire Hathaway shareholders for sixty years, three times longer than Bezos has been writing his letters.

Buffett is still writing letters at the age of ninety. His experience gives him a perspective few people have. According to Buffett, the secret to clear and simple writing is to picture your audience. "I've always had the image that I'm talking to my sisters, Doris and Bertie,"[9] Buffett says. "Berkshire is pretty much their whole investment. They're smart, but they're not active in the business, so they're not reading about it every day. I pretend they've been away for a year and I'm reporting to them on their investment."

Buffett begins drafting his letters with the salutation "Dear Doris and Bertie." Just before he's ready to publish, he replaces their names with a formal greeting: "To the shareholders of Berkshire Hathaway."

Buffett's letters are accessible, readable, and entertaining. By picturing his audience, Buffett puts himself in their shoes, speaking to them in language they'll easily comprehend. As Buffett sat down to draft his 2018 letter, he imagined that his sisters were thinking about selling their shares. His job was to convince them to hold on.

Read Buffett's 2018 letter and you'll see how he made complex financial information accessible to Doris and Bertie. The letter made headlines for its now-famous "focus on the forest" metaphor.

Buffett said that analyzing the complex financial details of each company in Berkshire's massive portfolio would be a mind-numbing task given their complexity. Fortunately for investors, it wasn't necessary to evaluate each company to estimate whether Berkshire was worth keeping. Buffett said investors need to know that individual businesses are "trees," ranging from twigs to redwoods. "A few of our trees are diseased and unlikely

to be around a decade from now," Buffett acknowledged. "Many others, though, are destined to grow in size and beauty."[10]

Buffett devoted the rest of the letter to taking investors on a journey through the five categories or "groves" that make up Berkshire's portfolio: noninsurance business ("the most valuable grove in Berkshire's forest"), marketable equities, controlling interest in several businesses, cash, and insurance.

Buffett chose to use the tree metaphor as a mental model to simplify complex financial information. He said it's easier for people to wrap their minds around a grove of trees than it is for them to understand the relationship among ninety businesses with nearly four hundred thousand employees. In chapter 5, you'll learn much more about how to employ metaphors as mental shortcuts. Buffett is considered the king of metaphor in business communication, but Jeff Bezos is close to taking the crown.

COACHING DRILL

If you're working on a complex topic, take a page from Warren Buffett's approach to writing his famous financial letters. Get to know your audience before you write by asking yourself three questions.

Who is your target audience? Buffett thinks about writing for his sisters, Doris and Bertie.

What do they need to know? Avoid telling them everything *you* know. What do they need to know that they don't know already?

Why should they care? Nobody cares about your ideas. They care about how your idea will help them lead a better life.

Who are your Doris and Bertie? Once you really know your audience—who they are, what they need to know, and why they should care—you're ready to take the next step toward simplifying your message. If step one was *knowing* your audience, step two is *selecting* the right messages for them.

TWENTY-SEVEN YEARS OF INNOVATION IN JUST 620 WORDS

Simplicity is an act of selection, not compression. You've heard of speakers who are "in the weeds," meaning they're getting far too granular and detailed. As a speaker, you can avoid falling into the weeds if you've done the hard work of removing the weeds ahead of your presentation.

On February 2, 2021, Bezos announced in an email to employees that he was stepping down as Amazon's CEO and handing the reins to AWS chief executive Andy Jassy. Bezos explained that he'd chair Amazon's board of directors and remain very involved in the company's new products and early initiatives.

Bezos's email scores a grade level of 7.8 for its simple structure, words, and sentences. But the real secret to its simplicity lies in the information Bezos chose to highlight. If Bezos had decided to talk about everything Amazon had accomplished from 1994 to 2021, it would have been the world's longest email. That simply wouldn't do for a leader who prides himself on creating a frictionless experience. By carefully selecting what to leave in and what to keep out, Bezos covered twenty-seven years of innovation in an email of just 620 words.

"Invention is the root of our success,"[11] Bezos wrote. "We've done crazy things together, and then made them normal. We pioneered customer reviews, 1-Click, personalized recommendations, Prime's insanely-fast shipping, Just Walk Out shopping, the Climate Pledge, Kindle, Alexa, marketplace, infrastructure cloud computing, Career Choice, and much more."

And much more. Three words that understate the scope of initiatives and innovations Bezos chose to leave out.

"If there's one reason we have done better than our peers in the internet space, it is because we have focused like a laser on customer experience,"[12] Bezos once said. From Day One, Bezos understood a fundamental rule of human behavior—people will align around shared goals, visions, and priorities when they are expressed simply, concisely, and consistently.

DON'T GET LOST IN A SEA OF DATA

Stephen Moret is glad he studied Amazon's guiding principles and vision. In April 2017, Amazon put out the word that it was looking for a location outside of Seattle to build its second headquarters. It invited regions across the country to submit their bids. Amazon received 238 submissions.

Moret, Virginia's top economic development official, saw a huge opportunity to develop his state's economy. But he knew the odds were stacked against him. A consulting agency gathered data from twenty categories to analyze Virginia's viability. The results didn't bode well. Virginia didn't match the generous incentives other states offered, nor could Virginia compete with low expenses in more affordable markets.

"We knew Amazon would get hundreds of proposals," Moret told me. "We had a limited opportunity to break through, so we needed to be clear on the things that made us distinctive."[13]

The team began crafting the Northern Virginia (NOVA) pitch by working backwards, researching the company's needs as a starting point (*Working Backwards* is an Amazon writing and decision-making technique you'll learn more about in chapter 10). They discovered that Amazon valued a solid and sustainable talent pipeline. Moret's team persuaded government and private entities to commit $1.1 billion to expand computer science education and build a new innovation campus at Virginia Tech. Moret overcame initial skepticism by pointing out that, even if Virginia lost the bid, a region known for its tech talent would attract companies from across the country.

Although the final NOVA pitch came in at nine hundred pages (including detailed appendix material), Moret challenged the team to make "the real story fit onto a page."

Moret's team simplified NOVA's story into six carefully and deliberately selected key messages:

- North America's top producer of tech talent.
- A global and inclusive region.
- America's only metro area leading public and private sector innovation.
- A stable and competitive partner with a legacy of exceptional governance.
- A portfolio of trophy sites to match the scope, speed, and scale of HQ2.
- A new model of economic development for the twenty-first century.

"Focusing on six points forced us to make sure we were making a compelling case," Moret says. "If you have to distill the case you're trying to make into a few points, what would those points be? Make sure those points are clear, bulletproof, and supportable. Don't get lost in a sea of data."

Moret assembled a team that accomplished what most observers said could never happen. On November 13, 2018, Amazon announced that

Northern Virginia would be home to its second headquarters. Moret's team won the largest private economic project in U.S. history. Amazon's second headquarters will create twenty-five thousand new jobs and bring in upward of $500 million a year in revenue for Virginia.

If you talk to Moret, you'll soon figure out why he's successful at unifying hundreds of people with diverse—and sometimes competing—interests to work together for the common good. He refuses to take credit, always shining the spotlight on the five hundred others involved in the pitch. But make no mistake, Moret was the team's quarterback. Smart leaders keep things simple because simple things lead to smart decisions.

"If you have a competence nobody else has, a hip-pocket skill, you become more valuable," says Indra Nooyi, the former CEO of PepsiCo who currently sits on Amazon's board of directors.[14] Nooyi also identifies her "hip-pocket skill" as the ability to make the complex simple.

"Anytime things were too complex, it always came back to me. People would ask, 'Indra, you simplify it first. You tell us how to navigate through this extremely complex problem.' That was my skill then. It still is today."

According to Nooyi, "If you want to be a leader and you cannot communicate effectively, forget it. In the digital world, people think texting and tweeting is communicating. It's not. You've got to be able to stand in front of employees and get them to go places they never thought they could get to. You need to have enormous communication capabilities. You cannot over-invest in communication skills."

You will always meet people who refuse to simplify their message. They're infatuated with their intellect, captivated by their credentials, and enchanted with their experience. They would never choose a short word to replace a long one. Why should they? They're sesquipedalians. Yes, it's a real word. A sesquipedalian is fond of using multisyllabic words that are tough to pronounce and hard to understand. Don't let them intimidate you. The billionaire founder of a private investment firm once told me the biggest weakness he sees among business graduates applying at his firm is a failure to translate their work and ideas into plain English. "Their presentations are comprehensive and highly technical, and utterly incomprehensible and entirely unmemorable."

Put in the hard work to keep the message simple, and your simple message will become your superpower.

2

A MODERN SPIN
ON ANCIENT WORDS

Short words are best, and old words when short are best
of all.

—Winston Churchill

A revolution rocked the publishing world in November of 2007. Amazon's
launch of its e-reader, the Kindle, took off like a rocket.

The first devices sold out in five hours as customers devoured the selection of ninety thousand available titles. Today, Kindle customers can
choose from more than six million titles. Amazon commands 80 percent of
all ebook sales in the U.S.

About 25 percent of U.S. adults read ebooks. Even if you're not part
of that group and you prefer print or the fast-growing category of audiobooks, you know how to access and read ebooks. But in 2007, most people
had not seen such a device. Bezos highlighted a few of its features in his
shareholder letter.

> If you come across a word you don't recognize, you can look it up easily. You
> can search your books. Your margin notes and underlinings are stored on
> the server-side in the "cloud," where they can't be lost. Kindle keeps your
> place in each of the books you're reading, automatically. If your eyes are
> tired, you can change the font size. Most important is the seamless, simple
> ability to find a book and have it in 60 seconds. When I've watched people
> do this for the first time, it's clear the capability has a profound effect on
> them. Our vision for Kindle is every book ever printed in any language, all
> available in less than 60 seconds.[1]

Ninety-two percent of the words in the preceding passage are one or two syllables. In fact, the majority of words that Bezos chose to describe the Kindle—76 percent—are just one syllable.

Great speakers use short words to explain new ideas.

Short, simple words trace their origin to an event that looms large in the minds of the English people. About 940 years before the Kindle changed the way people read, the Battle of Hastings changed the way people speak.

In 1066, William the Conqueror lived up to his moniker and sailed across the English Channel from France along with seven thousand Norman invaders. He introduced new words to the ruling class, an early version of French based on Latin (Norman French). The Norman Conquest had a major effect on the English language, and its impact is felt to this day.

Although the new Norman ruling class spoke in "fancy" language, the remaining 97 percent of the country's people, the "common" folk, continued to use Old English, the earliest recorded form of the English language, tracing its roots to the fifth century. After 1066, Norman French became the language of English nobility while short, ancient words remained the language of the people.

Today, 80 percent of the words we speak in English fall into two camps: Germanic (a combination of Old and Middle English) and Latinate. The remaining 20 percent of English words come from a combination of Greek and other origins that have crossed continents (e.g., *tobacco* and *potato* from America and words like *bungalow* and *guru* from the Far East). Technology is also responsible for a small percentage of words, like *googling*.

How can you tell the difference between the more ancient words of the English language and those words with a Latin origin? It's easy once you get the hang of it. The ancient words are short and often have one syllable. Latin-based words are longer with more syllables. When someone speaks in "plain English," they're likely using ancient words. When a speaker is long-winded, confusing, and complicated, they're likely using too many words of Latin origin.

If you *need* something, you're speaking in plain English. If you *require* it, you're using fancy language.

If you report to a *boss,* you're speaking in plain English. If you report to a *superior,* you're using fancy language.

If you say your neighbor's property is *next* to yours, you're speaking in plain English. If you say their property is *adjacent* to your house, you're using fancy language.

Ancient words of Germanic origin are informal and conversational. Latinate words are often formal and stuffy. Table 2.1 shows more examples comparing formal phrases with their informal counterparts.

Table 2.1: Formal Phrases Compared to Simpler Versions

Formal	Characters	Informal	Characters
He engaged in a deliberate prevarication.	36	He told a lie.	11
I perceive something in the distance.	32	I see something.	14
Let's engage in a conversation.	27	It's time to talk.	15
You are required to purchase any item you damage.	41	If you break it, you buy it.	22

In this chapter, you'll learn a simple language device to inspire, persuade, and motivate: Combine ancient words and fancy ones. When Patrick Henry wrote, "Give me liberty or give me death," he combined *liberty,* a noun derived from the Latin word *libertas,* with a short word of Old English origin, *death.* Henry's words unified the American colonists and sparked a revolution.

A combination of Latinate and Germanic words fall somewhere in between a legal textbook and a children's book like *Fun with Dick and Jane.* When Jane says, "Run, run," and Dick says, "Look, look," it only makes for interesting reading to the mind of a six-year-old. On the opposite end, text and presentations comprised solely of Latinate words are baffling and bewildering, confusing and complicated. Simply put, fancy words put people to sleep.

How do you decide when to pick a short word instead of a long one? The answer is simple. Use short words to talk about hard things: a crisis, a complex idea, or a big idea that you want listeners to remember.

COACHING DRILL

Put your message to the test. Select a sample of text from one of your presentation scripts. How many words or phrases are fancy, Latin-based? You can use an online etymology dictionary to identify the origin of words.

Look for simpler, shorter words to replace the formal ones. You'll find that favoring short words will cut most of the jargon from your speech, words that confuse your audience. As a result, your sentences will be tight, clear, and strong. Replace long words with short ones and you'll be far more persuasive.

PICK SHORT WORDS IN A CRISIS

"The shorter words of a language are usually the more ancient," Winston Churchill once said. "Their meaning is more ingrained in the national character, and they appeal to greater force."

Erik Larson is the bestselling author of historical narratives like *Dead Wake*, about the sinking of the *Lusitania* in World War I and *The Splendid and the Vile*, about the early months of Churchill's role as England's prime minister in World War II. Larson told me that Churchill put a lot of care into the words he chose to communicate to the public. In a memo titled "Brevity," Churchill urged government administrators to replace lengthy "woolly phrases" with single words that were more conversational. Churchill said, "The discipline of setting out the real points concisely will prove an aid to clear thinking."[2]

Clear thinking and clear messaging is what we needed when the coronavirus pandemic brought the world to a halt. In March of 2020, health agencies around the globe issued national quarantine orders and ran campaigns to encourage people to take precautions to reduce the spread of COVID-19. Across English-speaking countries from the U.S. to the UK and from Canada to Australia, citizens were told to: Stay Home. Stop the Spread. Save Lives.

The government in the UK ran print and radio ads aimed at protecting the National Health System from being overwhelmed: "Stay home. Stop the spread." Australians were advised: "Stop the spread and stay healthy." Canadians were instructed: "Stay home, wear a mask, and wash your hands."

In a crisis, short words are urgent, attention-grabbing, and easy to grasp.

Imagine if the campaigns had used traditional bureaucratic jargon. The message might have sounded like this:

> For the preservation of public health and safety, all citizens who do not
> engage in essential activities that impact critical infrastructure are hereby
> ordered to remain in their residence in order to mitigate the propagation of
> the novel coronavirus and to minimize morbidity and mortality.[3]

I didn't make up that paragraph. It's from the executive order issued in the state of New York announcing the stay-at-home guidelines
on March 16, 2020. It's legal language, not the everyday language of
real people. Most health care communicators know the difference. When
they communicate in a crisis, they choose words of ancient origin like
stay, home, and *lives.*

What about non–English speaking countries? Do simple words apply
in a crisis? They sure do.

The COVID-19 pandemic threw Japan into a tailspin because the
country had to deal with the added psychological and economic blow
of postponing the 2020 Tokyo Olympics. A meeting of health experts in
March concluded that three conditions were responsible for transmitting
the virus: enclosed spaces with little ventilation, crowded spaces where it
was impossible to maintain social distancing, and conversations in prox-
imity to another person.

"Behavior modification" was critical, and only effective communication would persuade the public to take precautions. Health authorities
launched a campaign urging people to avoid the "Three Cs: Closed Spaces,
Crowded Places, and Close-Contact Settings." The three Cs were so easy
to remember that even young Japanese schoolchildren knew to avoid
closed, crowded, and close-contact settings.

Global health experts are trained in crisis communication. The first rule
they learn is to make the message clear and concise. Much of the research
in the field of crisis communication is based on "mental noise theory." It
means that in times of crisis, stress is high and emotions are charged. In
these situations, people are less likely to hear information accurately, understand it, and remember it.

The solution to cutting through the noise is to craft a message that can
be spoken in seven to nine seconds or printed in twenty words. That's why
you'll often see crisis messages in groups of three with the shortest words
possible. If your clothes catch fire, it's easy to remember to "stop, drop,

and roll." In earthquake-prone areas of the U.S., children are taught to
"drop, cover, and hold on."

Pick the shortest words to deliver a message in a crisis. During the pandemic, we all heard the same instructions over and over: stay home, wear
a mask, and stay six feet apart. You'll know when you've found the most
ancient words to express a message when there's no shorter word to say the
same thing.

HOW TO EXPLAIN COMPLEX IDEAS TO THE MOST PEOPLE

As your idea grows in complexity, the length of your words should shrink.

Let's turn to the legal field as an example. Lawyers have a love affair
with words of French and Latin origin. That's why legal contracts are
filled with words you would not use in everyday conversation: *heretofore,*
indemnification, and *force majeure.*

Shawn Burton decided it was time for a change. The innovation that he
brought to GE's legal department came in the form of communicating in
plain English. Burton, the general counsel for GE's aviation division, began an article in the *Harvard Business Review* with this observation: "What
do you call a dense, overly lengthy contract that is loaded with legal jargon
and virtually impossible for a nonlawyer to understand? The status quo."[4]

Burton says that the majority of legal contracts are "full of unnecessary and incomprehensible language." Burton led a three-year effort to
promote contracts written in plain language instead of arcane legalese or,
as *Webster's* dictionary defines it, "the language used by lawyers that is
difficult for most people to understand."

The problem with legal jargon frustrated the company's sales teams. Contracts of more than one hundred pages in length and nearly three dozen
definitions took up far too much time to read, comprehend, and negotiate.
Burton, who learned about plain English in law school, came up with a
simple test: "If someone in high school couldn't pick this up and understand it without any context, it wasn't plain enough."[5]

Rewriting contracts wasn't easy. Burton's legal team spent a month on
the first draft, but they succeeded in reducing seven contracts into one.
Statements and paragraphs that required more than one page were reduced
to one or two sentences. One contract had a sentence of 142 words. By
replacing many of the Latin-based phrases with simpler versions, the sen-

tence weighed in at 65 words—still hefty, but the exercise slimmed the length by more than half.

Best of all, there was no more need for an appendix because all 33 words that required a definition had been eliminated.

Everyone agreed that the final contracts were shorter and easier to read. Gone were words like *indemnification, heretofore, whereas,* and *forthwith.* Some even found the new contract "jarring" because they realized the simpler the language, the easier it was to understand. "Legal concepts that historically had been made complicated in contracts were explained in lay terms. Sentences were short and written in the active voice,"[6] said Burton.

The effort paid off. The first 150 plain-language contracts took 60 percent less time to negotiate. According to Burton, the new contracts sped up deals, improved customer satisfaction, and saved money.

Burton calls his initiative "brilliant contracting." The strategy *is* brilliant, but not new.

About 150 years before GE's plain-language initiative, a prairie lawyer by the name of Abraham Lincoln had stumbled upon the strategy.

"The key to Lincoln's success was his uncanny ability to break down the most complex case or issue into its simplest elements,"[7] writes historian Doris Kearns Goodwin. Although Lincoln's arguments were logical and profound, they were easy to follow. How? "He aimed for intimate conversations with jurors, as if conversing with friends." Goodwin quotes one of Lincoln's peers, Henry Clay Whitney, who observed that "Lincoln's language was composed of plain Anglo-Saxon words."

Good ole Abe had it right all along.

Let's return to Amazon. Not the Amazon of Seattle but the "Amazon of South Korea."

In March of 2021, Coupang went public. Bom Kim started the company in 2010 after dropping out of Harvard Business School after only six months. There's no need to worry about him, though. He adopted some of Amazon's principles to revolutionize e-commerce in his part of the world and is now worth $8 billion, according to *Forbes.*

When Kim talks about his company's obsession with service, large selection, and low price, we're reminded of the principles that made Amazon successful. The young entrepreneur also pulls a page from the Bezos playbook and uses plain talk and simple words to explain new ideas.

In Kim's IPO road-show presentation, he explained the speedy service he named "rocket delivery." It is remarkably fast. Coupang's advanced logistics systems allows it to deliver millions of items and fresh groceries within hours, 365 days a year.

Here's how Kim explains the service: "Order as late as midnight and wake up to find your item when you wake up. Place your order. Head to bed. Wake up to find your items at your door like Christmas morning. Does your child need a tutu for ballet practice? Order by midnight and have it arrive at dawn before they're off to school. Or order headphones at night and use them on your commute the very next day."[8]

Kim's pitch receives a score of 90 for reading ease, which means it's "very easy" for most people to understand. The higher the score, the shorter the sentences and words. The passage returns a grade level of 3 and contains no passive sentences. There's almost no simpler way to say the same thing.

Kim's words, however, hide enormous complexity. He doesn't say that the company "leverages machine learning to anticipate demand and to forward deploy the inventory closer to customers." He doesn't explain "dynamic orchestration," a technology that sorts through hundreds of millions of combinations of inventory and route options to predict the most efficient path for every order. He avoids a discussion of the integrated system that enables the company to "optimize upstream processes to decrease inefficiencies downstream."

The average customer doesn't care how an order gets to the door. They don't care to know which AI, logistics, or software platforms the company uses to provide the experience. And while they don't care to understand "dynamic orchestration," they are impressed with the outcome: The technology allows Coupang to deliver 100 percent of orders by the next day or within hours.

Kim told CNBC that he "envied" Amazon's business model and was inspired by the way Bezos articulated the company's vision and benefits. Kim has become an excellent communicator. Many customers can recite the company's simple, memorable mission statement: "To create a world where customers wonder, how did I ever live without Coupong?"

APHORISMS COMPRESS POWERFUL IDEAS

We've all heard the quote "If it ain't broke, don't fix it." Some entrepreneurs have put a new spin on the old adage and created their own:

"Move fast and break things." These are aphorisms—pithy sayings, as-
tute observations, pearls of wisdom, or nuggets of advice. Every aphorism contains a different message, of course, but they're almost always
short:

- As you sow, so shall you reap.
- A chain is only as strong as its weakest link.
- There is nothing good or bad, but thinking makes it so.
- Rome wasn't built in a day.
- Don't judge a book by its cover.

A long, confusing adage would be hard to remember. People can't follow advice if they can't recall it. Short sentences and simple words are
best for new or thought-provoking ideas.

Philosopher and bestselling author of *The Black Swan,* Nassim Nicholas Taleb, says that an aphorism's power lies in its ability "to compress
powerful ideas in a handful of words."

In Taleb's book *The Bed of Procrustes,* he explains that aphorisms,
maxims, proverbs, and short sayings are examples of the earliest literary
forms. "They carry the cognitive compactness of the sound bite . . . with
some show of bravado in the ability of the author to compress powerful
ideas in a handful of words—particularly in an oral format. . . . aphorisms
require us to change our reading habits and approach them in small doses;
each one of them is a complete unit, a complete narrative disassociated
from the others."[9]

Some aphorisms are bland platitudes that repeat commonsense ideas
that you've heard many times. But according to Taleb, others are "crisp,
commoditized ideas" that trigger the moment of discovery and have "ex-
plosive consequences."

Aphorisms that force you to think about the world in a new way stand
the test of time because they are handed down from generation to generation. In much the same way, Bezos wants his strategies to be passed from
current employees to new ones, so the entire company remains aligned
around a common goal. And that's why Bezos packages his advice in the
form of proverbs and aphorisms which, by definition, are short phrases
that contain a lot of wisdom. Short words are easy to say, easy to read, easy
to remember, and easy to repeat.

FAMOUS JEFF-ISMS

Let's take a closer look at some of the most famous "Jeff-isms" (Bezos's most memorable sayings) and examine why he chooses certain words over others. You'll find examples in table 2.2 along with notes on why the quotes are popular.

Table 2.2: Bezos Aphorisms

Aphorism	Notes
"Get big fast."	Three words that register a Flesch reading ease score of 100 points. It can't be written in a simpler way.
"You don't choose your passions. Your passions choose you."	Once again, this quote has a reading score of close to 100, a nearly perfect sentence. It has the added power of a rhetorical device called *chiasmus,* a fancy word for inverting the same phrase in two successive sentences like JFK's famous line, "Ask not what your country can do for you, ask what you can do for your country."
"You can work long, hard, or smart, but at Amazon.com, you can't choose two out of the three."	Bezos made this observation in 1997, and it's stuck ever since. Except for *Amazon,* every word is one syllable.
"In short, what's good for customers is good for shareholders."	Bezos gave this advice in 2002. We know it's a short summary of a big principle because he says so.
"Life's too short to hang out with people who aren't resourceful."	Bezos could have used *associate* or *fraternize,* but chose the common phrase *hang out.*
"If you can't feed a team with two pizzas, it's too large."	A reading ease score of 100 means there is no simpler way to express this concept that can—and has—filled entire books.
"Your brand is what others say about you when you're not in the room."	Once again, a concept that can fill a book on brand building, written almost entirely in one-syllable words.
"It's always Day 1."	Very easy to read, remember, and repeat.

COACHING DRILL

Use the Flesch-Kincaid test to simplify your writing. Several writing platforms offer the service, including Grammarly and Microsoft Word, which has added readability scores to its popular software. Under Word's options, you'll find a spelling and grammar tab. Check the box that says "Show readability statistics," and it will display the readability and reading level of the document. Amazon teaches its employees to aim for a "readability" level of 50 or higher and a grade level of 8. This chapter has a readability score of 59 and a Flesch-Kincaid grade level of 8, which means it's simple enough for a broad range of readers to clearly understand its content.

THE SAGE OF OMAHA

A *sage* is defined as a profoundly wise person. They can be found in every part of the world, including Omaha, Nebraska, where the brightest financial sage on the planet makes his home.

Billionaire Warren Buffett is the king of metaphor, as we saw above. He's also the prince of pithy quotes. Most of Buffett's famous quotes contain wisdom that has filled entire books on the subject, which explains why we like to read and share short expressions that reveal essential truths. These sayings enlighten, educate, and inspire in a sentence or two. Table 2.3 provides a sample of quotes from the profoundly wise Sage of Omaha.

Table 2.3: Buffett Aphorisms

Aphorism	Notes
"Be fearful when others are greedy and greedy when others are fearful."	This quote from Buffett's 1996 shareholder letter has two things in its favor: short words—he uses *greed* not *avarice*—and, once again, the rhetorical tool of inverting a word or phrase. The line is short and catchy and has the added benefit of being pleasing to the ear. In short, it works.
"It's not how you sell 'em, it's how you tell 'em."	In Buffett's 2016 letter, he doesn't even bother spelling out entire words. That's why his sayings are often called "folksy wisdom." He writes the way people talk.
"It's better to hang out with people better than you."	In the sentence following this quote, Buffett rephrased it: "Pick out associates whose behavior is better than yours and you'll drift in their direction." The shorter sentence stuck.
"I don't look to jump over 7-foot bars: I look for 1-foot bars that I can step over."	An entire sentence of one-syllable words with the exception of the word *over*.
"If you buy things you do not need, soon you will have to sell things you need."	Another all one-syllable sentence.

Aphorism	Notes
"You never know who's swimming naked until the tide goes out."	Tides that *subside* don't pack the same punch as ones that roll out or go out.
"For 240 years it's been a terrible mistake to bet against America, and now is no time to start."	Word choice is key. Buffett chooses the shorter *bet* over *wager* and *start* over *commence*.
"America's best days lie ahead."	This sentence is even shorter than the first version. Imagine if Buffett had written: "America is well-positioned to capitalize on future growth opportunities." If you go bold, keep it short.

Short, catchy phrases are to leadership what song hooks are to music. A *hook* is a powerful songwriting tool that makes a song unforgettable. The academic way to describe the phenomenon is "involuntary musical imagery." In plain language, it's an earworm.

GREAT COMMUNICATORS WRITE FOR THE EAR

The earworm is the section of a song that you sing in the shower because it's catchy and easy to remember. While there are a number of ways to write a catchy hook, the fundamental rule is that it has to be simple and repeatable. Most radio-friendly hooks are just three to five seconds long. The hook stands out, and when it's repeated over and over, it's more likely to stick in your head.

In 1972, Bill Withers wrote the hook *Lean on me / when you're not strong.* He had no idea it would land on *Rolling Stone*'s list of the five hundred greatest songs of all time.

"To me, the biggest challenge in the world is to take anything that's complicated and make it simple so it can be understood by the masses,"[10] Withers told an interviewer years later. "I'm a stickler for saying something the simplest possible way because simple is memorable. If something's too complicated, you're not going to walk around humming it to yourself because it's too hard to remember . . . The key is to make somebody not only remember it, but recall it over and over and over again."

Withers said country music is one of his favorite genres because the songs tell a story in simple lyrics. Withers made his observation long before country sensation Luke Combs arrived on the scene, but the two musicians share a love for turning complex story lines into short hooks.

Combs has set streaming records on the Billboard charts because of his clever, irresistible hooks that are often the titles of his song: "She Got the Best of Me," "When It Rains It Pours," "What You See Is What You Get," and "Beer Never Broke My Heart."

"I'm definitely very critical when it comes to the songwriting,"[11] Combs says of his process. "I'm a super, super perfectionist . . . Even the small words are super important."

If you don't think a music-like hook can help you communicate as a leader, I have three words for you: *Yes, it can.* Barack Obama didn't use a songwriter with a love for lyrics; he used a speechwriter with an ear for the lyrical.

Jon Favreau worked with Obama on the 2008 speech that put the Illinois senator on the map. Together, they resurrected a three-word phrase Obama had used in a political ad years earlier: "Yes We Can." In rhetorical terms, they turned the phrase into an *epistrophe,* a repetition of words at the end of a sentence. The phrase acts as a hook, the sing-along part of the speech. It became a refrain that audiences began to know by heart. *The Washington Post* called it a "lyrical catchphrase."

In one speech, Obama repeated the hook twelve times.

For when we have faced down impossible odds, when we've been told we're not ready or that we shouldn't try or that we can't, generations of Americans have responded with a simple creed that sums up the spirit of a people: Yes, we can. Yes, we can. Yes, we can.

It was a creed written into the founding documents that declared the destiny of a nation: Yes, we can.

It was whispered by slaves and abolitionists as they blazed a trail towards freedom through the darkest of nights: Yes, we can.

It was sung by immigrants as they struck out from distant shores and pioneers who pushed westward against an unforgiving wilderness: Yes, we can.

. . . And, together, we will begin the next great chapter in the American story, with three words that will ring from coast to coast, from sea to shining sea: Yes, we can.[12]

Obama's speeches were rhetorical songs, stories told in the rhythm of music. His ideas filled the verses while "Yes, we can" made up the chorus, the sing-along, the memorable catchphrase.

Good communicators are clear and concise; great communicators make music for the ear.

3

WRITING THAT DAZZLES, SHINES, AND SPARKLES

Writing, invented thousands of years ago, is a grand whopper of a tool, and I have no doubt that it changed us dramatically.

—Jeff Bezos

The sportswriter Red Smith once said, "Writing is easy. You simply sit down at the typewriter, open your veins, and bleed."

Putting pen to paper is easy. Writing meaningful words is hard.

Expressing your ideas in written form is like "pushing against the wind in soft, muddy ground with a wheelbarrow full of bricks,"[1] the comedian Jerry Seinfeld once told podcaster Tim Ferriss. "Writing is a painful and arduous process but, in comedy, you either learn to write or you will die. It saved my life and made my career. Stand-up comedy is really the profession of writing."

Your career might not rely on writing as much as Seinfeld's, but writing is a critical skill in almost every level of every profession. Nearly every piece of communication intended to inform, persuade, or motivate begins its journey in the form of the written word: an inspiring college essay that moves an applicant to the top of the pile, a memorable presentation that wows the audience, a succinct email that moves the reader to action, and a TikTok or Instagram caption that drives engagement. Strong writing skills are also a requirement for getting hired at Amazon and climbing the career ladder into a leadership position. Few companies value writing as highly as Amazon, and few people evangelize the skill as passionately as Bezos.

Writing is a skill, which means you can improve with regular practice. Seinfeld has created systems to help him write, techniques that business professionals can also use to elevate their writing skills. First, Seinfeld approaches the craft like an athlete trains for a sport. He puts in the reps and writes every day, even if the ideas don't turn into comedy gold. "No one starts out great,"[2] he says. "The ones who are great put a tremendous number of hours into it. It's a game of tonnage."

Second, Seinfeld sets a time limit on his writing. When Seinfeld's daughter told her dad that she planned to spend the entire day writing a project, he responded, "No, you're not. No one can write all day. Shakespeare can't write all day. It's torture. Give yourself an hour." Seinfeld reminded his daughter that writing is one of the most difficult tasks a human can attempt. To summon an idea from your brain and your spirit and to transfer it to a blank page doesn't come naturally to most of us. "People tell you to 'just write' like you're supposed to be able to do it. The greatest people in the world can't do it. If you're going to do it, you should first be told that what you are attempting to do is incredibly difficult."

Now that we've established that good writing is hard work, I'll avoid making it harder by giving you a list of "rules" to follow. Rules are rigid and, for many people, evoke painful memories of struggling to write a school essay. Rules are also constricting. They don't apply in the very same way to every business-writing platform. Memos, emails, texts, blogs, tweets, LinkedIn posts, and other social media platforms have their own styles and reader expectations.

Dwayne "The Rock" Johnson posted one of the most popular Instagram images of 2020, a photo from his secret wedding in Hawaii. He wrote:

> Our Hawaiian wedding was beautiful and I want to thank our incredible staff for their outstanding work. To carry out my #1 goal of complete privacy, no wedding planners or outside resources were hired. Everything you see was created by hand, by staff and family only. The end results were spectacular and Lauren and I will forever be grateful for helping our hearts sing on this day.

Johnson's text is sweet and gracious. I was one of the fifteen million people who "liked" it. I think it's perfect, but grammarians would find plenty wrong with it. I ran Johnson's text through grammar software and found that it violated several of those pesky rules. For instance:

- A comma should be added after the word *beautiful* because the next word, *and,* is a coordinating conjunction in a compound sentence.
- The sentence that starts with the subordinate phrase *to carry about my #1 goal of complete privacy* contains a dangling modifier and should be rewritten.
- The phrase *no wedding planners or outside resources were hired* should be rewritten in the active voice.
- The word *end* in the phrase *the end results* is redundant and should be eliminated.
- There should be a comma after *spectacular* because, once again, it separates a coordinating conjunction *and* in a compound sentence.

Johnson's post doesn't follow several "rules," and yet I wouldn't change a thing. Yes, rules serve a purpose, and you should understand the rules of grammar to develop your writing skills. But rules imply that there's a right answer and a wrong one. I wrote this book to help you navigate the gray area where persuasion and clear communication thrive. You might have the best idea and use proper grammar, but if you're not successful at convincing others to take action on your idea, you have failed to *persuade*. You might have the best solution to a problem, but if you can't convey clearly both the meaning and emotion you seek, you may lose your audience. The most effective method of expressing your ideas is the method that works. And what works might break some of the formal "rules."

So let's replace *rules* with *tools* and *strategies*. Tools are flexible. We choose the right tool for the job. A strategy combines art and science, and persuasion is very much a skill that requires knowledge of both art and science. Yes, learn the rules, but don't let them get in your way.

Very few business books tackle the subject of writing unless it's the sole topic of the title. Many CEOs who write books talk about leadership skills, but other than paying lip service to the importance of writing, they avoid giving specific tips on how to write more effectively. They simply don't feel qualified to offer such advice, even though many of them are exceptional writers. We've been conditioned to think that good writers have tapped into some sort of magic that eludes the rest of us. Nonsense. I'll repeat it—writing is a skill that you can sharpen with knowledge and practice.

Figure 3 shows a plot graph of all twenty-four shareholder letters that Bezos wrote as CEO of Amazon. By using Grammarly's readability feature,

I was able to identify the grade level for each letter. The Bezos letters range from eighth grade to "some college required." Remember, the lower the grade, the easier it is to understand the material. A full 70 percent of letters that scored highest for writing quality appeared after 2007, a decade after Bezos began communicating to shareholders through the written word. One former Amazonian who worked closely with Bezos told me that this graphic is another example of his relentless pursuit of the exceptional. Bezos is a student of communication. He reads, tweaks, gathers experts, and sharpens his skills year after year. Writing skills are no exception.

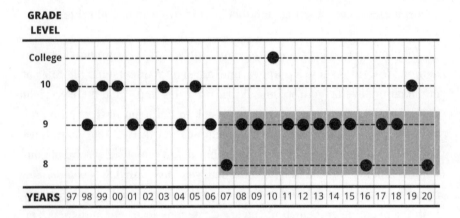

Since we can all strive for the exceptional and improve our writing skills, I went back to school before I began working on this book. I reread some of my favorite writing books and interviewed some of the top experts in the field. At first, I just wanted to understand why the twenty-four Bezos shareholder letters are considered models of simplicity and clarity. But as I talked to the experts, they stirred my passion for the art of writing. Most important, they helped me identify several simple writing strategies that influential business leaders use to stand apart. I turned to several authors and writing experts such as Gary Provost, Roy Peter Clark, and Gill, a British YouTube sensation.

In the rest of this chapter, I'll offer seven writing tips from these instructors and other experts. Their strategies will elevate your writing skills. You'll also learn how Jeff Bezos and other effective business leaders follow many of these principles to sell their ideas.

1. BEGIN SENTENCES WITH SUBJECTS AND VERBS

The subject of a sentence is the person or thing that performs the action (verb). Think of subjects and verbs as the locomotive of a train, pulling along the rest of the railcars. A good writer starts with the strongest element of the sentence and lets everything else branch to the right.

Roy Peter Clark offers the following example: "A writer composes a sentence with subject and verb at the beginning, followed by other subordinate elements, creating what scholars call a right-branching sentence."[3] In the preceding sentence, Clark starts with the subject and the verb closely connected: *writer composes.* Try to avoid a long separation between the subject and verb. Here's a weak version of Clark's sentence: *A writer who wants to be really good at the craft should* compose *a sentence with a subject and verb at the beginning.*

If you're struggling to write a good sentence, start with a subject and a verb. It'll lighten the load.

Let's see how Bezos starts sentences with subjects and verbs that pull the rest of the sentence. The subjects and verbs are in bold.

- "**Amazon's vision** is to **build** Earth's most customer-centric company, a place where customers can come to find and discover anything and everything they might want to buy online."[4]
- "**We live** in an era of extraordinary increases in available bandwidth, disk space, and processing power, all of which continue to get cheap fast."[5]
- "**Our energy** at Amazon **comes** from the desire to impress customers rather than the zeal to best customers."[6]
- "**We designed** Amazon Prime as an all-you-can-eat free program."

The subjects and verbs at the beginning of each of these sentences act as the locomotive pulling the rest of the thought.

2. ORDER WORDS FOR EMPHASIS

The British call a period a *full stop*. It's a perfect image for the period's role in punctuation. The period acts as a stop sign, drawing a reader's eye to the words that come next.

Many writing instructors suggest putting your strongest stuff at the beginning (the locomotive) and save an interesting word for the end (the caboose). Hide the weaker material in the middle.

Consider this famous line from Shakespeare's *Macbeth*: "The Queen, my lord, is dead." Shakespeare could have kept the subject and verb together by writing, "The Queen is dead, my lord." Instead, he starts with the subject and leaves the shocker for the end, just before the full stop. In Clark's words: "Shakespeare stuck the landing."[7]

Bezos structures many of his sentences with a strong locomotive pulling the weaker words in the middle before sticking the landing. Look at the following two sentences from his 1998 letter:

"We love to be pioneers, it's in the DNA of the company, and it's a good thing, too, because we'll need that pioneering spirit to succeed."[8] *It's a good thing, too,* makes the sentence conversational and advances his point, but it's stronger to end with *spirit to succeed.*

"Setting the bar high in our approach to hiring has been, and will continue to be, the single most important element of Amazon's success." Once again, Bezos puts the weaker phrase *will continue to be* in the middle. *Setting the bar high* and *Amazon's success* are the two most important concepts, which come after and before full stops.

In real estate, it's all about location. Apply the same strategy to your message. You might have built a beautiful house (a compelling idea), but a bad location will hurt its value. Quintilian, a Roman oratory instructor, believed that rearranging the words of a sentence could enhance its rhythm and move the reader/listener.

Effective writers think about where to place their words for greatest impact. Start with the strongest words, leave weaker ones in the middle, and end strong.

3. USE THE ACTIVE VOICE (MOST OF THE TIME)

John F. Kennedy loved Ian Fleming's James Bond books. According to Clark, "The power of Fleming's prose flows from active verbs."[9] For example, in JFK's favorite book, *From Russia with Love*, verbs energize the action: "Bond *climbed* the few stairs and *unlocked* his door and *locked* and *bolted* it behind him."

If the subject of the sentence performs the action, it's an active sentence. If the subject receives the action, it's a passive one. Here's an example:

Jeff Bezos founded Amazon in 1994. (Active)
Amazon was founded by Jeff Bezos in 1994. (Passive)

The active sentence is clearer and uses fewer words to say the same thing. In addition to being wordier, passive sentences muddle the message and confuse the reader as the message grows in complexity. The passive voice also sows distrust. Leaders often hide behind passive sentences to avoid taking responsibility. The joke among journalists is that a leader who wants to avoid blame says, "Mistakes were committed by some staffers." People hunger for leaders who take responsibility, and those who do use active sentences: "I made mistakes. The buck stops with me. Blame me."

Many writing experts agree that converting passive sentences into active ones will energize your writing. Stephen King blames the passive voice for ruining "just about any business document ever written." In his bestselling classic *On Writing Well*, William Zinsser says, "Use active verbs unless there is not a comfortable way to get around using a passive verb. The difference between an active-verb style and a passive-verb style—in clarity and vigor—is the difference between life and death as a writer."[10] And in the classic *The Elements of Style,* William Strunk writes, "The active voice is usually more direct and vigorous than the passive. For example, 'I shall always remember my first visit to Boston' is better than, 'My first visit to Boston will always be remembered by me.' The latter sentence is less direct, less bold, and less concise."[11]

In business writing, strive to use the active voice as much as possible. Sentences written in the active voice are easy to understand, get to the point faster, and shorten the number of words needed to express an idea.

The following sentence is active: The boy kicked the ball. The boy is the subject because he performs the action. Kicked is the verb because it expresses the action. The ball is the object of the sentence because it receives the action. Subject-Verb-Object. The sentence is short, simple, and precise. It leaves no doubt about who did what. It's better than the passive, muddled, clunky version of the same idea: The ball was kicked by the boy.

Grammarly only spotted one problem in the previous paragraph. It identified "The ball was kicked by the boy" as a passive sentence. Grammarly's recommendation: "Your sentence may be unclear and hard to follow. Consider rephrasing." Grammarly is right. Your writing will be stronger if you consider rephrasing passive sentences as active ones.

Reading headlines in high-quality business publications is an excellent way of getting the hang of writing in the active voice. For example, while I was writing this chapter, I noticed the following headline in the form of subject-verb-object: **Fed Raises Rates**. The rest of the article explained why the U.S. Federal Reserve Bank raised rates, how much rates rose, and what the action means to the average consumer. But if you only read the three-word headline in the active voice, you'll get a lot of information.

Here are more headlines that came across my desk (verbs are in italics):

Intel *invests* $20 billion in Ohio.

Home sales *hit* 15-year high.

Pandemic *blurs* economic outlook.

Inflation *accelerates* at the fastest pace in a decade.

TikTok *dances* past Google for top spot in web traffic (one of my favorites).

Writing in the active voice produces results that will compound over the course of your career. Imagine trying to gain admission to Harvard Business School, the number one business school in the world. More than ten thousand people apply, and about 11 percent are admitted. Harvard admissions officers acknowledge they look for candidates whose writing dazzles and shines. "An applicant must be able to communicate, in a relatively short amount of space, something that makes them human," says one Harvard executive director of admissions.[12] "Good communicators use simple language and short sentences to get their point across." This admissions director, as well as many college consultants, advise candidates to use the active voice to structure most of the sentences in their essays. The active voice conveys action and creates a stronger emotional impact. Stay active to stand out.

The next step to dazzling your readers is to unleash dynamic verbs on your audience.

4. UNLEASH STRONG VERBS

Strong verbs pack a punch. According to Clark, "Strong verbs create action, save words, and reveal the players."[13] Strong, meaningful, illustrative verbs demonstrate confidence and certainty. "Verbs, words of action, are the primary source of energy in your sentences,"[14] writes Gary Provost in *100 Ways to Improve Your Writing*. "They are the executives; they should be in charge." Provost says "weak" verbs are the opposite of strong ones: weak verbs are not specific, are not active, and are unnecessarily dependent on adverbs for their meaning. For example, in the sentence "The fox walked rapidly through the woods," *walked* is a verb that depends on an adverb *rapidly* for its meaning. A stronger sentence is, "The fox dashed through the woods."

"If you choose strong verbs and choose them wisely, they will work harder for you than any other part of speech,"[15] according to Provost. "More important, strong verbs will pack your paragraphs with the energy, the excitement, and the sense of motion that readers crave."

Deliver words your audience craves.

Bezos often chooses the active voice and strong verbs to describe Amazon's success. "The most radical and transformative of inventions are often those that *empower* others to *unleash* their creativity—to pursue their dreams," Bezos once said. In his 1999 letter, Bezos wrote, "We *listen* to customers, *invent* on their behalf, *personalize* the story for each of them, and *earn* their trust."[16]

"In many ways, Amazon.com is not a normal store,"[17] Bezos wrote in his 2002 letter. "We *turn* our inventory 19 times in a year. We *personalize* the store for each and every customer. We *trade* real estate for technology. We *display* customer reviews critical of our products. You can *make* a purchase with a few seconds and one click. We *put* used products next to new ones so you can choose. We *share* our prime real estate—our product detail pages—with third parties, and, if they can *offer* better value, we *let* them."

Choose strong verbs to energize your writing. Let's see how Jeff Bezos used action verbs to highlight several accomplishments in his 2009 shareholder letter:

- "We *added* 21 new product categories around the world."[18]
- "The apparel team continued to *enhance* the customer experience."

- "The shoes and apparel team *created* over 121,000 product descriptions."
- "Amazon Web Services *continued* its rapid pace of innovation."

Consider the verbs that propel your writing. Make your content dynamic.

In 2013, Bezos took readers on a tour of Amazon's initiatives. Each step of the tour began with an active sentence and a strong verb. For example:

- "Customers love Prime."[19]
- "Thanks to Audible Studios, people drive to work listening to Kate Winslet, Colin Firth, Anne Hathaway, and many other stars."
- "The Amazon App store now serves customers in almost 200 countries."
- "We [AWS] launched 61 significant services and features . . . the development teams work directly with customers and are empowered to design, build, and launch based on what they learn."

In 2016 Bezos revisited the Day One metaphor with a series of strong verbs.

Staying in Day 1 requires you to *experiment* patiently, *accept* failures, *plant* seeds, *protect* saplings, and *double down* when you see customer delight.[20]

5. AVOID VERB QUALIFIERS AND "WEASEL WORDS"

Persuasive leaders sound assertive when they use the active voice and prefer action verbs. They avoid muddling the message with "verb qualifiers" that are weak and wishy-washy (Amazonians call them "weasel words"). Here are some examples of verb qualifiers:

- Sort of
- Tend to
- Kind of
- Seemed to
- Could have

Let's reimagine some of Bezos's famous quotes with qualifiers. The first statement is what Bezos actually said and the second statement is the reimagined "weak" version.

Assertive: "At Amazon we obsess over the customer."

Weak: "At Amazon we tend to think that if we're preoccupied with the customer and actually obsess about them, we could probably be more successful over the long run."

Assertive: "Missionaries make better products. They care more."

Weak: "I sort of think that missionaries tend to make better products. They seem to care a bit more."

Assertive: "The keys to success are patience, persistence, and obsessive attention to detail."

Weak: "I kind of think that the keys to success are probably things like being really patient, very persistent, and sort of having a very obsessive attention to tiny details."

Assertive writers and speakers pay attention to words that are easy to remove. Common adverbs are a good place to start. Adverbs modify words—many of them end in *ly* and are easy to remove without degrading the sentence. You don't *really* need them. I mean, you don't need them. Are you *extremely* shocked or just shocked? Did the blast *totally* destroy the building, or did it destroy the building?

The late David Cornwell, who went by the pen name John le Carré, let verbs do the heavy lifting in his British spy novels. "I don't use adjectives if I can get away with it. I don't use adverbs,"[21] he told an interviewer for *60 Minutes*. "Get rid of anything extraneous."

"The adverb is not your friend," Stephen King once wrote. "The road to hell is paved with adverbs."

Adverbs aren't useless, of course, but they're often redundant or unnecessary in business writing.

6. VARY SENTENCE LENGTH

By all means, strive to condense your writing, but don't get hung up on keeping every sentence to as few words as possible. Break up the pattern.

Imagine if I had written this entire book in six-word sentences:

Jeff Bezos is a good communicator. His message is clear and concise. Bezos also simplifies complex, complicated ideas. Now the writing is growing stale. You're getting bored with the pattern. Short sentences are great, in doses. Your eyes and ears crave variety.

Great writers vary the length of their sentences to engage readers. They write short sentences, medium sentences, and much, much longer ones. According to Clark, "Long sentences create a flow that carries the reader down a stream of understanding, a steady advance. A short sentence slams on the brakes."[22]

Clark advises writers to "fear not the long sentence." Bezos doesn't fear the long sentence; he embraces it.

In the first sentence of his 2010 shareholder letter, Bezos writes: "Random forests, naïve Bayesian estimators, RESTful services, gossip protocols, eventual consistency, data sharding, anti-entropy, Byzantine quorum, erasure coding, vector clocks . . . walk into certain Amazon meetings, and you may momentarily think you've stumbled into a computer science lecture."[23]

Long sentences work best to list items or describe scenes. The key is to mix it up.

Here are two more examples of Bezos using a variety of short and long sentences in his shareholder letters.

- **1998:** The last 3½ years have been exciting. **(8 words)** We've served a cumulative 6.2 million customers, exited 1998 with a $1 billion revenue run rate, launched music, video, and gift stores in the U.S., opened shop in the U.K. and Germany, and, just recently, launched Amazon.com Auctions. **(38 words)** We predict the next 3½ years will be even more exciting.[24] **(12 words)**

- **2014:** A dreamy business offering has at least four characteristics: **(9 words)** Customers love it, it can grow to very large size, it has strong returns on capital, and it's durable in time—with the potential to endure for decades. **(28 words)** When you find one of these, don't just swipe right, get married.[25] **(12 words)**

The 2000 Amazon shareholder letter contains my favorite example of combining short sentences with long ones. Note how each sentence grows (a little more) in length.

Ouch. **(1 word)**. It's been a brutal year for many in the capital markets and certainly for Amazon.com shareholders. **(16 words)** As of this writing, our shares are down more than 80% from when I wrote you last year. **(18 words)** Nevertheless, by almost any measure, Amazon .com the company is in a stronger position now than at any time in its past.[26] **(21 words)**

The four sentences in this paragraph average 14 words in length, but they're not distributed evenly: 1, 16, 18, and 21 words, respectively.

Let's see how Bezos used a long sentence to provide a list in 2009, followed by shorter sentences.

The financial results for 2009 reflect the cumulative effect of 15 years of customer service improvements: increasing selection, speeding delivery, reducing cost structure so we can afford to offer customers ever-lower prices. **(32 words)** We are proud of our low prices, our reliable delivery, and our in-stock position on even obscure and hard-to-find items. **(20 words)** We also know that we can still be much better, and we're dedicated to improving further.[27] **(16 words)**

7. CONSTRUCT PARALLEL STRUCTURES

In the last example, Bezos relied on a grammatical device called *parallel construction*: using the same pattern to express two or more ideas, which gives the ideas the same level of importance.

For example, Bezos wrote that improvements are "increas*ing*," "speed*ing*," and "reduc*ing*." In the next sentence, Bezos wrote, "We are proud of our *low prices,* our *reliable delivery,* and our *in-stock position* on even obscure and hard-to-find items." The nonparallel form of the sentence would read: "We are proud of Amazon's lowest prices, the fact that customers get their products delivered reliably, and find most of their items to be in stock when they want them." Parallel construction adds power and cuts words.

Parallel construction makes a sentence smoother. For instance, I like running, golfing, and reading. I can also say that I like *to* run, *to* golf, and *to* read. It's not parallel to say that I like running, to play golf, and buying books to read.

A parallel message is satisfying to read and pleasing to hear. In many cases, the same text can be read or spoken with equal effect.

In his first shareholder letter in 1997, Bezos wrote: "We will continue to focus relentlessly on our customers."[28] Bezos followed the structure in a series of bullet points.

- We will continue to make investment decisions in light of long-term market leadership considerations rather than short-term profitability considerations or short-term Wall Street reactions.
- We will continue to measure our programs and the effectiveness of our investments analytically . . .
- We will continue to learn from both our successes and our failures.
- We will make bold rather than timid investment decisions . . .
- We will share our strategic thought processes with you when we make bold choices . . .
- We will work hard to spend wisely and maintain our lean culture.
- We will balance our focus on growth with emphasis on long-term profitability and capital management.
- We will continue to focus on hiring and retaining versatile and talented employees, and continue to weight their compensation to stock options rather than cash.

COACHING DRILL

In this chapter, I've offered simple writing strategies that will put you far ahead of your peers. But there's always more to learn from brilliant writing instructors whose books have a permanent place on my bookshelf. Here are a few titles that will elevate your writing skills.

Writing Tools: 55 Essential Strategies for Every Writer by Roy Peter Clark
Writing to Persuade by Trish Hall
On Writing Well by William Zinsser
100 Ways to Improve Your Writing by Gary Provost
On Writing by Stephen King

Keep in mind that when it comes to building your writing, speaking, and presenting skills, you're never done learning. Microsoft CEO Satya Nadella says you'll meet two types of people in the business world: know-it-alls and learn-it-alls. The know-it-alls don't last very long in the digital economy, where the pace of change is unlike anything we've seen in human history. In this environment, the learn-it-alls are the ones who shine. They adapt, grow, and thrive no matter what changes come their way. The great thing about writing is—while there's a lot to learn—there are a lot of teachers eager to guide us.

4

THE LOGLINE:
YOUR BIG IDEA

Amazon's mission is to be Earth's most customer-centric company.

—Jeff Bezos

Ouch.

With just one word, Jeff Bezos described the dot-com crash, a jarring stock market implosion that wiped out more than $5 trillion in wealth.

On March 10, 2000, the Nasdaq, an index mainly of tech stocks, hit a high of 5,132. What happened next sent a jolt of pain throughout the financial community, Silicon Valley, and millions of employees. Beginning in 1996, investors had started pumping money into speculative internet companies. No profits? No problem! Like all manias, this, too, would end. By April, one month after tech stocks had peaked, the Nasdaq lost 34 percent of its value. By October of 2002, the index had fallen nearly 80 percent.

Ouch.

It would take another four years for the index to claw its way back to the March 2000 level. Adjusted for inflation, however, it didn't recover for another seventeen years.

Ouch.

Silicon Valley alone lost two hundred thousand jobs.

Ouch.

Amazon's stock fell from $113 to $6 a share.

Ouch is right.

The word *ouch* originated as one of those ancient, short words you learned about in chapter 2. German immigrants who settled in Pennsylvania in the early 1800s introduced the word to America, a shorthand for crying out in pain. If you can find a single better word to describe the dot-com collapse, go right ahead, but I think that *ouch* speaks volumes.

Bezos didn't end his letter with one word, of course, but he didn't take much longer to get to his main message. Bezos covered a lot of ground in the following fifty-five words:

> It's been a brutal year for many in the capital markets and certainly for Amazon.com shareholders. As of this writing, our shares are down more than 80% from when I wrote you last year. Nevertheless, by almost any measure, Amazon.com the company is in a stronger position now than at any time in its past.[1]

Think about what Bezos accomplished in four short sentences.

- He grabbed the attention of Amazon's shareholders.
- He told them what happened.
- He offered them hope.
- He gave them a compelling reason to stick with the company.

Bezos gives a lot of thought to the first lines of his written or spoken material. First lines grab your audience's attention and set the tone for the rest of the discussion.

JAMES PATTERSON'S "DISTINCT ADVANTAGE"

According to James Patterson, the world's bestselling author, a great first line will give you "a distinct advantage" whether you're writing a book, sending an email, or delivering a presentation.

Among the many first lines that Patterson has written, the opening to his book *Private* is one of his favorites: *To the best of my understandably shaky recollection, the first time I died it went something like this.*

"That's a pretty cool first line, actually, if I do give myself some credit,"[2] Patterson recalled with a smile.

Patterson credits opening lines for helping to sell more than three hundred million books. He rewrites the first pages—and the first sentence—over and over until he feels they're strong enough to hook the reader. An opening line doesn't have to pull the reader *all* the way in, says Patterson, but if your reader or listener is quickly invested in the story, they'll stick around for the next part.

Amazon's senior leaders learned that they'd better get their boss invested in the idea and do it quickly. Bezos doesn't like to waste time and ends meetings abruptly if he loses interest.

Bezos holds his most important meetings at 10:00 A.M., when his focus and energy are highest. Like many CEOs, Bezos protects his time because he makes more meaningful decisions in one day than the average business professional makes in a year. When Bezos was running Amazon, he didn't just have responsibility for its e-commerce division, which shipped ten million packages a day. Bezos ran a company that provides cloud services for apps and websites that touch your life every day—from ordering a Lyft trip to streaming a Netflix movie, from booking an Airbnb to reading *The Washington Post,* and from attending a Zoom meeting to having conversations on Slack. In addition, he ran a company that produces movies, develops AI technology, and owns more than forty subsidiaries like Zappos, Whole Foods, and Audible. In this spare time, Bezos launched Blue Origin, a space exploration company. The guy's busy.

Most CEOs and senior leaders report that time is their scarcest resource. It's not uncommon for a CEO to get up to one thousand emails a day and a jam-packed schedule that's booked six months out. If you don't get to the point—and get to it fast—you'll lose their attention.

Many business professionals tell me stories of a time they made the mistake of preparing an excessive amount of material for busy leaders. Silicon Valley pioneer Andy Grove had a well-earned reputation for rebuking long-winded presenters. Even outsiders like the late Harvard professor and innovation guru Clay Christensen had to get used to Grove's legendary impatience. In his famous *Harvard Business Review* article "How Will You Measure Your Life," Christensen recalls meeting Grove for the first time.

Grove had read one of Christensen's papers on disruptive technology and invited the professor to Intel's headquarters in Santa Clara, California, to discuss the implications of his research. Christensen enthusiastically flew cross-country to share his findings.

"Look, stuff has happened,"[3] Grove said at the start of the meeting. "We have only 10 minutes for you. Tell us what your model of disruption means for Intel."

"I can't," Christensen said. "I need full thirty minutes to explain the model."

Grove let him begin, but after ten minutes, he interrupted the presentation and said, "Look, I've got your model. Just tell us what it means for Intel."

Christensen managed to squeeze in an extra few minutes. "OK, I get it. What it means for Intel is . . ." Grove then succinctly articulated how Christensen's model could help the company dominate the microprocessor market.

Christensen had to fight for every extra minute; it's not a situation you'd like to face. The fact is that CEOs, bosses, managers, clients, investors, and stakeholders are usually impatient. They may not cut you off after ten minutes, but rest assured they're giving you no more than ten minutes of their full attention. They're asking themselves a version of the same question Grove pointedly asked Christensen: *What does it mean to me?*

The people who work *for* you are also facing an increasingly demanding workload and more sophisticated distractions. Studies show that while the human attention span has remained constant since the 1800s, the number of things that compete for our attention has exploded exponentially. The human brain gets easily bored. We're constantly seeking alternative options to what we're doing at any given moment, a psychological fact that social media companies have leveraged to keep us hooked on their platforms.

In addition, the bombardment of digital noise that confronts us every minute of every day makes it tougher for any one message to stick. Five hundred hours of video are uploaded to YouTube every minute, 365 days a year. In 60 seconds, WhatsApp users send 42 million messages, Zoom hosts 208,000 meetings, Twitter users send 350,000 tweets, people send 188 million emails, and speakers give 25,000 PowerPoint presentations with an average of 40 words per slide.

Data never sleeps, but your audience does. They simply don't have the mental bandwidth to deal with the tsunami of information they're drowning in every minute of every day. As the volume of content continues to grow, our attention is increasingly fragmented, say researchers. And that's because we're novelty seekers, constantly looking for something "new." Today, not a second goes by when something new isn't available at our fingertips.

It turns out that the secret to catching a person's attention is not to cut through the noise but to boost the signal.

In the last thirty years, cognitive psychologists have reached fascinating conclusions about how people learn new concepts. For example, studies of effective teachers find that the best instructors organize information around big ideas. If you think about creating content in a hierarchical structure, the big idea opens your memo or presentation while details *support* your big idea.

When I was writing *Talk Like TED*, a book featuring the world's best speakers, I interviewed many experts whose TED speeches have gone viral. Nearly all of them had a similar reaction when they received the invitation: "How can I possibly squeeze everything I know into eighteen minutes?" The short answer is you can't.

Great TED speakers select one big idea they can express in bite-size messages. Brevity doesn't come from compressing a mountain of information into a short amount of time. Instead, brevity happens when you start with one big idea and carefully select the stories, examples, and data that support your big idea.

The next time you hear someone say, "Get to the point," what they're really asking is to see the big picture. It sounds so simple—just get to the point. But as you've learned, keeping things simple is hard work. So for help, let's turn to professional communicators—men and women who bring you the stories you love to watch.

THE LOGLINE

I adapted the logline concept from Hollywood screenwriters. When writers pitch screenplays to studios, they enter the meetings armed with a logline, a concise and compelling sentence that answers the question: What is my story about? A successful logline is twenty-five to thirty words that can be delivered in fifteen seconds or less.

Long before writers uploaded scripts to the cloud, screenplays were printed and stored in studio vaults. Then, studio executives wrote the title and one sentence about the movie on the spine, or log, of the script. Today, the logline is written in an email or delivered in a pitch meeting.

Try to name the movies behind these successful loglines:

A young man is transported to the past, where he must reunite his parents before he and his future cease to exist.

When an optimistic farm boy discovers that he has powers, he teams up with other rebel fighters to liberate the galaxy from the sinister forces of the Empire.

Two star-crossed lovers fall in love on the maiden voyage of the Titanic *and struggle to survive as the doomed ship sinks into the Atlantic Ocean.*

When his son is swept out to sea, an anxious clownfish embarks on a perilous journey across a treacherous ocean to bring him back.

You can probably guess each film, but, for the record, the answers are: *Back to the Future, Star Wars, Titanic,* and *Finding Nemo.*

Shonda Rhimes, *Grey's Anatomy* creator, says, "Pitching is the single most important thing that you can do once you've gotten in the door . . . If you are bad at it, it's a giant challenge. You have to figure out how to do it and do it well."[4]

Hollywood studio executives get dozens of pitches every week. If a writer fails to hook them—grab their attention quickly—the project is probably doomed. According to Rhimes, "A strong pitch captures the listener's imagination almost immediately."

The key to creating a winning logline is to take a page from Jeff Bezos—be customer-obsessed. For a screenplay writer, the customer (the audience) is a producer, director, or studio executive. While those audiences listen to a pitch, they're also thinking, *How can I market it?*

When Rhimes pitched *Grey's Anatomy,* she called it "sex in the surgery," a marketing-friendly comparison to a popular show at the time, *Sex and the City.* She says the logline worked as a sales tool because it gave executives a clear and concise idea of how they could market the show. Rhimes knew that the show would evolve from its original concept, but she had to convince the studio to buy it first. So she wrote the pitch with her audience top of mind.

A clear and concise logline will not necessarily sell the project on its own, but without it, a project has no chance of success. Successful loglines entice studio heads to stick around for the rest of the story.

Jimmy Donaldson doesn't sell films, but he creates content. Donaldson's YouTube channel, MrBeast, attracts more views than the season finales of *Seinfeld* or *Friends.* MrBeast has attracted more than sixty million subscribers.

Donaldson posted his first video at the age of thirteen and attracted only forty subscribers in his first year. Then, after a few years of trial, error, and carefully studying the algorithms that YouTube uses to recommend videos, Donaldson scored a viral hit in 2017. One day, he was bored and recorded himself counting to one hundred thousand. It took Donaldson forty-four hours to reach that number, and every minute of it is still on YouTube if you have a lot of time to kill. *The Huffington Post* posted an article about the stunt with the title "Watch This Guy Count to 100,000 for No Reason Whatsoever."

Although Donaldson's videos are now shorter, the stunts have grown more elaborate with the help of sponsored giveaways. For example, he surprised one of his subscribers with an outrageous gift in a video titled "I gave my 40,000,000th subscriber 40 cars."

Keeping the story line simple built one of the fastest-growing YouTube channels, according to consultant Derral Eves, who has worked with Donaldson. "If MrBeast can't explain a video concept in one sentence, he labels it as too complicated and scratches it,"[5] says Eves. "This content creation skill is highly overlooked and undervalued by most YouTube creators, but it's what sets great creators apart from the messages."

The following one-line titles garnered a combined two hundred million views, and the longest title is only fifty-four characters.

"I Gave People $1,000,000 But Only 1 Minute to
Spend It"
"I Opened a Restaurant That Pays You to Eat at It"
"I Opened a Free Car Dealership"

The first words that you hear Donaldson speak in his videos are the exact words in the titles, flashed across the screen in large text. In one sentence, the viewer knows exactly what they'll be seeing. Every week, Donaldson's videos attract more viewers than the Super Bowl. He starts with a logline, the big idea.

Strong loglines also attract investors in Silicon Valley, home to the world's leading venture capital firms. I've met with VCs who have backed start-ups with the names of Amazon, Apple, Airbnb, Google, PayPal, Twitter, YouTube, and many others. I have also worked with start-up CEOs and entrepreneurs to prepare them for IPO road shows, a series of presentations where executive teams pitch their companies to potential investors.

Investors are like Hollywood movie producers; they want to know the big picture before diving into the details. In short, what's the movie about? Below are several real loglines from start-up pitches.

- "Google organizes the world's information and makes it universally accessible." (10 words)
- "Coursera provides universal access to world-class learning so that anyone, anywhere has the power to transform their life through learning." (20 words)
- "Airbnb is a web platform where users can rent out their space. Travelers save money, hosts make money, and both share their cultures." (23 words)
- "Canva is an online design tool with a mission to empower everyone in the world to design anything and publish anywhere." (21 words)
- "Amazon is Earth's most customer-centric company." (6 words)

Don't make the mistake of pitching an idea or giving a presentation without a logline. One investor on the *Forbes* list of the world's billionaires once gave me this message to share with my readers: "If an entrepreneur cannot express their idea in one sentence, I'm not interested—period."

After you create a logline—the one big idea you want your audience to know—the question becomes where to introduce it. The U.S. military has put a considerable amount of research into answering this question. Their solution is taught as a communication technique throughout the branches and, as it turns out, at Amazon, too.

THE BOTTOM LINE UP FRONT

On a September day when the heat soared to a toasty 114 degrees in the desert of Yuma, Arizona, I met with a class of about a hundred U.S. Marine Corps aviators, the equivalent of the Navy's TOPGUN fighter pilots.

The pilots—the best aviators in the U.S. Marine Corps—were attending a seven-week program considered the most comprehensive aviation course in the world. During the Weapons and Tactics Instructor (WTI) course, aviators learn advanced technical and leadership skills in class and in the air. It may surprise you to know that verbal and written communication is considered an essential war-fighting skill. But of course, to-the-point, easily understood communication is essential to any enterprise that relies on coordinated expertise responding quickly and agilely to whatever challenges crop up.

Leaders in all U.S. military branches learn a communication strategy that applies to entrepreneurs, business professionals, and anyone who aspires to leadership in any field. It's called "Commander's Intent."

Commander's Intent is a statement that defines the mission commander's vision of a successful outcome: It must be clear, concise, and easily understood. It's the mission's big picture, the logline. The Commander's Intent should be easy to identify. First, it answers the five Ws: who, what, when, where, and why? Second, it's repeated at the beginning and end of the briefing. And third, it begins with the statement: "The single most important thing we must accomplish is . . ."

According to military communication instructors, Commander's Intent serves as a purpose statement that conveys the big picture clearly and concisely. According to one training manual, "Long narrative descriptions tend to inhibit the initiative of the subordinates." In other words, the men and women who carry out the mission need to understand the purpose of their mission in a brief, clear statement. Brevity clarifies, and clarity inspires.

Commander's Intent is not a list of bullet points; it's a written and verbal narrative with sentences that contain nouns and verbs. For example, "Our mission is to destroy the enemy's radar equipment at Objective Bravo to prevent the early detection of subsequent coalition air attacks." The sentence is written in the active voice and avoids vague orders like, "We will attack vigorously."

In the heat of battle, a concise and specific statement is faster to convey over radio than a lengthy announcement. As a result, the order is more likely to be accurately transmitted from person to person and far easier for subordinates to remember while they're under extreme stress.

When fighter pilots navigate mountainous terrain at seven hundred miles per hour, they don't have time to read or recall the mountains of detail they need to know to do their job successfully. By the time they see action, they've had years of experience and have spent thousands of hours in class, flight simulators, and training missions. They know how to do what they do. But knowing *how* to do something doesn't matter if they don't know *what* they're supposed to do and *why* they're doing it.

Think of yourself as a commander. Your mission is to inform and inspire a wide range of audiences, from individuals like customers, bosses, or hiring managers to teams of peers, investors, and employees. In one sentence, tell them what the movie's about.

Since Commander's Intent is the single most crucial phrase leaders communicate when it's time for action, they should make the statement at the beginning of a briefing. And that's why military leaders follow a precise and powerful communication technique called BLUF.

The acronym BLUF stands for *bottom line up front*. Although BLUF started as a writing technique in the U.S. Army, it is now taught in all military branches. While the U.S. Army can lay claim to coining the acronym, they're not the first to identify the need. During World War II, British prime minister Winston Churchill wrote a famous memo titled "Brevity," in which he argued for highlighting the essential points in lengthy documents. Churchill said most papers wasted time and energy because they buried the main points.

Stating the bottom line early has also found its way in every corner of Amazon, where it's taught in writing classes as BLOT (bottom line on top).

The bottom line up front (or on top) means what it says: it's the most crucial information your listener or reader needs to know. If they know nothing else but the bottom line, they'll know the big picture. It should be the first thing that your readers see in an email or hear in a presentation.

Amazonians write the bottom line in bold at the top of their emails. In one or two sentences, it tells the reader why they're on the email and why they should care about the rest of it. For example, in his first major policy announcement after becoming just the second CEO in Amazon's history, Andy Jassy sent a memo to Amazon's employees in late 2021 explaining the company's current thinking on back-to-work rules as the COVID pandemic began to subside.

The email's subject line read: "Updated guidance on where we work."

"Dear Amazonians," it began. "I want to update you on how we're continuing to evolve our thinking on where we work." In one sentence, along with the subject line, the topic of the email is clear.

Jassy then explains that the leadership team held several meetings to discuss the challenges and uncertainties of returning to the office. They agreed on "three things," he wrote:

> First, none of us know the definitive answers to these questions, especially long term. Second, at a company of our size, there is no one-size-fits-all approach for how every team works best. And third, we're going to be in a stage of experimenting, learning, and adjusting for a while as we emerge from this pandemic.

Jassy explained that for those who work in corporate roles, the decision on how many days a week they'd be required to show up in the office would be decided on the team level by individual directors. He added that decisions should be guided by Amazon's Leadership Principles—namely, "what will be most effective for our customers."

Here's an unspoken rule that you will not learn in business school: You're more likely to win over your boss or teammates with communication that saves time and energy, and gives them the bottom line up front. Studies show that you have fifteen seconds to grab a reader's attention in an email, document, or article. About 45 percent of readers will lose interest or drop out completely after fifteen seconds. If, however, you can grab and keep their attention past fifteen seconds (thirty-five words), they'll be more likely to stick around for the rest of the content.

AMAZON-STYLE PRECISION

If you'd like to write and speak with military-style or Amazon-style precision, your big idea must be clear, concise, and specific.

Clear. Amazon places a premium on clear communication. Amazonians are encouraged to follow these guidelines to clarify their verbal and written communication:

- Use the active voice to make it clear who is doing what.
- Avoid jargon.
- Strive for a Flesch-Kincaid grade level of 8 or lower.
- Make sure your idea passes the *So what?* test.

Since we've covered the first three communication tips, let's take a deeper dive into the *So what?* test. I use a version of it to help CEOs and executives uncover the logline for major announcements and presentations. Here's how it works.

First, accept that you're too close to your idea; you know details few others understand. Then, as you begin to craft a message, ask yourself: *So what?* Ask the question three times. You'll find yourself getting closer to the core message with each answer—the one thing your audience wants to know.

I've seen this process work for many companies, not just Amazon. Apple also uses it. Let's go behind the scenes of a hypothetical meeting at Apple as marketers and executives brainstorm the launch of a product—in this case, the M1 chip.

What are we announcing?
The M1, the first Apple chip specifically designed for the Mac.

So what?
It's Apple's first SOC (system on a chip).

So what?
It has sixteen billion transistors, making it the world's fastest CPU core.

So what?
The M1 chip is a gigantic leap forward for the Mac, delivering more power, faster performance, and longer battery life.

The final sentence is what CEO Tim Cook and other executives actually used to announce the first MacBook notebooks with Apple silicon.

This type of conversation is widespread in the early stages of creating a launch presentation. The experts in the room have worked on the product for months or years—they're smart but suffer from the curse of knowledge. They're not knee-deep in the weeds; they're in over their heads. Just as most people don't care about what's under the hood of a car, most computer buyers don't think about the engine that powers their system. The details are essential to communicate, but details are not loglines. Loglines deliver the big picture.

COACHING DRILL

Apply the *So what?* test to one of your presentations. Start with the topic of your conversation and answer the question, "So what?" Ask the question two more times until you craft a clear logline for your pitch or presentation.

Topic _____

So what? _____

_____

So what? _____

_____

So what? _____

_____

Concise. Communicating the Amazon way means writing memos, documents, and emails that are easy to read and understand. Amazonians are taught to keep sentences to twenty or fewer words. That means the writer must eliminate unnecessary words.

Vanessa Gallo coleads our business at Gallo Communications Group. Vanessa has a background in developmental psychology and uses her experience to help executives look and sound more assertive and confident. She parses the text of their presentations to eliminate extraneous words. Like a sculptor removes excess stone to reveal the masterpiece inside, removing excess verbiage reveals the full power of your message. Here's an example of how Vanessa streamlines messages. The original version is what a senior military instructor told students at the beginning of a class required to graduate from the program. Vanessa crafted a revised version that eliminated unnecessary words, got to the point, and provided clarity:

> **Original version:** "A lot of you are here because it's a requirement, but if you take the time to sit in class and it's gonna be a long class, right, because that's what we're working on in the summer, but if you take the time to sit in that class and do the work, you're doing yourself, your brain, your future self a favor." (62 words)

Revised version: "Most of you are here because it's a requirement. If you take the time to sit in class and do the work, you're doing yourself, your brain, and your future a favor." (32 words)

Jeff Bezos, leading by example, keeps his messages short and to the point. Take a look at the following three statements in table 4. In the first column, you'll see the actual words that Bezos wrote. In the second column, Vanessa and I created hypothetical, long-winded alternatives to his statements. The second column is the "bad" example, of course, but it reflects what we hear all too often from business communicators.

Table 4: Concise Quotes vs. Wordy Quotes

Shareholder Letter	Concise Bezos Quotes	Wordy Quotes
2018	"Third-party sellers are kicking our first-party butt. Badly."[6] (8 words; 1- and 2-syllable words)	"An interesting point to note—third-party sellers in our industry are outperforming us as first-party sellers by a noticeable margin, so much so that there is a substantial difference." (29 words; 6 words have three or four syllables)
2007	"I'll highlight a few of the useful features we built into Kindle that go beyond what you could ever do with a physical book."[7] (24 words; mostly 1- and 2-syllable words)	"During this next part of the presentation, I would like to review some of the dynamic features of the Kindle, a device we recently released with the intent to maximize this market that can execute more tasks than would be possible to execute reading physical books." (46 words; 7 multisyllabic words)

Shareholder Letter	Concise Bezos Quotes	Wordy Quotes
2005	"This year, Amazon became the fastest company ever to reach $100 billion in annual sales."[8] (15 words)	"Before I review the year and get into the details, I guess I should mention that Amazon reached $100 billion in annual sales. What's really impressive about that accomplishment is that we reached that number at a faster pace than any other company has been able to achieve." (48 words)

Specific. In writing classes, Amazonians learn to avoid vague language, or "weasel words."

Instead of saying "nearly all customers," be specific: "87 percent of Prime members." Instead of saying "significantly better," be specific: "an increase of 25 basis points." Instead of saying "Some time ago," be specific: "Three months ago."

Visit the Amazon newsroom for lessons in specificity. The logline (the first statement) in Amazon announcements usually contains precise information ranging from metrics and data to specific locations and target audiences. Here are a few examples (I bolded specific language):

- Amazon expands its Boston tech hub with plans to create **3,000 new jobs** to **support Alexa, AWS, and Amazon Pharmacy.**
- Amazon Launches **$2 Billion** Housing Equity Fund to Make Over **20,000 Affordable Homes** Available for Families in Communities It Calls Home.
- Amazon's new **one-million-square-foot** fulfillment center in **Oklahoma City** will create **500 jobs.**
- Amazon customers can now purchase **prescription medications** through the Amazon online store without leaving home. **Amazon Prime members** receive **free two-day delivery** and up to **80% savings** when paying without insurance, with new prescription savings benefit.
- Amazon is hiring **75,000 Employees** across Fulfillment and Transportation, with average starting pay of over **$17 Per Hour** and sign-on bonuses of up to **$1,000.**

BEZOS WORKS BACKWARDS

On February 2, 2021, more than one million Amazonians received an email memo from their boss. In twenty-two words, Jeff Bezos announced the most meaningful action he'd taken since launching the company. "Fellow Amazonians," he began.

> I'm excited to announce that this Q3 I'll transition to Executive Chair of the Amazon Board and Andy Jassy will become CEO.[9]

The reader knows what the email is about from the top sentence alone. Bezos works backwards: He opens with the most important takeaway—the logline—followed by details of the transition. Those details explain *why* he is making the change, *what* he will do next, and *how* the company he started twenty-seven years earlier has transformed the world.

Bezos's email provides a model of clear, concise, and specific writing, which you can see in figure 4.

Counts	
Words	620
Characters	2,959
Paragraphs	12
Sentences	47
Averages	
Sentences per Paragraph	4.7
Words per Sentence	13.1
Characters per Word	4.6
Readability	
Flesch Reading Ease	62.4
Flesch-Kincaid Grade Level	7.8
Passive Sentences	6.3%

Figure 4: Linguistic Analysis of Jeff Bezos Email

Clear: The email that Bezos sent begins with a logline, the big picture. If you stop reading after the first sentence, you should know most of the story. The entire email earns a grade level of 7.8 on the Flesch-Kincaid scale. Bezos writes most of the email (94 percent) in the active voice, which, as you'll recall from chapter 3, clarifies *who* is doing *what*.

Concise: The 620-word email can be read in just two minutes. That's a short amount of time to cover Amazon's twenty-seven-year history and preview the company's next steps.

Specific: The logline provides three specific points. Bezos will become executive chair; Andy Jassy will become the CEO; the transition will happen in Q3. Specific details follow:

- "In the Exec Chair role, I intend to focus my energies and attention on new products and early initiatives."
- "Today, we employ 1.3 million talented, dedicated people."
- "Invention is the root of our success. We pioneered customer reviews, 1-Click, personalized recommendations, Prime's insanely-fast shipping, Just Walk Out shopping, the Climate Pledge, Kindle, Alexa, marketplace, infrastructure cloud computing, Career Choice, and much more."

So what, exactly, will Bezos do next? Where will Bezos focus his energy? He explains in one sentence a logline that reporter Brad Stone stumbled upon while searching through a trash bin.

In 2003, Stone, working for *Newsweek*, conducted old-fashioned sleuthing to figure out what Bezos had planned for his new space company. Stone discovered an entry for Blue Operations LLC, an entity registered with a Seattle address matching Amazon's headquarters. He looked it up and found a vague website recruiting aerospace engineers.

Determined to be the first to break the news, Stone drove to an industrial zone south of Seattle to another address on the documents. He found a fifty-three-thousand-square-foot warehouse with the name BLUE ORIGIN printed on the door.

It was late on a weekend night. Stone couldn't see anything through the windows. Finally, after an hour of waiting in the car, he decided to walk across the street to a trash bin and carry as much as he could to the trunk of his car. Sifting through the items, Stone came upon a coffee-stained paper on which Bezos had written the first mission of Blue Origin:

To create an enduring human presence in space.

You can have the greatest idea in the world, but if you cannot express it in one clear, concise, and specific sentence, no one will pay attention.

5

METAPHORS THAT STICK

I named Amazon for Earth's biggest river; Earth's biggest
selection.

—Jeff Bezos, the Economic Club of Washington, D.C., 2018

Jeff Bezos ran Amazon for 9,863 days, but he always showed up to work
on day one.

"Day One" served as a metaphor for a start-up mindset. When Amazon
launched as an online bookseller, the company payroll covered about ten
people. By the time Bezos stepped aside from running Amazon's day-to-
day business some twenty-seven years later, the company had grown to
1.6 million employees. But a Day One leader, according to Bezos, always
reminds people to think and act like they're working in a start-up, finding
opportunities to learn, grow, innovate, and create.

The Day One metaphor made its first appearance in Amazon's first
shareholder letter as a public company in 1997: "This is Day 1 for the
Internet,"[1] Bezos proclaimed. He reminded shareholders who wondered
when Amazon would start showing a profit that, though e-commerce was
growing rapidly, online shopping was still in its early days. The real change
was yet to come.

The phrase "Day 1" appeared repeatedly in the annual letters Bezos
wrote for shareholders. In twenty-one letters, Bezos used the phrase
twenty-five times. In 2009, Bezos began closing every letter with the sentence "It's still Day 1." He changed one word from 2016 to 2020: "It *remains* Day 1." The 2019 letter was published in April of 2020, one month
into the COVID-19 pandemic. Bezos—addressing both shareholders and
employees—wrote, "Even in these circumstances, it remains Day 1."

By making reference to Day One with striking consistency, Bezos turned a metaphor from a figure of speech into a blueprint on how to think and act. To this day, the Day One metaphor is fully integrated throughout Amazon, acting as a shortcut to explain a mindset that embraces risk-taking, speed, curiosity, experimentation, failure, and continuous learning. The Day One message is hard to miss. Bezos named the Seattle building where he worked "Day 1 North." A plaque still greets visitors in the lobby. Bezos wrote the inscription that reads, "There's so much more stuff that has yet to be invented. There's so much new that's going to happen."

In 2016, Bezos answered a question that came up more than once at an all-hands meeting. Employees wanted to know: What does Day Two look like?

Bezos responded, "Day 2 is stasis. Complacency. The beginning of a slow and painful decline."[2]

The Day One metaphor has reached far beyond Amazon. It's become a management philosophy taught in business schools. A popular search term is "What is a Day 1 company?" There is no Day One company. It's not a physical thing. It's a mindset. It's an abstract concept that, like any good metaphor, acts as a shortcut to the transfer of knowledge.

In this chapter, you'll learn the neuroscience behind metaphors and why they're critical to convincing an audience. I'll take you on a brief history of metaphor as a persuasive tool and explain why 1980 was a watershed year for how we think about metaphor as more than a simple figure of speech. You'll learn why Bezos deliberately chooses his metaphors, and you'll meet other business communicators who rely on metaphors to turn abstract concepts into actionable ideas. Finally, you'll learn easy steps to find the right metaphor that will give your ideas the "clarity of angels singing."

GIVING LIFE TO LIFELESS THINGS

Let's start with the basics. What is a metaphor? A metaphor is a comparison between two otherwise unrelated things. That's the boring, standard definition of metaphor. I prefer a more exciting description offered by Ward Farnsworth, dean of the University of Texas School of Law and author of three books on classical writing. According to Farnsworth:

A metaphor can make unfamiliar things familiar, invisible things visible, and complicated things easier to understand. It can, as Aristotle said, give life to lifeless things. It can produce amusement by putting a subject into unexpected company. It can create feeling by boring it from the source to which the subject is compared. It can make a point riveting and memorable by the beauty of the comparison's fit. It can attract attention by the element of surprise. And it can do all this with wondrous economy, invoking a mass of imagery and meaning in a sentence or a single word.[3]

Metaphors are everywhere. You use them all the time, whether you know it or not. Are you *drowning* in paperwork? If so, you're sinking into a metaphor. Is your friend a *jewel*, a *shining star* with a *heart of gold*? If so, you're not just wading into the metaphorical pool. You're swimming in it.

On the fourteenth day of every February, Americans spend billions of dollars celebrating a timeless metaphor: the rose. Florists sell 250 million roses on that day; the most popular is the red rose, a symbol of love.

The legend of the red rose is traced to Aphrodite, the goddess of love in Greek mythology. She was said to be as beautiful as a red rose. Since then, poets have turned to the rose as an expression of love. When Shakespeare's Juliet says, "A rose by any other name would smell as sweet," she's acknowledging her love for Romeo despite the inconvenient fact that he comes from a rival family. Not to be outdone in the metaphor department, Romeo exclaims that "Juliet is the sun" because she radiates beauty and brings light to the darkness. Deep stuff.

Since many popular songs start their lives as poetry on paper, it's no coincidence that songwriters ride the metaphor wave to superstardom. Bret Michaels found the rose theme irresistible when he wrote "Every Rose Has Its Thorn." The rose signifies his career taking off, while the thorn is the damage his success had on his relationship. When Garth Brooks sings about "The Dance," he's not talking about line dancing at a Nashville honky-tonk. The dance is a metaphor for losing someone close to you. You would indeed have avoided the pain if you had never met that person, but you would have had to miss the happy times, too.

Of all the songs Garth has written, he says he receives the most letters about one in particular: "The River." When he sings about sailing his vessel "'til the river runs dry," he's not really the captain of a ship. He was a struggling singer who had a dream of making it big in country music. The dream is like a river, and Garth, the dreamer, is the vessel following the river where it goes. "Don't sit upon the shoreline . . . choose to chance the rapids and dare to dance the tide."

Jimmy Buffett can claim the most lucrative metaphor in popular music. When he initially sang of "Margaritaville," he wasn't thinking about a place. It's a state of mind, an anthem for a life philosophy. Once the song took off, it did turn into a real location—many of them. Margaritaville bars, restaurants, and products have made Buffett worth more than half a billion dollars.

Metaphors may not make you as rich as Bezos or Buffett, but if you can use language to create a state of mind—a feeling—for your listeners, you'll enrich your life and career.

We consume metaphors all day long. We write, sing, and even think in them. In 1980, the study of metaphor in cognitive science picked up steam with the publication of *Metaphors We Live By* by George Lakoff and Mark Johnson. Most people considered metaphor a literary device reserved for poetry and speeches. The authors argue that metaphor is more pervasive than that: "The way we think, what we experience, and what we do every day is very much a matter of metaphor."[4]

Lakoff and Johnson popularized the concept of conceptual metaphor theory, or CMT.[5] It means that our brain makes sense of our world by "mapping" one domain in terms of another. This finding leads to the fundamental rule of metaphor: It must contain a source domain and a target domain. The target is the abstract concept you're trying to get across; the source domain is the concrete thing you're using as a comparison. Source domains allow us to understand the abstract target and to communicate a lot of information in just a few words. Source domains usually fall into a few categories: motion, physical location, or spatial orientation.

For example, the concept of "life" is so abstract we have to think about it in terms of something more concrete to make sense of it.

We can use a motion comparison: *I'm on the fast track. It'll be smooth sailing from here.*

We can make a physical comparison: *I'm at a crossroad.*

We can employ a spatial orientation: *My life's looking up.*

COACHING DRILL

Search for comparisons outside your subject expertise, or "domain." See how many metaphors you can spot in books, articles, speeches, and presentations. Challenge yourself. Categorize the metaphors into motion, physical, or spatial comparisons. Being aware of the metaphors you see, hear, and read will spark creative ideas to help you write and deliver persuasive presentations.

It's almost impossible to describe a feeling, an abstract principle, or a complex idea without searching for an appropriate metaphor. According to art historian Nelson Goodman, "Metaphor permeates all discourse, ordinary and special . . . This incessant use of metaphor springs not merely from love of literary color but also from urgent need of economy."[6] In other words, metaphors act as mental shortcuts, condensing an enormous amount of information into one word or phrase. Metaphors allow you to paint a fast picture for your audience without getting bogged down in details.

Let's examine two metaphorical concepts that fueled Amazon's growth: two-pizza teams and the Amazon flywheel. In both cases, Bezos leveraged symbolic thinking and communication to inspire Amazon's leaders to think differently.

TWO-PIZZA TEAMS

After the tech bubble burst (another famous metaphor), Bezos took time off during the holidays to think and read. Weighing on his mind was the slowing pace of innovation at the company he had founded in the garage of his rented Seattle home. Although Amazon was a fast-growing company, engineers and product managers were frustrated with the complicated process of shipping code. Product development had been organized into a few significant divisions, and there were simply too many hands in the decision-making pie. "A hierarchy isn't responsive enough to change,"[7] Bezos said in a speech to the American Association of Publishers in March of 1999.

Bezos returned from his self-imposed retreat with a simple idea. If he organized teams as he had in Amazon's early days, each group could own their project road maps and software code, enabling them to move much more quickly. Bezos recalled that they could feed a whole team with two large pizzas. Bezos wrote his idea on a one-pager, and the two-pizza team was born.

The metaphor of a two-pizza team communicated volumes. It spoke
to the need for decentralized decision-making. It spoke to the need to
organize the company into small engineering teams that operated auton-
omously with only a loose connection between units. It spoke to the real-
ization that too much coordination among employees hindered speed and
agility. It even shortened a mathematical formula.

A famous equation called the "communication path formula" showed
that as teams grew larger, communication channels exploded among team
members, increasing the time required to share information and get the
work done.

The communication formula works like this:

$$N * (N-1)/2$$
N = the number of team members on a project.[8]

According to the formula, if you start with a small project team of
five people, there are ten possible channels of communication. Doubling
the group means the communication channels expand to forty-five. That
means a project manager expends 4.5 times the energy and time to keep
the team informed.

Bezos understood the formula, which was inspired by a book he had
read and recommended to his senior leadership team, Frederick Brooks's
The Mythical Man-Month.

Brooks, a computer scientist and high-tech veteran from IBM, argued
that throwing more bodies at a project didn't yield faster results. On the
contrary, an exploding increase in communication channels slowed down
the process.

According to Brad Stone in *The Everything Store,* Bezos hoped that
"freed from the constraints of intracompany communication, these loosely
coupled teams could move faster and get features to customers quicker."[9]
A well-designed two-pizza team had another powerful benefit: their nim-
bleness would allow them to course-correct if they detected mistakes or
had to make quick fixes.

As you can see, mathematicians and computer scientists had carefully
examined the strategy behind small teams. Entire books and arcane formu-
las were devoted to the subject. Bezos knew that he had to find a shortcut
to explain the concept.

Just as the time it takes to complete a project is directly proportional to a team's size, the speed with which an idea is adopted is directly proportional to its simplicity.

What could be simpler than two pizzas? The concept took off . . . until it hit a roadblock.

REPLACING TWO PIZZAS WITH SINGLE THREADS

Despite the promise of two-pizza teams, the metaphor had a shortcoming, according to former Amazon executives Bill Carr and Colin Bryar in their book, *Working Backwards*. Few people knew Bezos better than Carr and Bryar, who spent a combined twenty-seven years at Amazon and were on the ground floor for many of the most pivotal moments during the company's growth. On the subject of two-pizza teams, Carr and Bryar say small teams worked well in areas like product development, but they failed to increase speed or flexibility in other areas like the legal department or human resources.

The two-pizza metaphor was catchy and easy to understand. And yes, it was useful in some work environments, but not in others. Amazon's senior leaders figured out that the most significant predictor of a team's success was not necessarily its size but "whether it had a leader with the appropriate skills, authority, and experience to staff and manage a team whose sole focus was to get the job done."[10]

The model needed a new name—a new metaphor.

Since many of the company's leaders came from the fields of engineering and computer science, they mapped the new concept (target) to something similar in a source domain they knew well. They found what they were looking for in the term *single-threading*.

Computer programmers are familiar with threads: the processing of one command at a time. Many programming languages like JavaScript are *single-threaded*, which, by definition, means one line of code is executed at any given time. Applying the concept to leadership means that a team leader keeps a single-minded focus on one thing at a time: a new product, a new line of business, or a business transformation.

What started as teams that could be fed with two pizzas evolved into teams run by "single-threaded leaders," or STLs. According to Bryar and Carr, single-threaded leadership ushered in a new wave of innovation at Amazon because it allowed "a single person, unencumbered by competing responsibilities to own a single major initiative." The STL heads up a team that has the resources, flexibility, and agility to deliver on its goals.

The new metaphor triggered a surge of innovation like Fulfillment by Amazon (FBA). The idea was to give third-party sellers access to Amazon's warehouse and shipping services. Amazon would store, pick, pack, and ship on a merchant's behalf, eliminating logistics problems for these sellers.

Executives who worked in retail and operations loved the idea of FBA. But it languished for over a year because no one person had the bandwidth to manage all the details to turn the concept into reality. Enter Tom Taylor, a vice president at the company, who was asked to devote 100 percent of his focus to hiring and managing a team that would create FBA. The system worked for customers who wanted faster delivery and merchants who wanted a more flexible warehouse option to scale their businesses. One single-threaded leader solved a problem for millions of merchants and made millions of customers much happier.

A Google search for the term "single-threaded leader" returns more than five million references. The concept coined at Amazon has now become a popular management principle and shorthand for a leader who is 100 percent dedicated and accountable to a single initiative. That's the power of metaphor—it communicates volumes in a word or two and serves as a guide for employees as a company grows.

One hot Canadian start-up jumped on the single-threaded metaphor and rode it to riches.

Hopper is a mobile-only travel app that scored a record valuation in 2018 when it raised $100 million. The investment made Hopper the most valuable start-up in Canadian history.

According to Hopper CEO and cofounder Frederic Lalonde, a start-up in hypergrowth needs to look at everything differently: culture, messaging, marketing, and management. Lalonde is a voracious reader of business books and leadership methods. He recognized that the STL technique empowers leaders to act like owners, which leads to "hypergrowth velocity."

Single-threaded owners at Hopper are people who wake up and worry about one thing. The company has no product team, no engineering team, no data science team, no design team. Instead, Hopper is organized around small groups working on features or services to improve the customer experience. "It's like a loosely bound federation of internal start-ups with very strong multidisciplinary teams,"[11] says Lalonde.

Anyone at the company can grow into a leadership position. Once a leader is assigned with a single focus, they are in charge of building the team and putting the right people in place. The team might start with one or two technical people, providing just enough resources to begin building, iterating, and delivering something new to the customer. If the product or feature finds a market fit, the single-threaded leader has the authority to scale the team and grow the idea into a bigger business.

Lalonde credits the flexibility and speed of single-threaded leadership for helping the company double its growth during the COVID pandemic. As travel restrictions began to lift in the early part of 2021, Hopper was adding up to two hundred employees per quarter.

Hopper even adopted the two-pizza team metaphor, and added a twist.

In addition to the many books Lalonde consumed as he was building the company, he also studied behavioral science, where he learned that the most scalable organization in history—the one that grew the fastest—was the Roman Empire. Soldiers were placed into small teams of eight because that was the number of people who could fit into one tent. The Roman legion created "a distributed network" that ruled the Western world for five hundred years, says Lalonde.

And so, at Hopper, two-pizza teams have been replaced with Roman tents. Teams are organized into groups no larger than eight to ten people, with one leader who is accountable to the team's sole project.

While Roman tents and pizza teams are catchy and powerful management ideas, one former Amazon executive believes he discovered a more delicious metaphor—bagels.

THE DOZEN-BAGEL RULE

Former AWS executive Jeff Lawson adopted ideas from the Bezos blueprint when he started his company, Twilio.

Lawson joined Amazon in 2004 after the company had grown to five thousand employees. He asked the person who recruited him how much the company had changed since its early days when it had one hundred employees. Amazon, he was told, was "the same company with the same sense of urgency."

Lawson wanted to bring that sense of urgency to his start-up. He believed that small teams were the secret to making his goals come true. Lawson recalls that, despite its size, Amazon was structured like a collection of start-ups with small teams led by empowered, mission-driven leaders.[12] It was easy for Lawson to bring the small-team model to Twilio, which, after all, only had three founders, all of whom were software developers. If a customer reported a bug, Lawson could write the fix in five minutes. Three people made decisions quickly. They didn't even need two large pizzas. Three bagels would do.

In the early days of Twilio, the founders met for a meeting every Monday morning. Jeff would stop at a bakery for three bagels. As the company grew, so did the bagel order. Jeff bought half a dozen bagels, then a dozen, then three dozen. But Lawson began to notice the same trend that convinced Bezos to think in terms of smaller teams: At Twilio, the speed of innovation slowed down in direct proportion to the rising bagel orders.

At one point, thirty people reported to Lawson, the CEO. He noticed that the company wasn't running as efficiently as it did when they had fewer employees. Lawson, recalling the two-pizza metaphor from his Amazon days, came up with a solution to divide the group into three teams. One team supported existing products, while the other two focused on upcoming projects and internal platforms.

Instead of pizzas, Lawson's rule of thumb was that each team had to be small enough to be fed with a dozen bagels. As those three teams ballooned into 150 groups at Twilio, Lawson always kept the metaphor in mind: if a dozen bagels are not enough to feed the team, then it's grown too large. Today, Lawson likes to joke that Twilio is one of the most successful businesses nobody has ever heard of, even though it's likely you use its service without knowing it. Twilio's software is embedded in thousands of apps, from the text you get from an Uber driver to the code Netflix sends to your device before it lets you sign in. Building a company that consumers don't see required that Lawson think differently about communication in every step of the building process, from design to marketing.

Although Amazon found a better solution than two-pizza teams, the metaphor sparked conversations and ideas. You won't hear a lot about two-pizza teams at Amazon these days, but it's a handy metaphor that benefits start-ups and large enterprises alike.

Go ahead and pick a metaphor: single-threaded, two pizzas, a dozen bagels, or Roman tents. Better yet, come up with a new one that's unique to your culture and mission.

A two-pizza team might come up with ideas to make your company's flywheel spin faster. Ah, the flywheel. A chapter on metaphors wouldn't be complete without talking about the now famous flywheel—Amazon's secret sauce that powers its growth. It's also one of the most compelling metaphors in business history.

THE FLYWHEEL

In October of 2001, Jeff Bezos invited the author and business thinker, Jim Collins, to speak to members of Amazon's leadership team. Collins was about to release *Good to Great*, a book that would become a management classic. Bezos caught an early glimpse of the flywheel metaphor that Collins had uncovered in his research. Amazon adopted the concept to survive the dot-com crash and propel its growth for the next two decades.

A flywheel is a circular disk that rotates faster and faster as it collects energy. Collins says a flywheel is hard to get started. But after "pushing with great effort, you get the flywheel to inch forward,"[13] writes Collins. "You keep pushing, and with persistent effort, you get the flywheel to complete one entire turn. You don't stop. You keep pushing. The flywheel moves a bit faster. Two turns . . . then four . . . then eight . . . the flywheel builds momentum . . . sixteen . . . thirty-two . . . moving faster . . . a thousand . . . ten thousand . . . a hundred thousand. Then at some point—breakthrough! The flywheel flies forward with almost unstoppable momentum."

Bezos was taking notes.

On a napkin, Bezos sketched what would become known as the *virtuous cycle*. With "growth" at the center, the flywheel would be propelled by customer service, selection, and low prices. In a closed-loop system, the flywheel spins faster and faster as any or all of the inputs get better. For example, "customer service" can be improved by faster shipping, easier navigation, more selection, and so on.

According to Brad Stone, "Lower prices led to more customer visits. More customers increased the volume of sales and attracted more commission-paying third-party sellers to the site. That allowed Amazon to get more out of fixed costs like the fulfillment centers and the servers needed to run the website. This greater efficiency then enabled it to lower prices further. Feed any part of this flywheel, they reason, and it should accelerate the loop."[14]

Bezos was so enamored of the flywheel that he didn't include the concept in analyst presentations because he considered it the company's secret sauce. The flywheel made Amazon's consumer business the envy of the retail world.

Amazon's current leaders still refer to flywheels constantly in their conversations. As Amazon diversified beyond retail, the flywheel metaphor acts as the standard approach that each business division uses to fuel its growth, which, in turn, accelerates innovation in every other aspect of the organization.

For example, AWS, Amazon's cloud-computing division, does not sell products from third-party merchants, but it does sell unique tools for IT professionals. The more tools it creates, the more third-party developers it attracts. Tools lead to higher consumption of services and attract more enterprise customers. As it grows in scale, AWS provides lower prices for cloud services, attracting more developers, who create more tools, which draw in more enterprise customers.

Amazon Web Services appears to be very different from the consumer retail business, but Bezos pointed out their similarities in his 2015 letter. Remember, a metaphor is a device that shows how two different things are quite similar.

"Superficially, the two could hardly be more different,"[15] Bezos wrote. "One serves consumers and the other serves enterprises . . . under the surface, the two are not so different after all."

The two are not so different after all. Bezos is describing the principle behind metaphor's power. A well-chosen metaphor helps you translate words into concrete mental images. The flywheel effect sounds logical, but only with the help of a tangible object—the flywheel itself—does its potential become obvious.

COACHING DRILL

Metaphors act as shortcuts to understanding. They help your audience comprehend complex or abstract ideas. They are so effective, we use metaphors constantly in everyday conversation. But try to avoid worn-out clichés in your business presentations. Metaphors that are too familiar lose their impact. Here are some common figures of speech to avoid.

- The ball is in your court
- Bring to the table
- Think outside the box
- A drop in the bucket
- A perfect storm
- A fly in the ointment

Avoid reaching for the easy metaphor. If you've heard a figure of speech a thousand times, so has your audience.

HOW TO ADD METAPHOR TO YOUR COMMUNICATION TOOL KIT

Use metaphors to describe unique experiences or events. Before astronaut Chris Hadfield could take command of the International Space Station, he had to get there. He hitched a ride aboard a Soyuz rocket. About three hundred tons of kerosene and nitrogen fuel generated a million pounds of thrust to push the rocket past the gravitational pull of Earth and toward its destination.

Hadfield is one of only 240 astronauts who have been to the International Space Station. Most of us will never experience sitting atop a massive rocket as it hurls us into space. Hadfield, a skilled science educator, relies on familiar comparisons to explain what the rocket launch felt like. He brings us along for the ride when he describes a rocket launch.

Six seconds before launch, suddenly, this beast starts roaring like a dragon starting to breathe fire. And you can feel the rocket pulse with an overpowering amount of horsepower that's just starting to erupt underneath you. You're like a little leaf in a hurricane. You recognize that you're puny compared to what's about to happen. When the clock hits zero, that's when the big engines light, the big solid rockets beside you. It's as if there was an enormous accident, something just crashed into your ship as a huge pulse of energy goes through your entire spaceship. As those engines light, you feel like you're in the jaws of an enormous dog that is shaking you and physically pummeling you with power. You're helpless, but you're focused.[16]

Roaring beasts, fire-breathing dragons, eruptions, leaves in a hurricane, jaws of an enormous dog—these are concrete ideas to describe an unfamiliar experience.

Choose metaphors to breathe life into arcane topics. If you watch business news or follow the stock market, you've no doubt heard the phrase *economic moat*. Warren Buffett popularized the phrase at a 1995 Berkshire Hathaway meeting. A shareholder asked the question, "What are the fundamental rules of economics that you used to make money?"[17]

Buffett answered, "The most important thing we do is to find a business with a wide and long-lasting moat around it, protecting a terrific economic castle with an honest lord in charge of the castle."

The castle metaphor acts as a concise shortcut, a vivid explanation for a complex system of data and information that Buffett and his team use to evaluate potential investments. A deep moat gives a company unique advantages that make it hard for competitors to enter the business, protecting its market share. The castle draws its strength from an honest and decent knight—the CEO—protecting it. Buffett explains that the moat acts as a permanent and powerful deterrent to potential attackers.

Buffett revisited the castle metaphor in 2007 to explain one of the best performing investments ever: GEICO insurance. It offered low-cost products, enjoyed high name recognition thanks mainly to a famous gecko, and had a high profit margin.

Looking for castles with moats has proven to be a lucrative strategy for Buffett. Although GEICO is not a publicly traded company, one investment site estimates that Buffett made $40 billion on the investment, a return of 48,000 percent.

"GEICO is a jewel," Buffett once said. The billionaire just can't stop talking in metaphor.

Pay attention to the experts who appear frequently on television or whom reporters rely on for analysis. I spent fifteen years as a television news anchor, including a stint covering financial markets in New York City. I'll let you in on a secret: It's rare to find an expert who is also a great communicator. That's why a small group of personalities get an outsize amount of publicity. Economist Diane Swonk is one of them.

Diane Swonk's title is chief economist for Grant Thornton, but she says her chief role is to translate complex data into everyday language.

Swonk is in high demand as one of the world's most respected economists. She keeps a busy schedule of interviews, podcasts, and speeches as media outlets and government leaders turn to her for clear insights on the global economy. Her power skill is the power of metaphor.

Swonk told me she devotes forty hours a month to write her reports. She spends much of that time crafting analogies and metaphors to mine insights from a mountain of data.

During the COVID-19 pandemic, the U.S. government spent trillions of dollars to help struggling individuals and businesses survive the crisis. Trillions is a lot of money for people to wrap their heads around. In addition, the government introduced an alphabet soup of programs to distribute the money. Swonk helped viewers and readers make sense of it all. Here is a list of Swonk's most-quoted explanations. It should be no surprise that her most popular quotes are framed in a metaphor.

- "The economy went into an ice age overnight. We're in a deep freeze. It's going to take much longer to thaw the economy than it took to freeze it."
- "Covid is the iceberg, and we are trying to get the lifeboats."
- "We're going into the hardest mile of the coronavirus marathon."
- "The jobs report looks pretty ugly under the hood."
- "The Fed is running out of rabbits to pull out of a hat."

Swonk's gift is her ability to translate the arcane, complicated language of economics into words that are easy for people to understand. But she says that "gift" takes practice. "A colleague of mine once said, 'You make it look so easy.' They don't realize how much time it takes,"[18] Swonk told me. "But I am a diligent writer. The art of communication is something I've worked hard at because if you can't explain it, everything is lost in translation."

Don't let your message get lost in translation. Finding the right metaphor takes work, but it'll be worth the effort when you become famous for your communication skills.

COACHING DRILL

A simple metaphor format is "A is B" like "Time is money." The format works well to express complex ideas. Select a complex idea from your own subject area. Use the A is B format to explain it. Describe the comparison in conversational language.

Complex idea: _____ (A)

Familiar idea: _____ (B)

A is B format: _____ is _____

Example:

Complex idea: A good investment

Familiar idea: Castle with a moat

A is B format: A good investment is an economic castle with a deep moat around it to deter competitors.

Aristotle called the ability to master the metaphor a sign of genius. I hope this chapter has convinced you to unleash your inner genius and use deliberate metaphors to communicate your ideas.

Influential leaders use both metaphors and analogies to educate their audiences. Although metaphor and analogy are close cousins, there is a difference between the two. Bezos knows which one to reach for when he needs it. And in the next chapter, so will you.

6

A COMMUNICATOR'S "MOST FORMIDABLE" WEAPON

Midway between the unintelligible and the commonplace,
it is analogy which produces most knowledge.

—Aristotle

Bill Carr has a vivid memory of the meeting that transformed Amazon and launched the most exciting part of his career. While Carr doesn't recall everything that Bezos said at the all-hands meeting, one story stuck. It gave Carr the confidence to move forward on an initiative that he was initially reluctant to accept.

After four years of rising through the ranks at Amazon to become vice president of Worldwide Media, Carr's boss invited him to head the company's new digital media business. Carr didn't feel like he had much of a choice since Bezos had blessed the move himself. Nonetheless, Carr felt terribly disappointed because his career seemed to be taking off. As director of Amazon's books, music, and video, Carr ran a division that accounted for 77 percent of the company's global revenue. Carr was now being tapped to lead the company's smallest initiative. Digital ebooks, for example, represented under 1 percent of the entire book category. Although Amazon had launched a search-inside-the-book feature, it had almost zero experience in delivering digital products and services. It also hadn't built a hardware product. But Amazon crushed the e-commerce space.

Why change now? Carr thought.

Carr got his answer at the all-hands meeting.

"I remember the meeting like it was yesterday,"[1] Carr says.

"A lot of people had questions and concerns: Why was Amazon investing in an area it knew little about? Why should Amazon distract itself from the one thing it was great at? Why should the company build its own devices? What does Amazon know about digital media services?"

After listening to their comments and concerns, Bezos delivered his response in the form of an ancient and effective rhetorical device—analogy.

Bezos said, "We need to plant many seeds because we don't know which one of those seeds will grow into a mighty oak."[2]

The oak analogy was a brilliant choice.

An oak tree lives up to one thousand years, and Bezos is all about long-term thinking. An oak tree is large, and Amazon is all about offering a large variety of products. An oak tree is also resilient and strong, values Bezos associates with the brand. One oak tree produces millions of acorns during its lifetime. Each acorn contains a seed, most of which are eaten by animals. But every year, a few acorns fall to the ground, take root, and grow into mighty oaks.

"It's an analogy most people can relate to,"[3] Carr says. "It really helped people make sense of the decision Bezos was making. You can literally picture it in your head—the planting of seeds, giving them water, nurturing them, watching them grow. You can even picture that one or two of those seeds will grow into a mighty oak tree and you'll be sitting under it in future years."

Some of those seeds did grow into mighty businesses that go by the names of Kindle, Amazon Music, Amazon Studios, and Alexa.

"Jeff Bezos is a masterful communicator,"[4] Carr told me. "Analogy is superpowerful."

Bezos is the master of metaphor and the king of analogies.

An analogy, like its close relative the metaphor, is a figure of speech comparing two unrelated things to highlight their similarities. Its purpose in communication is to transfer knowledge from one person to another. Although an analogy can contain a metaphor, it's a more elaborate explanation than a single metaphor.

We like receiving information in the form of an analogy because we think in analogy. "Analogies are pervasive in human thought,"[5] says psychologist Diane Halpern. "Whenever we are faced with a novel situation, we seek to understand it by reference to a familiar one."

Our brains are constantly processing the world by associating the new or unknown with something familiar. When we're presented with a new idea, our brains don't ask, "What is it?" Instead, our brains ask, "What is it *like*?"

THE EUREKA MOMENT

Without analogous thinking, it would be nearly impossible to have a creative idea. Most major scientific breakthroughs begin with analogy. For example, the event that gave us the eureka moment was the result of analogous thinking.

In the third century B.C., a mathematician named Archimedes had a puzzle to solve. A goldsmith had made a crown for King Hiero, who had reason to believe the goldsmith had fooled him, making a crown of gold and silver. Could Archimedes prove it? After thinking long and hard about it, Archimedes was frustrated and took a bath to relax.

As he lowered himself into the tub, some water spilled over the edge. He realized that the water displaced by his body was equal to the weight of his body. Since gold was heavier than other metals the crown maker could have used, like silver, Archimedes could use the same experiment to figure out if the crown was made of pure gold. It wasn't. Archimedes was so excited that he ran down the street without getting dressed, shouting, "Eureka!"

Cognitive scientists cite Archimedes to prove that analogy is critical to the way we think. Our brains map the underlying structure of a known topic (Archimedes's bathtub) onto a target or unknown subject (the crown).

By providing a common framework through which to see an idea in a new light, analogies facilitate the exchange of information from one person to another. An analogy makes the abstract concrete.

Some analogies are better than others. Halpern conducted an experiment to find out which analogies are the most effective.[6] She gathered 193 volunteers ranging in age from seventeen to sixty-four. They read three scientific passages and answered questions about the material as soon as they had finished. One week later, they answered a second set of questions about the same information.

The experiments covered topics like the lymphatic system and electrical current. The participants were divided into three groups: some read about the topics in passages that contained no analogies, some read passages with "near-domain" analogies, while others read "far-domain" analogies.

A near-domain analogy comes from the same branch of science the audience already knows. A far-domain analogy compares one topic to another topic in a completely different area. The far-domain analogy for the lymphatic system compared it to the flow of water through the spaces of a sponge. The near-domain analogy compared the lymphatic system to the movement of blood through veins.

In the electricity passage, the far-domain analogy compared electricity to a water hose. The voltage is like the pressure that pushes the water through the hose. The current is like the diameter of the hose (the wider it is, the more electricity flows through it), and resistance is like sand in the hose that slows down the flow of water. The near-domain passage described electricity flowing through an electrical circuit.

The purpose of the experiment was to test people on their ability to recall what they had read. At first, the research did not find a significant difference among any of the groups immediately after reading the material. But when Halpern retested everyone one week later, she found significant differences. The people who read passages with far-domain analogies were able to recall much more of what they read and demonstrated a better understanding of the material. In scientific terms: "When the similarity relationship is more obscure, as in a distant domain analogy, subjects are required to seek underlying relationships in order to render it meaningful." Put simply, Halpern had discovered that ideas far outside of the subject matter leave a deeper imprint on a person's mind.

Halpern's experiment isn't the only one in the field. In educational studies, students who read technical material containing far-domain analogies tend to score higher on tests that measure comprehension than students who read the same material with no analogies. Far-domain analogies such as "The heart is like a system of buckets and pumps" or "The circulatory system is like a railway" are memorable and easy to understand.

If you want your audience to remember, retain, and understand your idea, use an analogy far removed from the topic area. If you tell me that life is like a living organism, I might not pay much attention. But if you tell me that life is like a box of chocolates, I'd be curious to learn why. Forrest Gump knew the difference between a lousy analogy and a good one.

> **COACHING DRILL**
>
> The first step to leveraging the power of analogy in your writing and communication is to be aware of just how prevalent analogies are in our everyday language. Take note of how many analogies you encounter in conversations, books, articles, and videos. Pay extra attention to popular writers and speakers who cover complex topics. You'll find that they're more likely to use analogies to transfer their knowledge.

THE HANDSTAND ANALOGY

Starting, growing, and running a business requires constant learning and feedback. Jeff Bezos could have said as much in his 2017 letter, but instead he chose an analogy that's as far away from the e-commerce domain as one can imagine—learning how to do a handstand.

"A close friend recently decided to learn to do a perfect free-standing handstand,"[7] Bezos wrote.

No leaning against a wall. Not for just a few seconds. Instagram good. She decided to start her journey by taking a handstand workshop at her yoga studio. She then practiced for a while but wasn't getting the results she wanted. So, she hired a handstand coach. Yes, I know what you're thinking, but evidently this is an actual thing that exists. In the very first lesson, the coach gave her some wonderful advice. Most people, he said, think that if they work hard, they should be able to master a handstand in about two weeks. The reality is that it takes about six months of daily practice. If you think you should be able to do it in two weeks, you're just going to end up quitting.

Running a business and doing a handstand are different topics in different domains, but they share structural similarities. Starting a business is harder than it looks. Hiring the best talent is harder than it seems. And writing an outstanding six-page memo is harder than you think.

Bezos continued with the handstand analogy as a reminder that achieving excellence in any skill, especially writing, doesn't happen overnight. It takes time.

"Here's what we've figured out,"[8] Bezos said.

Often, when a memo isn't great, it's not the writer's inability to *recognize* the high standard, but instead a wrong expectation on *scope*: they mistakenly believe a high-standards, six-page memo can be written in one or two days or even a few hours, when really it might take a week or more! They're trying to perfect a handstand in just two weeks, and we're not coaching them right. The great memos are written and re-written, shared with colleagues who are asked to improve the work, set aside for a couple of days, and then edited again with a fresh mind. They simply can't be done in a day or two. A great memo probably should take a week or more.

THE LIGHT BULB WAS THE FIRST "KILLER APP"

In 2003, Bezos electrified a TED audience with an analogy that shaped his thinking.

The internet bubble had attracted hordes of investors who poured trillions of dollars into money-losing companies. The index that tracks technology stocks peaked on March 10, 2000. It wouldn't reach that level again for fifteen years. The stock market plummeted 80 percent, sending investors and analysts looking for a comparison.

One famous analogy that began circulating was California's gold rush, a fitting story since Silicon Valley was ground zero for the dot-com boom. Bezos acknowledged that the analogy seemed to fit on its face but, while "tempting" to use, he had another one in mind.

"It's hard to find the right analogy to describe an event,"[9] Bezos said. "But how we react to events, the decisions we make today, and what we expect from the future depends very much on how we categorize events."

First, Bezos demonstrated why people reached for the gold rush comparison.

"For one thing, both were very real. In 1849, in that gold rush, they took over $700 million worth of gold out of California. It was very real. The internet was also very real. This is a real way for humans to communicate with each other. It's a big deal."

Both the gold rush of the 1850s and the internet followed the same trajectory: "Huge boom. Huge boom. Huge bust. Huge bust."

Bezos kept describing the similarities. "A lot of hype accompanied both events. Newspaper ads blared, 'Gold! Gold! Gold!'"

The stories fueled people's excitement. Many left good jobs to strike it rich. "If you were a lawyer or a banker, people dropped what they were doing, no matter what skill set they had, to go pan for gold."

Bezos said that some doctors even left their practices, and he showed a newspaper photo of a man named Dr. Toland riding a covered wagon to California. "The same thing happened on the internet," he added with a smile. "We got DrKoop.com."

The fallout also had its similarities. It came suddenly and left a lot of carnage in its wake. Bezos displayed a photo of the White Pass Trail, an infamous area during the Klondike gold rush. It's a mountain pass on the border of Alaska and British Columbia. It was called White Pass Trail until thousands of pack animals died along its rugged path. Today, it's known as Dead Horse Trail.

"Now, here's where our analogy with the gold rush starts to diverge, and I think rather severely," Bezos continued. "In a gold rush, when it's over, it's over."

Instead of a gold rush, Bezos chose a more precise comparison, "a better analogy that allows you to be incredibly optimistic." He decided to replace the gold rush comparison with the advent of electricity.

Once again, as all analogies do, it required an explanation. Recall from chapter 5, a metaphor is saying that one thing is another, *A is B*. In this case, if Bezos had said, "The internet is electricity," it wouldn't make sense. An analogy almost always starts life as a metaphor, but it needs a storyteller to bring it to life.

Bezos explained that prospectors had looked under just about every stone in California by 1849. All the gold had disappeared. Electricity is different. Once the infrastructure had been installed, companies began using electricity to make all sorts of appliances. The innovations never ended.

According to Bezos, the light bulb was the first "killer app." Next came electric fans, and electric irons, and vacuum cleaners, followed by an appliance that sparked envy among neighbors: the washing machine.

"Everybody wanted one of these electric washing machines,"[10] Bezos said.

He displayed a photo of the 1908 Hurley washing machine, which looks more like a cement mixer than the elegant top-loading machines you can buy today at Home Depot. They were dangerous, too. "There are gruesome descriptions of people getting their hair and clothes caught in these devices," Bezos said.

"We are at the 1908 Hurley washing machine stage with the internet," Bezos added. "That's where we are. We don't get our hair caught in it, but that's the level of primitiveness of where we are. We're in 1908."

If you think of the internet in terms of the gold rush, according to Bezos, then "you'd be pretty depressed right now because the last nugget of gold would be gone. But the good thing is, with innovation, there isn't a last nugget. Every new thing creates two new questions and two new opportunities."

Choosing a better analogy takes time and thought. But the payoff can be tremendous, in terms of clarifying your own thinking as well as that of those who work for you. And it can give you the confidence that you are on the right path even when most people believe otherwise. Choosing a better analogy didn't just electrify Bezos's presentation, it gave him the confidence to handle his critics. Bezos showed a series of headlines about Amazon that had appeared in the press:

ALL THE NEGATIVES ADD UP TO MAKING THE ONLINE
EXPERIENCE NOT WORTH THE TROUBLE (1996)
AMAZON.TOAST (1998)
AMAZON.BOMB (1999)

Just as people would use electricity for more than light, Bezos argued, they would use the internet to do more than visit a web page or place an order.

Bezos concluded: "If you really do believe that it's the very, very beginning, if you believe it's the 1908 Hurley washing machine, then you're incredibly optimistic. And I do think that that's where we are. And I do think there's more innovation ahead of us than there is behind us. We're very, very early."

Bezos was right, and his analogy proved to be spot-on. Anyone who had invested in Amazon on the day of the TED Talk—and held on to it until Bezos stepped aside as CEO—would have seen the value of their investment rise by 15,000 percent. Carefully consider the analogies you use to frame an event. The right one might make you rich.

Your message doesn't have to change to change how you deliver the message. What should change is the method you use to translate your idea into language everyone understands. Reach for an analogy when you're speaking about an arcane topic that's unfamiliar to many people in your audience.

Dr. Werner Vogels is the legendary chief technology officer at Amazon and one of the chief architects of AWS, the world's biggest cloud-computing platform. He once said the role of a CTO is to bridge the world of technology and business, a role that requires clear and simple explanations. After all, the cloud would be useless if people don't know how to use it, Vogels says.

In 2006, Vogels and his team at AWS announced the launch of S3, a "Simple Storage Service" that allowed customers to store and retrieve data easily from the web. The service jump-started the cloud revolution, but it was so far ahead of its time that the original S3 press release didn't even refer to "cloud computing."

Vogels says that while S3 made storing data on the internet easy, building it wasn't easy. Amazon's developers landed on an entirely new system that used "objects, buckets, and keys" to create a service that was scalable, reliable, and affordable. If you're not a computer programmer, it's unlikely that those terms mean anything to you, so Vogels picked something familiar—a library—to explain how the system worked.

"One analogy for the S3 team built is the classic library,"[11] Vogels said.

In our S3 library, books are objects. Objects can be any form of data: a photo, a piece of music, a document, a call center exchange. Objects are stored in buckets. In the library analogy, buckets exist like the art history or geology section in a library. Buckets are how you classify and organize all the objects inside. Buckets can contain a single object or literally millions of objects or topics. Think of the keys as our library's card catalogue. Keys contain a bit of unique information about each of those objects within a bucket. Every object in a bucket has exactly one key. You use keys to head to the right bucket and find the right object.

The analogy helped to explain how the storage system was built to scale as the demand for data grew exponentially. On the fifteenth anniversary of the service in 2020, Vogels announced that one hundred trillion objects reside in S3 buckets. "While this doesn't make it easy to wrap our heads around," he added, "100 trillion is about equal to the number of synapses in the human brain or cells in the human body."

Vogels is constantly searching for comparisons to bridge the languages of technology and business.

Analogy is an ancient communication device, but its power to educate is more important than ever today as the world's information grows in volume and complexity. Enhance your language with carefully chosen analogies and you'll electrify your audiences.

Analogies and metaphors are the building blocks of stories, so it shouldn't come as any surprise that great storytellers use these figures of speech to make connections between familiar and unfamiliar things. In part 2, we'll explore the art of crafting stories to educate, persuade, motivate, and inspire. Great storytellers get accepted into the world's most elite universities. Great storytellers get hired for top jobs. Great storytellers attract investors for their start-ups. And great storytellers inspire others to do the impossible.

Part II

BUILD THE STORY STRUCTURE

7

EPIC STORYTELLING IN THREE ACTS

Jeff Bezos has never outgrown his wonder years . . . His interest in narrative and storytelling not only comes from Amazon's roots in the bookselling business; it is also a personal passion.

—Walter Isaacson

Picture the opening scene of a movie on the life of Jeff Bezos. The screenplay might begin with a terrifying event that came close to ending his life:

OPENING
EXTERNAL SCENE. MOUNTAIN IN SOUTHWEST
TEXAS—10:00 A.M.

The audience hears the whirring of helicopter blades over the rugged, jagged terrain of Cathedral Mountain in Southwest Texas.

CUT TO: The chopper is lifting off. It's a five-seat ruby-red Gazelle. Suddenly, a strong wind throws the helicopter off balance.

CUT TO: Extreme close-up of the panic on the faces of three passengers as the pilot tries to regain control. The passengers are Jeff, a billionaire, accompanied by an attorney, a cowboy, and a pilot nicknamed "Cheater."

Cheater is fighting frantically to keep control as the chopper struggles to clear a tree line. The chopper bucks like a rodeo bronco. It clips a mound of dirt and topples over. The rotor blades snap off and splinter into shards that come dangerously close to slicing into the cabin. The chassis rolls and tumbles into a creek. It lands upside down in a creek partially filled with water.

CUTAWAY: A sign near the crash site reads, "Calamity Creek."

Silence.

CUT TO CRASH: Creek water gushes into the cabin. The cowboy inadvertently gets a mouthful as he jostles to free himself from the seat belt that saved his life. The attorney is pinned underwater. The others scramble to save her. When her head rises above water, she gasps for breath. She feels intense pain in her back, but she's alive.

The passengers climb out of the helicopter and gather on the creek bank. They all have cuts, bruises, and soreness. They look at the chopper lying on its side in the creek. They know they're lucky to be alive.

Jeff turns to the cowboy and says, "You were right. We should have used horses."

FADE OUT as the billionaire who had cheated death lets out a full-throttled laugh that booms through the canyon.

The details of this story are true. The crash happened at 10:00 A.M. on March 6, 2003. The winds were gusty and unpredictable in the higher elevations of Southwest Texas during that time of year.

Jeff Bezos was riding in the chopper, along with his attorney, Elizabeth Korrell, and real-life cowboy Ty Holland, a local rancher who knew the backcountry better than anyone. Holland's experience with the wind patterns in the area in the made him nervous. Earlier that morning, Holland had suggested the group avoid taking a chopper and ride horses instead.

The locals knew about Charles "Cheater" Bella. Cheater's role in a prison break cemented his reputation. According to the *El Paso Times,* on July 11, 1997, Bella "was part of a botched attempt to fly three inmates from the Penitentiary of New Mexico near Santa Fe. He said he was forced to do so at gunpoint."[1] Bella flew the same helicopter he piloted in the movie *Rambo III* with Sylvester Stallone.

Some stories write themselves.

We later learned why Bezos was touring the remote area. He was scouting locations for his space company, Blue Origin. It would launch its first test flight two years after the accident. In July 2021, Bezos and his brother, Mark, became the first humans his company would launch into space.

Although Bezos was building the company in secret, his enthusiasm for storytelling showed up in the company's establishing documents. Bezos bought land under strange-sounding corporate entities like Zefram LLC, named for Zefram Cochrane, a *Star Trek* character who invented technology allowing humans to travel at warp speed, faster than light. Bezos asked his friend, science-fiction author Neal Stephenson, to act as the principal advisor on the new venture.

"Jeff's interest in narrative and storytelling not only comes from Amazon's roots in the bookselling business; it is also a personal passion,"[2] says author Walter Isaacson. "As a kid, Bezos read dozens of science fiction novels each summer at a local library, and he now hosts an annual retreat for writers and moviemakers . . . he connects this love of the humanities and his passion for technology to his instinct for business."

Isaacson's observation applies to most influential leaders—they share a passion for storytelling. Billionaire investor and former Amazon board member John Doerr told me that entrepreneurs who make real change are leaders who reach both the head and the heart. The most direct path to the heart is through stories. And not just any story, says Doerr, but a story that has an arc, a structure that engages the listener.

In this chapter, I'll reveal a proven, time-tested blueprint that great stories have followed over thousands of years across countries and cultures. You'll learn how to apply the same storytelling structure used to make Hollywood blockbusters and to create a mesmerizing business presentation. And you'll see how Bezos and other business storytellers follow the template to craft speeches and public presentations. Once you learn the model's simple steps, you'll be able to adapt it so you, too, can wow your audiences.

Let's begin by exploring the structure that makes storytelling as simple as one-two-three.

THE THREE-ACT STRUCTURE

More than two thousand years ago, Aristotle, the father of persuasion, identified the three parts of a story. A story, he said, must have a beginning, middle, and end. Aristotle's observation makes sense to us because it mirrors the journey of our lives: We're born. We live. We die.

Okay, fair enough. I think we can all accept Aristotle's basic outline that a story has a beginning, middle, and end. But it's not very helpful unless and until we learn exactly how to create content to fit into those parts.

You're probably wondering: If most stories have the same three parts, then why aren't they all alike? The answer lies in their common structure. A story has three parts, but what's in the three parts makes all the difference. The key is learning just how much fun you can have *within* the structure.

Structure doesn't confine creativity; structure unshackles it.

Aristotle is the father of persuasion, but Syd Field is the godfather of screenwriting. According to *The Hollywood Reporter,* Field was the most sought-after screenplay teacher in the world. Field didn't invent the three-act structure that serves as the foundation of almost every one of your favorite films; he identified it as the foundation of all *good* stories.

Act 1 is the setup. As its name implies, the first act of a screenplay sets up the story: introduces and establishes characters, launches the story's central premise, illustrates the world in which the characters live, and creates relationships between the main character and others who inhabit their world. The first few minutes of act 1 are critical, not only in movies but in business presentations. The opening scene must hook your audience, enticing them to pay attention to the rest of the story.

Act 2 is the challenge. In the middle of the story, the hero is tested, encounters villains, obstacles, and conflicts that stand in the way of achieving their dream. Overcoming these hurdles moves the story forward and keeps the audience invested and engaged. Screenwriter Aaron Sorkin says he worships at the altar of intention and obstacle: somebody wants something, and someone stands in their way. Syd Field put it best: "Without conflict, you have no action; without action, you have no character; without character, you have no story; and without story, you have no screenplay."[3]

Act 3 is the resolution. In the third and final act, the hero finds a solution to their problem, achieves their dream, and—this is critical—*transforms* themselves or the world for the better. They return from their adventure with a treasure, often in the form of newfound wisdom.

Don't confuse the three-act structure with a formula. Structure is a model that reveals the construction of a good story in any form—movies, novels, and business presentations. A formula implies that the output is the same each and every time. A formula strips content of its creativity; a structure unleashes creativity.

Star Wars: **A classic three-act story.** Although I can pick almost any successful movie to demonstrate the three-act structure, I'll stick to the film franchise most people recognize. The original 1977 George Lucas creation, *Star Wars: A New Hope,* is a classic example of three-act story-telling.

Act 1: We learn about the young farm boy Luke Skywalker. We see where he lives and what his life is like before the adventure begins. We make an emotional investment in the character as we learn about his hopes, dreams, and frustrations—the qualities that make him relatable to us, even though he lives in a galaxy far, far away.

We also meet most of the main characters who accompany Luke on his adventure or get in his way: Darth Vader, Leia, Obi-Wan Kenobi, R2-D2, and C-3PO. Han Solo and Chewy get their introductions early in act 2.

The premise of the story is revealed in the first ten minutes of act 1. The rebel forces must defeat the evil Empire to bring peace to the galaxy. Darth Vader captures Princess Leia, who cleverly hides the technical plans to destroy the Death Star in the memory banks of R2-D2.

Act 2: Luke faces a series of ever-menacing obstacles and villains who stand in the way of achieving his goal to rescue the princess and get the plans into the hands of the good guys. Standing in his way are Vader, stormtroopers, and a close call with a hideous creature who lives in the trash.

Act 3: The final duel between Luke (the protagonist) and Darth Vader (the antagonist). Luke destroys the Death Star and restores peace to the galaxy. Luke and his friends receive medals for aiding the Rebel Alliance, and everyone lives happily ever after—until the next episode.

You'll find the three-act structure followed to the letter in almost every film or show on Netflix, YouTube, Amazon Prime, Disney+, or your favorite streaming service. Even director James Cameron, who likes to deviate from the model from time to time (*Terminator* is five acts with a coda), says he starts writing with the three-act structure in mind. It's good to know the rules before you break them, says Cameron. Figure 7 is a visual display of

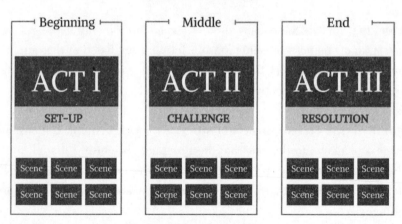

Figure 7: Three-Act Structure

how the three-act structure lends itself to creating a journey from beginning to end.

Here's the key to using this model as a blueprint to building a presentation: Most stories follow the three-act structure, but not all stories that follow the three-act structure are good. The difference between a story and a great one lies in a story's scenes, or "beats."

Essential scenes, or "beats." Beats are events that drive a story forward. They create the suspense, tension, and excitement that audiences adore. By building the following four beats into your pitches and presentations, your audience will be riveted to every word.

Catalyst: In screenplay writing, the catalyst is often called the "inciting incident," an event that disrupts the status quo, starts the adventure, and drives the story forward. Writers of romantic comedies are experts in crafting this scene. In *Notting Hill,* Anna (Julia Roberts) and William (Hugh Grant) bump into each other on a street corner. William spills orange juice on the front of Anna's blouse but, conveniently, his apartment is nearby. The sparks fly and the adventure begins.

Always consider the catalyst when you're creating a presentation. What was the spark that lit your passion for the idea? It might have been an event that you experienced, a problem you encountered, a mentor who inspired you, a book you read, or a trip you took. Howard Schultz visited a café in Milan, which inspired him to start Starbucks. Something happened that prompted you to think the way you do. Share the catalyst with your audience.

Debate: Even heroes have their doubts. They need to do some soul-searching or confer with other characters before choosing to embark on their journey. Change is scary. Since most people prefer the status quo, we can relate to others who want things to stay the same. But we love to see those outliers who find the courage to follow their dreams and seek a life of adventure. The classic example of this beat occurs thirty-five minutes into *Star Wars*. After seeing a very cool hologram from Princess Leia asking for help, Luke Skywalker has no intention of joining Obi-Wan Kenobi on the adventure. Once Luke sees the full evil of the Galactic Empire, however, he changes his mind. He wants to learn the ways of the Force and become a Jedi like his father. There's no turning back.

Before you decided to embark on your adventure, was there a moment of doubt? More important, what gave you the confidence to pursue your goal? How did you overcome the critics and naysayers who said you would never accomplish what you set out to do?

Netflix cofounder Marc Randolph told me that the most common reaction he received when he told people about his idea was, "That will never work." He began to think that maybe they were right. But his passion for problem-solving, confronting real problems, and testing solutions kept him motivated. You've probably been in a similar situation, a time in your life when someone told you, "That will never work." How you overcame those internal doubts or critics is a critical scene to include in your story.

Fun and Games: This is the fun part of a screenplay or business presentation. These beats are easy to spot and necessary to break up the tension. We don't always want to see the main character struggle. We crave lighter moments. These scenes are quirky, surprising, or funny escapades. Fun and games appear in every *Harry Potter* film. For example, when Harry arrives at Hogwarts, Harry is sorted into Gryffindor, where he explores the castle and plays on the house Quidditch team.

Most people get bored quickly in business presentations because there's little or no entertainment value. Find the fun. Sara Blakely credits her ability to find humor in a situation for her success at pitching SPANX. With no experience in fashion, no business school experience, and just $5,000 in savings, Blakely wasn't feeling very optimistic about her prospects. But when she couldn't find a suitable undergarment to wear at a party, she cut the feet out of a pair of pantyhose and felt great about the way they made her look. Blakely tells that story and many other funny anecdotes about funding and building her company. It's should come as no surprise that Blakely made humor one of SPANX's core values.

<u>All Is Lost:</u> This is my favorite scene in a film and, yes, in a business presentation. In a movie, it's the scene when two star-crossed lovers lose all hope that they'll ever be together, or the heroes in *Star Wars* are inches away from being crushed in the compactor. The main character is as far as possible from achieving their dreams—or so it seems. But how they climb out of the "dark night of the soul" is what gives a story its power to inspire.

James Dyson frequently tells the story of "failing" 5,126 times before he successfully built the first bagless vacuum, a product that would make him a billionaire. The odds were stacked against him. He was running out of time and money. But with every failure, Dyson learned something that brought him closer to his goal. The lesson he learned is that failure is to be welcomed, not feared.

COACHING DRILL

Consider your own presentation. Identify essential scenes or "beats" that you can incorporate into the narrative. These scenes keep the action moving and the audience engaged. Find events in your life or in your business that fall into one of these categories:

Catalyst: _____

Debate: _____

Fun and Games: _____

All Is Lost: _____

IT'S STILL DAY ONE

We've covered the three-act structure and the beats that turn a good story into a great one. Now let's examine how Jeff Bezos applies the structure to the Amazon story.

The COVID pandemic prevented Jeff Bezos from appearing in person for a congressional hearing on July 29, 2020. But though Bezos delivered the speech remotely from his Seattle office 2,700 miles away, he owned the room in a speech *The Wall Street Journal* called "inspiring, powerful, and compelling." The newspaper took the unusual step of quoting 350 words directly from the testimony. Although Bezos had included many metrics about Amazon in his speech, the newspaper chose to excerpt only those words where Bezos shared stories. "It's hard not to stand up and cheer," according to the article. After the speech, a CNBC anchor said, "Wow. That was inspiring. What a great story." Your audience will not remember everything about your presentation. They will not retain all the information and data you delivered. But they will remember the stories you tell.

The Bezos speech in the U.S. House of Representatives offers an excellent example of the three-act structure in action, along with scene beats. All of the following text is from one speech, which demonstrates how closely Bezos adheres to the storytelling structure.

Logline. I'm Jeff Bezos. I founded Amazon 26 years ago with the long-term mission of making it Earth's most customer-centric company.[4]

ACT 1

My mom, Jackie, had me when she was a 17-year-old high school student in Albuquerque, New Mexico. Being pregnant in high school was not popular in Albuquerque in 1964. It was difficult for her. When they tried to kick her out of school, my grandfather went to bat for her. After some negotiation, the principal said, "OK, she can stay and finish high school, but she can't do any extracurricular activities, and she can't have a locker." My grandfather took the deal, and my mother finished high school, though she wasn't allowed to walk across the stage with her classmates to get her diploma. Determined to keep up with her education, she enrolled in night school, picking classes led by professors who would let her bring an infant to class. She would show up with two duffel bags—one full of textbooks and one packed with diapers, bottles, and anything that would keep me interested and quiet for a few minutes.

My dad's name is Miguel. He adopted me when I was four years old. He was 16 when he came to the United States from Cuba as part of Operation Pedro Pan, shortly after Castro took over. My dad arrived in America alone. His parents felt he'd be safer here. His mom imagined America would be cold, so she made him a jacket sewn entirely out of cleaning cloths, the only material they had on hand. We still have that jacket; it hangs in my parents' dining room. My dad spent two weeks at Camp Matecumbe, a refugee center in Florida, before being moved to a Catholic mission in Wilmington, Delaware. He was lucky to get to the mission, but even so, he didn't speak English and didn't have an easy path. What he did have was a lot of grit and determination. He received a scholarship to college in Albuquerque, which is where he met my mom. You get different gifts in life, and one of my great gifts is my mom and dad. They have been incredible role models for me and my siblings our entire lives.

You learn different things from your grandparents than you do from your parents, and I had the opportunity to spend my summers from ages four to 16 on my grandparents' ranch in Texas. My grandfather was a civil servant and a rancher—he worked on space technology and missile-defense systems in the 1950s and '60s for the Atomic Energy Commission—and he was self-reliant and resourceful. When you're in the middle of nowhere, you don't pick up a phone and call somebody when something breaks. You fix it yourself. As a kid, I got to see him solve many seemingly unsolvable problems himself, whether he was restoring a broken-down Caterpillar bulldozer or doing his own veterinary work. He taught me that you can take on hard problems. When you have a setback, you get back up and try again. You can invent your way to a better place.

Debate

At the time, I was working at an investment firm in New York City. When I told my boss I was leaving, he took me on a long walk in Central Park. After a lot of listening, he finally said, "You know what, Jeff, I think this is a good idea, but it would be a better idea for somebody who didn't already have a good job." He convinced me to think about it for two days before making a final decision. It was a decision I made with my heart and not my head. When I'm 80 and reflecting back, I want to have minimized the number of regrets that I have in my life. And most of our regrets are acts of omission—the things we didn't try, the paths untraveled.

Fun and Games

I took these lessons to heart as a teenager and became a garage inventor. I invented an automatic gate closer out of cement-filled tires, a solar cooker out of an umbrella and tinfoil, and alarms made from baking pans to entrap my siblings.

ACT 2

The initial start-up capital for Amazon.com came primarily from my parents, who invested a large fraction of their life savings in something they didn't understand. They weren't making a bet on Amazon or the concept of a bookstore on the internet. They were making a bet on their son. I told them that I thought there was a 70% chance they would lose their investment, and they did it anyway. It took more than 50 meetings for me to raise $1 million from investors, and over the course of all those meetings, the most common question was, "What's the internet?"

Unlike many other countries around the world, this great nation we live in supports and does not stigmatize entrepreneurial risk-taking. I walked away from a steady job into a Seattle garage to found my startup, fully understanding that it might not work. It feels like just yesterday I was driving the packages to the post office myself, dreaming that one day we might be able to afford a forklift.

Amazon's success was anything but preordained. Investing in Amazon early on was a very risky proposition. From our founding through the end of 2001, our business had cumulative losses of nearly $3 billion, and we did not have a profitable quarter until the fourth quarter of that year.[5]

All Is Lost

Smart analysts predicted Barnes & Noble would steamroll us, and branded us "Amazon.toast." In 1999, after we'd been in business for nearly five years, Barron's headlined a story about our impending demise "Amazon.bomb." My annual shareholder letter for 2000 started with a one-word sentence: "Ouch." At the pinnacle of the internet bubble our stock price peaked at $116, and then after the bubble burst our stock went down to $6. Experts and pundits thought we were going out of business. It took a lot of smart people with a willingness to take a risk with me, and a willingness to stick to our convictions, for Amazon to survive and ultimately to succeed.

ACT 3

Fortunately, our approach is working. Eighty percent of Americans have a favorable impression of Amazon overall, according to leading independent polls. Who do Americans trust more than Amazon "to do the right thing?" Only their primary physicians and the military, according to a January 2020 Morning Consult survey. In Fortune's 2020 rankings of the World's Most Admired Companies, we came in second place (Apple was #1). We are grateful that customers notice the hard work we do on their behalf, and that they reward us with their trust. Working to earn and keep that trust is the single biggest driver of Amazon's Day One culture.

The company most of you know as Amazon is the one that sends you your online orders in the brown boxes with the smile on the side. That's where we started, and retail remains our largest business by far, accounting for over 80% of our total revenue. When customers shop on Amazon, they are helping to create jobs in their local communities. As a result, Amazon directly employs a million people, many of them entry-level and paid by the hour. We don't just employ highly educated computer scientists and MBAs in Seattle and Silicon Valley. We hire and train hundreds of thousands of people in states across the country such as West Virginia, Tennessee, Kansas, and Idaho. These employees are package stowers, mechanics, and plant managers. For many, it's their first job. For some, these jobs are a stepping stone to other careers, and we are proud to help them with that. We are spending more than $700 million to give more than 100,000 Amazon employees access to training programs in fields such as healthcare, transportation, machine learning, and cloud computing. That program is called Career Choice, and we pay 95% of tuition and fees toward a certificate or diploma for in-demand, high-paying fields, regardless of whether it's relevant to a career at Amazon.

In the speech's closing scene, Bezos uses the Amazon origin story as a metaphor for entrepreneurship in America: "It's not a coincidence that Amazon was born in this country. More than any other place on Earth, new companies can start, grow, and thrive here," Bezos said. "Our country embraces resourcefulness and self-reliance, and it embraces builders who start from scratch. And even in the face of today's humbling challenges, I have never been more optimistic about our future."

This speech has a setup, a challenge, and a resolution. Bezos set up the ordinary world he lived in before the adventure began. The values he learned in the ordinary world taught him values that would serve him well in the second act when he confronted tests, trials, obstacles and challenges. He overcame those challenges in the third act to transform the world.

Jeff Bezos takes a lot of pleasure in the fun and games section of the Amazon story. He has a stable of anecdotes to pull from, depending on the audience. Here are two examples:

The concept for Amazon came to me in 1994. I came across this startling statistic that web usage was growing at 2,300 percent a year. I decided I would try and find a business plan that made sense in the context of that growth, and I picked books as the first, best product to sell online. I called a friend, and he recommended his lawyer to me. He said, "I need to know what name you want the company to have for the incorporation papers." I said—this is over the phone—"Cadabra. Like *abracadabra*." He said, "Cadaver?" And I was like, OK, that's not going to work. So I said, "Go ahead with Cadabra for now, and I'll change it." Three months later, I changed it to Amazon for Earth's biggest river, Earth's biggest selection.[6]

The first month, I was packing boxes on my hands and knees on the hard cement floors, with somebody else kneeling next to me. I said,

"You know what we need? Kneepads. This is killing my knees." This guy packing alongside me said, "We need packing tables." I was like, "That's the most brilliant idea I've ever heard." The next day I went and bought packing tables, and it doubled our productivity.[7]

Humor is disarming. Humor is charming. Humor builds connection and trust. Find anecdotes that bring a smile to your face, and it's likely your audience will enjoy them, too.

BECOME A STUDENT OF STORY

Bezos is an effective storyteller because he studies narrative. Like other famous entrepreneurs, Bezos has suggested that superior technology and a solid business model are largely meaningless without a story to sell it. And Bezos knows a good story when he sees it.

During a tense meeting about the direction of Amazon Studios in 2017, Bezos expressed frustration with the quality of original programming coming out of the division:

"Iconic shows have basic things in common,"[8] Bezos said.

According to people who attended the meeting, what happened next proves that Bezos has a deep understanding of the ingredients that make up an epic story. Bezos provided the following list of storytelling elements without referring to notes or documents. He knew them by heart:

- A heroic protagonist who experiences growth and change
- A compelling antagonist
- Wish fulfillment (the protagonist has hidden abilities, such as superpowers or magic)
- Moral choices
- Diverse world-building (different geographic landscapes)
- Urgency to watch next episode (cliffhangers)
- Civilizational high stakes (a global threat to humanity like an alien invasion or a devastating pandemic)
- Humor
- Betrayal
- Positive emotions (love, joy, hope)

- Negative emotions (loss, sorrow)
- Violence

After the meeting, Bezos demanded that studio executives send him regular updates on the projects under development. The updates had to "include spreadsheets describing how each show had each storytelling element; and if one element was missing, they had to explain why."[9]

The storytelling of Amazon's original shows began to improve in quality, and Amazon Studios turned out massive global hits such as *Tom Clancy's Jack Ryan,* a spy thriller starring John Krasinski. It provided the international hit Bezos had craved.

Amazon Prime Video is available in over two hundred countries. Shows like *Jack Ryan* feature carefully calibrated storytelling to engage a global audience. In every episode, you'll find each of the twelve ingredients Bezos identified. Jack Ryan is an unsung hero, an analyst who feels like a cog in the machine and who's dealing with his own trauma. The show's creators purposely avoided making the protagonist superhuman—keeping him humble makes the character more relatable. Instead, they put even more thought into the villains Ryan encountered. "When you tell any story, your hero is only as good as the antagonist that he's facing. We put a lot of time and energy into creating a complex, multi-layered antagonist."[10]

If you want to see how quickly an effective story structure can reel you in, watch the pilot episode from season one of *Jack Ryan.* Although one-hour television dramas typically have five parts, those parts still fall within the ancient three-act structure.

The pilot episode opens with a teaser, a shocking or surprising scene that grabs hold of you and doesn't let go. I chose the helicopter crash as a teaser in the faux Bezos screenplay that opened this chapter. Following the teaser, the audience meets the show's main characters. In *Jack Ryan's* pilot episode, we get to know most of the main characters who remain for the rest of the eight-part series. There's even a scene when Ryan's new boss at the CIA walks into a conference room and says, "Let's go around the table. Introduce yourselves and tell me what do you."

We also learn more about our hero's values. In one scene, Ryan puts his principles above money, refusing to go along with an insider trading scheme.

There's plenty of confrontation in the show's second act, from heated verbal arguments to surprise attacks and terrifying battles.

In act 3, Ryan resolves several conflicts (his relationship with his boss and a close call with death in a terrorist interrogation outpost).

And just when you think it's over, every episode ends with a cliffhanger.

While every epic story follows a structure, the stories contained within that structure are as diverse as the number of humans who have lived before us and who will come after us. Everyone has a story. *You* have a story, and it deserves to be heard.

In the next chapter, you'll hear from four entrepreneurs who started with nothing but an idea, and today, their companies are valued at a combined $320 billion. You'll see how each of them learned to craft an origin story that follows the three-act structure. Every entrepreneur and leader should learn to tell a compelling story. Your audience is wired for story. They crave story. And they're waiting for you to deliver a story that will set their imagination ablaze.

8
ORIGIN STORIES

Telling effective stories is not easy. Yet when it succeeds, it
gives Sapiens immense power, because it enables millions
of strangers to cooperate and work towards a common goal.

—Yuval Noah Harari

Storytelling is a trust-building skill that played a major role in the development of our species.

According to Yuval Noah Harari in *Sapiens,* "Trade cannot exist without trust, and it is very difficult to trust strangers."[1] Stories are the glue that binds us together in families and groups, says Harari, "giving Sapiens the unprecedented ability to cooperate flexibly in large numbers. That's why Sapiens rule the world."

Anthropologists say that when our ancestors gathered around campfires after a long day of hunting and gathering, they would spend eighty percent of their time sharing stories. Those men and women who had mastered the art of storytelling were widely admired among the tribespeople and often seen as the group's leaders. Storytellers used this skill to earn trust, influence behavior, encourage cooperation, and build a strong culture based on shared values.

Remarkably, nearly all epic tales—from the earliest-known stories of Gilgamesh to the founding myths behind the world's most admired brands—follow the stages outlined in Joseph Campbell's *The Hero's Journey.* Campbell, a mythology professor, discovered that heroic tales across time and cultures follow a similar cycle. He called the shared journey a *monomyth,* a standard template for heroic stories. Heroes in ancient texts followed the journey, as do modern movie heroes from Jack Ryan to Harry Potter, from Katniss Everdeen to Luke Skywalker.

Campbell did not invent the formula; he identified it.

The Hero's Journey tracks perfectly with most entrepreneurial success stories: A hero or heroine lives in an ordinary world and gets a call to adventure (a problem, challenge, or idea). They face doubts and doubters. They also meet mentors who prepare them to face the unknown. The hero ultimately crosses the threshold when the road trip begins and the wagon wheels start rolling. They leave the comfort and safety of their current home to pursue the adventure. Along the journey, they encounter tests, obstacles, allies, and enemies. Their ordeal gets worse. They face a near-death experience, fall into an abyss, and hit rock bottom. But as Campbell said, it's when they stumble that heroes find the real treasure, the secret to achieving their dreams. After escaping danger, the hero emerges triumphant and is transformed by the experience. Most important, they return from their adventure with an "elixir," a lesson or treasure that will benefit others.

If you listen carefully to the speeches and presentations of skilled communicators like Jeff Bezos, you'll recognize almost every step of the Hero's Journey.

Bezos was born in the very ordinary world of Albuquerque, New Mexico, to a young mother who was still in high school. As he gets older, Bezos meets a mentor, his grandfather, who teaches him the values the ambitious boy will need to succeed in his quest. Bezos receives a call to adventure when he learns that the internet is growing by 2,300 percent a year. He faces doubters in the form of a boss who tells him to give up on his dream. Bezos crosses a threshold, literally, when he gets into a car with his wife, McKenzie, and embarks on a road trip to Seattle. He survives a near-death experience when the dot-com collapse wipes out much of Amazon's value. But during that ordeal, he comes up with ideas that unleash the company's growth (renting out cloud services and opening up the platform to third-party sellers). He even returns with an "elixir." In the closing sentences of Bezos's speech to a U.S. congressional committee, he said, "The rest of the world would love even the tiniest sip of the elixir we have here in the U.S. Immigrants like my dad see what a treasure this country is."

Storytelling is not something we do. Storytellers are who we are.

Entrepreneurs who excel in storytelling understand the Hero's Journey, but they don't feel obligated to hit each and every one of its stages. Campbell identified seventeen stages of the Hero's Journey. Later, in the 1990s, Christopher Vogler, a screenwriter for Disney, condensed Campbell's formula into twelve stages, an easier template for Hollywood filmmakers to follow.

Although the Hero's Journey inspires everything from screenwriting to video-game production, any storyteller can adapt the mythic structure to suit their own needs. They can skip stages or rearrange them. If your purpose is business storytelling, it's critical to remember that, regardless of the stages of the Hero's Journey, the overarching narrative is still presented in three acts. The Hero's Journey *overlays* an intricate character arc onto the three-act structure.

If you want to steal scenes from the Hero's Journey to move the action along, that's perfectly fine. The most important thing to remember is that your audiences crave stories, and the three-act structure is the template they love.

In the rest of this chapter, I'll provide examples of Hero's and Heroine's Journeys that successful entrepreneurs have told publicly to educate customers, raise money, pitch ideas, build trust, and wow their audiences. You'll see that, while the stories change, their structure remains the same.

GOLIATH, MEET DAVID

Act 1: Marc and Reed shared a carpool to work. Marc, a serial entrepreneur, pitched ideas to Reed on a typical drive: customized dog food, customized shampoo, personalized surfboards. Reed shot them down. Except for one.

In January of 1997, Reed was irritated because Blockbuster had charged him a forty-dollar late fee for a VHS copy of *Apollo 13*.

"What if there were no late fees?"[2] he wondered aloud.

With that question, the idea for Netflix was born. But the entrepreneurs would face formidable obstacles and near-death experiences as they embarked on their adventure.

Act 2: Marc Randolph and Reed Hastings soon learned that sending VHS movies through the mail would be too expensive. Fortunately, a new invention called DVDs brought down the mailing costs. In May

1998, Marc and Reed launched Netflix, the world's first online DVD rental store.

A crisis struck two years later. With only three hundred thousand subscribers, Netflix was losing money. In 2000 alone, the company had lost $57 million. Additional sources of funding were drying up as a result of the dot-com crash. So the two entrepreneurs set aside their pride and arranged a meeting with Blockbuster.

Blockbuster was a thousand times the size of Netflix, Reed reminded Marc as they stepped into the cavernous meeting room where they would face Blockbuster CEO John Antioco.

Reed made the pitch: Blockbuster could buy Netflix for $50 million, and Netflix would run the online division of the combined business.

It was clear to Marc that Antioco was struggling to contain his laughter. The meeting quickly went downhill after that. Sullen and shaken, Marc and Reed boarded a plane back to California. Before parting ways, Marc turned to Reed and said, "Blockbuster doesn't want us. So it's obvious what we have to do now. We're going to have to kick their ass."

Goliath, meet David.

Act 3: The two entrepreneurs triumph over Blockbuster, which had grown complacent. The Blockbuster culture did not emphasize innovation and, therefore, failed to adapt to the new method of consuming entertainment—streaming. On the other hand, Netflix had pivoted from the DVD-by-mail business to an internet streaming service with two hundred million subscribers in 190 countries. Netflix also became a major producer of TV shows and movies around the world.

The Netflix three-act story takes about three minutes to tell. But it's not the whole story. Not even close. It doesn't cover the hours that Randolph spent researching ideas that never worked out. It doesn't cover the months of analysis, hundreds of hours of discussions, and marathon meetings before the company's launch.

"The whole story is messy, but people's eyes will glaze over if you tell them everything,"[3] Randolph said when I visited him in Santa Cruz, California. "Silicon Valley loves a good origin story. Investors, board members, reporters, and the public like to hear them. Having these emotionally true stories is a huge advantage. When you're trying to take down a juggernaut, the story of your company's founding can't be a three-hundred-page book. It has to fit into three or four short paragraphs. Reed's origin story, which he often repeats, is branding at its finest."

The Netflix origin story is simple, clear, and memorable. It captures the essence of the company's vision, innovation, and resilience. The story gave Reed and Marc a narrative they used for years to persuade customers, investors, and partners to back their vision.

ENTREPRENEUR OVERCOMES ONE HUNDRED REJECTIONS TO BUILD A $40 BILLION BRAND

Act 1: While attending college in Perth, Australia, Melanie Perkins taught Adobe Photoshop to make extra money. The students struggled to learn the basics. The software was expensive and complicated. In 2007, Melanie had a brainstorm: to start a web-based service that made design ridiculously simple for anyone. At that moment, the idea for Canva was born.

Act 2: Canva was based thousands of miles from Silicon Valley. Investors were hard to reach and lacked interest. Melanie pitched the idea to one hundred investors and heard *no* one hundred times. But she didn't take no for an answer.

In one memorable event, Melanie had learned to kite surf to meet potential funders who had picked up the hobby. In May 2013, she was invited to pitch her idea at a competition sponsored by Richard Branson on his private island in the British Virgin Islands, where many of the investors also kite surfed. She joined them one morning but went off course and was left stranded when her thirty-foot sail deflated. As Perkins waited for hours to be rescued, suffering in pain from an encounter with a coral reef, she reminded herself that the risk was worth it—an investment would fuel the growth of the company she had started six years earlier.

The kite surfing story that Perkins often shares reflects her core values of grit and persistence, teaching us something about what drives her (the heroine of the story). It also provides some "fun and games" in the middle of the narrative.

Act 3: Perkins finds a resolution to her struggle in the third act when she discovers that investors are reluctant to fund the start-up because they did not understand the reason it exists. Perkins' pitch was rejected more than 100 times because she spent too much time focusing on *how* Canva worked instead of explaining *why* she came up with the idea. She had no first act. Once Perkins began to share the origin of her idea—the frustration creators had with existing design tools—she said everything changed. "A lot of people can relate to being completely overwhelmed with Photoshop or design tools,"[4] Perkins told me. "It became important to tell that part of the story, especially for investors, because if they didn't understand the problem, they wouldn't understand why customers would need our solution. The story was transformative."

Fueled by her mission to democratize design and a reimagined pitch deck, Melanie convinced investors to back her idea. Actors Woody Harrelson and Owen Wilson became ardent supporters, in addition to former Apple evangelist Guy Kawasaki. In 2019, an $85 million investment valued Canva at $3.2 billion. And that was just the beginning. A massive investment of $200 million in 2021 made Canva a $40 billion company. Today, Perkins owns the world's most valuable female-founded and female-led start-up. And with more than fifty million active users in 190 countries, Perkins is fulfilling her mission to empower the world to design.

REVOLUTIONIZING TRAVEL

Act 1: Brian and Joe, two friends from design school, were looking for ways to cover the cost of their ruinously expensive San Francisco apartment. In 2007, they saw an opportunity. An international design conference was coming to town, and every hotel was sold out. They quickly created a website, hoping to rent air beds in their apartment to attendees. Three designers took them up on their offer.

When Brian and Joe told people what they were doing, they thought the idea sounded crazy. "Strangers will never stay in each other's homes," they said. But something unexpected happened that first weekend. Brian and Joe treated their guests like old friends from out of town, connecting them to a unique slice of San Francisco that they could never have experienced on their own. The attendees came to town as outsiders but left feeling like locals.

The experience left Brian and Joe feeling something special, too. The idea for Airbnb was born.

Act 2: Nate Blecharczyk, a software engineer, joined Brian Chesky and Joe Gebbia to design a platform. But the three founders faced a bigger design problem: How do they make strangers feel comfortable enough to stay in each other's homes? The key was trust. The solution they designed combined host and guest profiles, integrated messaging, two-way reviews, and secure payments built on a technology platform that unlocked trust. Their ideas eventually led to hosting at a global scale that was unimaginable at the time.

Act 3: Today, the idea of house and apartment sharing does not seem so crazy after all. More than 4 million hosts now offer everything from a private room in their home to luxury villas, from one night to several months at a time. In more than 220 countries and regions worldwide, Airbnb hosts have welcomed over 825 million guest arrivals and have earned a combined $110 billion.

Airbnb has enabled home-sharing at a global scale and created a new category of travel. Instead of traveling like tourists and feeling like outsiders, guests on Airbnb can stay in neighborhoods where people live, have authentic experiences, live like locals, and spend time with locals in approximately one hundred thousand cities around the world.

Airbnb transformed the world for hosts and guests—and the lives of its founders. Brian, Joe, and Nate are now worth a combined $30 billion.

Airbnb cofounder and CEO Brian Chesky is a skilled storyteller. I remember speaking at a venture capital event at an exclusive resort north of San Francisco. Chesky was also a speaker. He spoke of the Hero's Journey and how Airbnb facilitated experiences for people to write their own stories. Jeff Jordan, a partner at venture capital firm Andreessen Horowitz, recalls thinking that Airbnb was "the stupidest idea" when he first heard about it. But that was before he met Chesky, who captivated Jordan with Airbnb's backstory as well as a memorable analogy: Airbnb was the marketplace for space just as eBay was the marketplace for stuff, Chesky said.

"I went from complete skeptic to complete believer in twenty-nine minutes," Jordan says. "Every great founder can really tell a great story."

Jordan was "blown away" by Chesky's pitch in the form of narrative. Chesky had an ability to weave a start-up story with a dramatic arc that had a beginning, middle, and end. His story also had ups and downs, tension and relief, and a compelling vision that tied it all together. The story Chesky pitched paid off when Airbnb went public in December 2020. Airbnb is now active in over two hundred countries, and with a net worth of about $15 billion, Chesky is no longer worried about paying this month's rent.

AN ORIGIN STORY IN ONE HUNDRED WORDS

Origin stories should follow a three-act structure, but they don't have to be long. For example, Warby Parker was founded in 2010 by a group of entrepreneurs who had a vision to disrupt the traditional eyewear industry. Order eyeglasses from the company, and you'll find a cleaning cloth in the case. It doesn't have the company logo; it has a story instead. The story fits on the cloth because it's under one hundred words:

> Once upon a time, a young man left his glasses on an airplane. He tried to buy new glasses. But new glasses were expensive. "Why is it so hard to buy stylish glasses without spending a fortune on them?" he wondered. He returned to school and told his friends. "We should start a company to sell amazing glasses for non-insane prices," said one. "We should make shopping for glasses fun," said another. "We should distribute a pair of glasses to someone in need for every pair sold," said a third. Eureka! Warby Parker was born.[5]

Act 1 is the setting. Our hero leaves his glasses on an airplane.

Act 2 is the conflict, the problem. Our hero finds that new glasses are expensive. So he goes on a quest to solve the problem and attract others to join the adventure.

Act 3 is the resolution. The hero and his allies start a company that makes shopping for eyeglasses fun and inexpensive, and makes the world a better place.

The entire Warby Parker history can be read "in less time than it takes to wash a dish, clean a smudge off your glasses, or consume six baby carrots at a responsible chewing pace."[6]

If you visit the Warby Parker website, you'll find an extended version of the story with additional details and explanations. For example, the founder who lost his glasses, Neil Blumenthal, spent his first semester of grad school without them, "squinting and complaining." The rest of the cofounders had similar experiences and were shocked at how hard it was to find a pair of great frames without breaking the bank. The story goes on to explain why prices in the eyewear industry are so high. It also includes information about the "get-a-pair, give-a-pair" program that distributes free eyeglasses to those in need. These details are interesting but not necessary for every audience. For most customers, a one-hundred-word story is enough to build trust.

COACHING DRILL

Build your origin story. Every start-up has one. Every company has one. What's yours? What person, thing, or event ignited your big idea? Tell the story in three acts: In act 1, tell us about your life before you embarked on your adventure. What was the problem or event that catalyzed your ideas? In act 2, talk about the challenges you faced. What obstacles got in the way of seeking the treasure you desired? Build the tension by reminding your audience how close you came to failure. In act 3, reveal the resolution. How did you overcome these hurdles, and how did you turn adversity into success? What lessons did you learn, and how did the experience transform you, the company, and the world for the better?

Your audience wants a neatly packaged origin story. And you have one to share.

You have a story to tell, a story that's unique to you and reflects your values. Share your story as often as you can. Do not expect your customers, investors, employees, or partners to know your company's story. You might get tired of telling it, but others want to hear it.

Storytelling is deeply embedded within the Amazon culture. In the next chapter, you'll learn how Bezos turned narrative into Amazon's competitive advantage, unleashing the most innovative period of the company's history.

9

THE NARRATIVE INFORMATION MULTIPLIER

This is the weirdest meeting culture you will ever encounter.

—Jeff Bezos

Every senior leader who worked at Amazon on Wednesday, June 9, 2004, remembers the email that popped into their inbox at 6:02 P.M.

Many Amazonians were enjoying the warmer-than-average summer day. It was seventy-six degrees, and "the mountain was out," as Seattleites say when the majestic peak of Mount Rainier is in clear view. Seattle summers are short, and residents look forward to days when the sun doesn't set until 9:00 P.M.

And then the email hit.

The message was "simple, direct, and earthshaking," according to Colin Bryar, the executive who sent it on behalf of his boss. The subject line read:

No PowerPoint presentations from now on at S-Team.

A sudden chill had blown in, ruining the warm summer evening for those executives who had spent weeks finalizing their PowerPoint slides for the following Tuesday's meeting. Bryar fielded a flurry of phone calls and a deluge of emails.

"Are you kidding?" executives asked. No, he wasn't.

Bezos had banned PowerPoint at Amazon's senior leadership meetings. Members of the teams who planned to present their ideas at the next meeting could still do so. They'd only have to make one change: replace PowerPoint slides with a short narrative memo.

No kidding.

JEFF'S SHADOW

Bryar was known as "Jeff's shadow," the second person to hold the position after Andy Jassy, who would become Amazon's CEO seventeen years later. Officially, "Jeff's shadow" was a technical advisor, a role similar to the president's chief of staff in the White House. If you've watched *The West Wing*, you know nobody talks to the president without going through the chief of staff. A team that wanted to get time with Bezos would have to schedule the meeting with Bryar, who would then prepare them for a conversation with the boss.

When Bezos asked Bryar to be his technical assistant, Bryar said he'd need the weekend to think about it. The challenges coursed through his head:

> *My time won't be my own.*
> *I'll meet with five to seven teams a day.*
> *I'll spend ten hours a day with my boss.*
> *Jeff will expect me to contribute ideas right away.*

The demands of the job would be enormous, and so would the benefits. Bezos was handing Bryar an opportunity to learn more than he could ever imagine. Bryar would have a front-row seat to one of history's most visionary business leaders. He'd watch as Bezos, in a single day, made more monumental decisions than the average professional will make in their entire career.

Bryar accepted and shadowed Jeff for the next two years.

During Bryar's tenure, narrative memos gave life to Amazon Prime, Amazon Web Services, Kindle, Fulfillment by Amazon, and many other features, products, and services that touch your life every day.

Narrative is to Amazon what an engine is to a Ferrari. A Ferrari is instantly recognizable, of course, but what makes it special is what lies under the hood. Narrative writing isn't solely responsible for Amazon's success, but it powers the engine of innovation.

THE ESSAY THAT CHANGED EVERYTHING

Why did Bezos feel an urgent need to dispense with PowerPoint, the communication tool that had become ubiquitous throughout the organization?

Inspiration struck Bezos in the form of a thirty-page essay he had brought along to read on a business flight. Bryar was seated next to Bezos, reading the same article. Both men were looking for a way to improve decision-making at senior executive meetings. They found their answer in the works of ET, not the movie character but a Yale professor who made an argument that was out of this world.

In *The Cognitive Style of PowerPoint*, Edward Tufte, a pioneer in the field of data visualization, argues that the traditional style of delivering slides with bullet points "usually weakens verbal and spatial reasoning, and almost always corrupts statistical analysis."[1] Tufte's criticism appears in the first paragraph and gets more vicious throughout the paper.

Tufte writes, "In day-to-day practice, PowerPoint templates may improve 10 percent or 20 percent of all presentations by organizing inept, extremely disorganized speakers, at a cost of detectable intellectual damage to 80 percent. For statistical data, the damage levels approach dementia." According to Tufte, "PowerPoint allows speakers to pretend they are giving a real talk, and audiences to pretend that they are listening."

Tufte challenges the reader to imagine an expensive and widely used drug that claims to make them beautiful. "Instead the drug had frequent, serious side effects: making us stupid, degrading the quality and credibility of our communication, turning us into bores, wasting our colleagues' time. Those side effects, and the resulting unsatisfactory cost/benefit ratio, would rightly lead to a worldwide product recall."

Tufte *really* hates PowerPoint. Or does he?

I've carefully studied the same paper that Bezos and Bryar read on the plane in 2004, the essay that triggered a massive change at Amazon and many other companies that adopted Amazon's narrative strategy. Since many former Amazonians admit to blatantly ripping off the six-page blueprint and introducing it at their own start-ups, it's worth exploring Tufte's analysis of PowerPoint and where he identified its limitations.

Tufte directed his criticism at the typical PowerPoint presentation, which replaces sentences and paragraphs—verbal discussion—with word fragments and bulleted lists. According to Tufte, "By leaving out the narrative between the points, the bullet outline ignores and conceals the causal assumptions and analytic structure of the reasoning." A list of bullet points is a presenter's way of compressing language into brief phrases. Bulleted outlines "might be useful now and then," Tufte writes, "but sentences with subjects and verbs are usually better."

Tufte believes that in the wrong hands, bullet points can kill, literally. He backs up his claim with the final report on the 2003 disaster of the space shuttle *Columbia*. The shuttle disintegrated upon reentering Earth's atmosphere at eighteen times the speed of sound. All seven astronauts were killed.

When *Columbia* lifted off two weeks earlier, a piece of foam used to insulate the external fuel tank had broken off and struck the leading edge of the left wing. The hole it made in the wing remained undetected, leaving the shuttle incapable of withstanding the intense heat that occurs upon reentry.

NASA officials could see the small foam debris break off in a frame of video eighty-two seconds after *Columbia*'s launch. They requested an assessment of the damage from engineers at Boeing, the company that designed and built the shuttle. The engineers quickly prepared three reports in PowerPoint with a total of twenty-eight slides.

Tufte analyzed one slide that he called "a PowerPoint festival of bureaucratic hyper-rationalism." It had six different levels of hierarchical bullets, each containing short statements in cascading order (see figure 9).

The slide's title painted an optimistic picture for NASA officials who had to determine what action to take. The lower-level bullet points in tiny font buried the shuttle's actual damage. Engineers had written the bullets

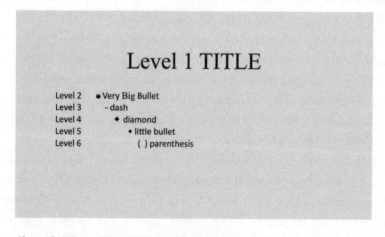

Figure 9: What a "PowerPoint Festival of Bureaucratic Hyper-rationalism"
Slide Looks Like

in small sentence fragments to fit the material on the slides. In the absence of complete sentences, the bullet-pointed fragments obscured the information's real meaning.

"Satisfied that the reports indicated that the Columbia was not in real danger, the officials made no further attempts to assess the threats," writes Tufte.

Boeing's engineers attempted to tell a story of what had happened, but PowerPoint is not a storytelling tool.

In its final report, the *Columbia* Accident Investigation Board reached the following conclusion: "The endemic use of PowerPoint illustrated the problematic methods of technical communication . . . as information gets passed up an organization hierarchy, key explanations and supporting information is filtered out. In this context, it is easy to understand how a senior manager might read this PowerPoint slide and not realize it addresses a life-threatening situation."

The investigation convinced Tufte that bulleted lists broken up into fragments to fit a template does real damage to decision-making. "PowerPoint will not do for serious presentations," says Tufte. "Serious problems require serious tools."

Jeff Bezos consumed every page of Tufte's essay. He realized that Tufte had found a better alternative, a "new" way of sharing ideas that dates back five thousand years—expressing an idea in complete sentences and paragraphs. "Replace PowerPoint slides with paper handouts showing words, numbers, data, graphics, and images together," Tufte advised.

Bezos explained the reason for making the switch: "The reason writing a good 4-page memo is harder than 'writing' a 20-page Powerpoint is because the narrative structure of a good memo forces better thought and better understanding of what's more important than what, and how things are related. Powerpoint-style presentations somehow give permission to gloss over ideas, flatten out any sense of relative importance, and ignore the interconnectedness of ideas."[2]

GOOD INTENTIONS NEVER WORK, GOOD MECHANISMS DO

One of the pithy Jeff-isms that has become part of the Amazon lexicon is: "Good intentions never work, you need good mechanisms to make anything happen."

The saying—now popular at Amazon—is a shortened version of a slightly longer explanation Bezos offered at an all-hands meeting in February 2008. "Often, when we find a recurring problem, something that happens over and over again, we pull the team together, ask them to try harder, do better—essentially, we ask for good intentions. This rarely works,"[3] Bezos said. "When you are asking for good intentions, you are not asking for a change because people already had good intentions. But if good intentions don't work, what does? Mechanisms work."

A mechanism is a repeatable process, a tool that aligns actions and decisions to Amazon's Leadership Principles. To work properly, a mechanism is introduced, adopted, and "audited" to make sure it works as designed. For example, "two-pizza teams" and "single-threaded leaders," which we discussed earlier, are examples of mechanisms. Another Amazon mechanism, born of frustration, is now credited for many of Amazon's greatest innovations. The mechanism is *narrative*.

A narrative is simply a written document that forces clarity of thought. Narratives come in different forms. The two primary forms that Bezos popularized at Amazon are the subjects of this chapter and the next, forms anyone can adopt to elevate the quality of their communication: the six-pager and the press release / frequently asked questions (PR/ FAQ).

The process of writing narratives allows you to refine, clarify, and articulate your ideas. Best of all, anyone can do it.

The first Amazon attempts at writing narratives were "laughably poor," Bryar recalls. Executives who didn't think they could explain their ideas in four pages ignored the guideline and submitted forty pages of prose. When they were told to stick to the limit, they found clever ways of circumventing the rules like single spacing text, narrowing margins, and shrinking font sizes. Clever, but not effective. Bezos caught on quickly.

Bezos and his senior leaders eventually decided that memos with a maximum length of six pages would suit their needs. Supporting details could be attached as an appendix, but the memo itself could be no longer than six pages. This raises a critical point. A narratively structured memo should be long enough to express the idea—and not a sentence more. If two pages are all it takes to share an idea, then stick to two.

A two-pager or a six-pager serves the same purpose—forcing presenters to clarify their thinking. The act of writing narrative memos with titles, subheadings, sentences, verbs, nouns, and paragraphs is harder than filling slides with bullet points. Narratives force "the writer to think and synthesize more deeply than they would in the act of crafting a Power-Point deck,"[4] says Bryar. "The idea on paper will be better thought out, especially after the author's entire team has reviewed it and offered feedback. It's a daunting task to get all the relevant facts and all one's salient arguments into a coherent, understandable document—and it should be."

There's no formal template for writing a narrative that will impress Bezos, but there are proven strategies for creating an impressive narrative.

Adopt and adapt the following strategies. Remember, the narrative process is behind every major Amazon innovation since 2004—every success that's fueled Amazon's growth and made Bezos one of the wealthiest people in the world. It worked for him. It will work for you.

FIVE STRATEGIES FOR WRITING GREAT NARRATIVES

1. Focus on narrative, not "six-pagers." The key to adopting and benefiting from Amazon's six-pager is to keep the focus on where it belongs: the narrative. A narratively structured memo requires "topic sentences, verbs, and nouns, not just bullet points," says Bezos.

The "six-pager" refers to a unique format that fits the needs of Amazon's decision-making process in senior leadership meetings. There's no rule even at Amazon that a narrative memo must be six pages. Any written communication, whether an email or internal memo, should be no longer than is necessary. In many cases, a one-page memo does the job. Let's turn to Procter & Gamble for an example.

You might not recognize the name *Richard Deupree*, but you're familiar with the TV format he invented: the soap opera.

As the CEO of Procter & Gamble in the 1930s, Deupree ignored calls to cut back on marketing during the Great Depression. Instead, he doubled down on a new medium—radio. The company's candle sales had started to decline with the invention of the light bulb, so it focused on boosting sales of another popular product—soap. Deupree sponsored daytime serial dramas that provided escapist entertainment for millions of Americans who were out of work. Procter & Gamble (P&G) used the platform to push sales of Ivory soap—and hence, the "soap opera" was born.

Deupree also introduced the "one-page memo" to P&G's leadership teams. According to management expert Tom Peters, "Deupree strongly disliked any memorandum more than one typewritten page in length. He often would return a long memo with an injunction: 'Boil it down to something I can grasp.' If the memo involved a complex situation, he sometimes would add, 'I don't understand complicated problems. I only understand simple ones.' When an interviewer once queried him about this, he explained, 'Part of my job is to train people to break down an involved question into a series of simple matters. Then we can all act intelligently.'"[5]

And it's true—the ability to simplify has the power to transform everything. So how did P&G train its employees to meet their boss's exacting standards? The process of writing a one-page memo evolved at P&G to include five elements. This easy-to-follow format in table 9 explains each element:

Table 9: Elements of P&G's One-Page Memo[6]

Element	Description	Notes
Idea Summary	In one sentence, what are you proposing? See the logline in chapter 4 for tips on how to express your main idea in one sentence.	"P&G Good Everyday is a new consumer rewards program, featuring our trusted brands, that helps turn everyday actions into acts of good for you, your family, the community and the world."
Perspective	A situation summary that presents facts, trends, issues.	"P&G has been working to make a positive impact for more than 180 years. Our family of household brands has had a longstanding commitment to doing what is right: making a positive community impact, supporting gender equality, driving diversity and inclusion, and promoting environmental sustainability in the world."
How It Works	Explain the details of your proposal. How, what, who, when, where?	"The P&G Good Everyday is a rewards program for people who want to make an impact."

Element	Description	Notes
Key Benefits	Deupree challenged presenters to express three benefits of their idea, ideally benefits that proved to have strategic and profitable value for the company. See the rule of three in chapter 16 for an explanation of this powerful communication strategy.	"When you join the P&G Good Everyday rewards program and take simple actions through the website, P&G will donate to the cause of your choice, so you can help make a difference, too. Engage through quizzes, surveys, or scanning receipts, earn rewards, and P&G automatically makes donations to the causes you care about at no cost to you."
Next Steps	What actions need to be taken, by whom, and by when?	"We can accomplish more together. With P&G Good Everyday, you can combine your desire to do good with P&G's ongoing efforts to help solve challenges around the world. To sign up, visit the P&G Good Everyday website."

The one-pager is so engrained in the P&G culture that it's still followed as a blueprint for emails, memos, sales and marketing pitches, and even as a model for the company's television commercials.

2. Stick to headings and subheadings. Returning to Edward Tufte's essay, he says that "scientists and engineers—and everyone else for that matter—have communicated about complex matters for centuries without hierarchical bullet outlines."

Tufte reminds us that renowned physicist Richard Feynman wrote a six-hundred-page book covering complex topics like thermodynamics and quantum behavior, and he did it with only two levels of words: titles and subheadings.

"Richard Feynman was an amazing scientist, but more importantly, he was an amazing teacher," says Bill Gates. "He could explain things in a fun and interesting way to anyone. He's the only one who really succeeded in explaining quantum physics in a clear way. Taking something that's a little mysterious to most people and using very simple concepts to explain how it works, that's classic Feynman."[7]

Feynman had experienced a personal run-in with bullet points when he served on the commission investigating the shuttle *Challenger* explosion in 1986. Feynman wrote, "Then we learned about 'bullets'—little black circles in front of phrases that were supposed to summarize things. There was one after another of these little goddamn bullets in our briefing books and on slides."[8]

Feynman delivered a now-famous demonstration of what caused the 1986 *Challenger* shuttle explosion. He didn't need slides or bullet points to make a persuasive argument. A cup of ice water ran circles around PowerPoint.

In what's become known as the "O-ring ice water demonstration," the Nobel Prize–winning physicist proved his theory that low temperatures on the night of launch reduced the resiliency of rubber O-ring seals in the solid rocket boosters. The failure led to the shuttle's explosion seventy-three seconds after liftoff.

During a media-packed hearing, Feynman, the physicist and performer, brought sample material from the rubber O-ring and dropped it in a cup of ice water. The rubber became rigid, demonstrating its inability to seal properly at low temperatures, just as the O-ring had failed to seal properly on the morning of the launch.

Feynman admitted that he was reluctant to go through with the demonstration on the night before his testimony. "No, that would be gauche,"[9] he thought. But then Feynman recalled physicists whom he admired for their "gutsiness and sense of humor." His heroes communicated information simply when everyone else tried to keep it complicated. The other speakers invited to offer their explanations about the *Challenger* disaster brought binders of briefing books with charts, slides, and tiny bullet points. Feynman's simple demo "startled the commission," according to newspaper headlines.

Feynman was a genius, a scientist whose name is celebrated alongside Einstein's, Galileo's, and Newton's. Feynman earned a reputation as "the great explainer" because he translated complex topics into plain, simple language. Feynman popularized a technique for learning new things: Write the concept on a sheet of paper in your own words, the words you would use to explain the topic to someone else. Write the explanation in complete sentences with nouns and verbs—not bullet points. Feynman once said, "You can recognize truth by its beauty and simplicity."

3. Don't rush it. As you might recall from chapter 6 on analogies, Bezos once compared writing to learning to do a handstand. It looks easy but takes weeks, even months, of practice. The same tip applies to narratively structured memos. Good writing takes time. Don't expect to become an expert overnight, and give yourself plenty of time (if possible) to refine what you create.

You can't rush narratives because clear writing reflects clear thinking. The biggest mistake narrative writers make is not spending enough time on the actual writing process. According to Bezos, if you put in the time to make it great, your idea will be brilliant, thoughtful, and have "the clarity of angels singing." There's no higher praise.

4. Collaborate to communicate. The tradition at Amazon is to submit six-pagers with no names on them. It sends the signal that good writing is a team effort and that no one author is solely responsible for writing a document.

The difference between a great memo and an average one is "squishy," Bezos wrote in his 2017 letter. "It would be extremely hard to write down the detailed requirements that make up a great memo. Nevertheless, I find that much of the time, readers react to great memos very similarly. They know it when they see it. The standard is there, and it is real, even if it's not easily describable."[10]

Although great writing is hard to describe, Bezos says there's no question that teamwork elevates a document's quality. Do you need to be an extremely skilled writer to write a world-class memo? "In my view, not so much," says Bezos. As long as you work as a team, he adds. "The football coach doesn't need to be able to throw, and a film director doesn't need to be able to act. But they both do need to recognize high standards for those things and teach realistic expectations on scope. Even in the example of writing a six-page memo, that's teamwork. *Someone* on the team needs to have the skill, but it doesn't have to be you." Left unsaid is that if the best writer on the team *is* you, you'll become that person everyone wants on their team.

"Writing a good six-page evidence-based narrative is hard work,"[11] says Brad Porter, who worked at Amazon for thirteen years. As one of only a handful of "distinguished engineers," Porter's job was to accelerate the development of ambitious projects like Prime Now, Amazon's lightning-fast delivery service that gets a product to a customer's door just one hour after placing the order.

"Precision counts," says Porter. "It can be hard to summarize a complex business in six pages, so teams work for hours preparing the document for these reviews. But that preparation does two things. First, it requires the team writing the document to really, deeply understand their own space, gather their data, understand their operating tenets, and be able to communicate them clearly. The second thing a great document does is enable our senior executives to internalize a whole new space they may not be familiar with within thirty minutes of reading."

5. Hold study hall. At Amazon, everyone gets a printed copy of the document when they enter the meeting, and not a moment sooner. The attendees then read the material in silence. If attendees are remote, of course, they're allowed to read the paper on a computer, but it's ideal to read the memo together in the same room. Bezos refers to the time spent silently reading as "study hall."

At Microsoft, which adopted the Amazon narrative idea, documents are uploaded to a collaborative platform like SharePoint, where readers make their comments in real time. With this method, everyone can see each other's comments. When someone supports a point, they'll write "+1," which means, "I agree." In just a moment, you'll learn why and how the Amazon narrative made its way into Microsoft.

Regardless of format—printed copies or online documents—those who did not work on the memo shouldn't be allowed to read it ahead of time.

For years, new hires at Amazon were taken aback by the "eerie silence" during the first twenty minutes of a meeting. After exchanging greetings, the room goes silent while everyone reads the prepared memo. At an average reading pace of three minutes a page, a six-page memo should take about eighteen to twenty minutes for everyone to finish. That leaves the remaining forty minutes for discussion, assuming a typical one-hour meeting.

Amazonians adapt the memo length and discussion time for the type of meeting they're holding. Let's say you attend a meeting that's scheduled for thirty minutes. After exchanging pleasantries and catching up with your peers for a couple of minutes, you sit down and silently read a two-page memo. After another six minutes or so, everyone looks up from the document they've finished reading, leaving twenty minutes to discuss the idea, challenge the arguments, question the tactics, provide feedback, ask questions, and determine the next steps.

For the record, if you're in a meeting with Bezos, there's a good chance he'll be the last one to finish reading. Bezos has an uncanny ability to arrive at insights nobody in the room saw coming. "He assumes each sentence is wrong until he can prove it otherwise,"[12] says Bryar. "He's challenging the content of the sentence, not the motive of the writer."

If it sounds stressful, it is, according to Amazonians who have experienced the narrative experience. Jesse Freeman, a developer who spent five years at the company, said preparing the narrative memo was the most challenging and intense part of his job. "It felt like writing a master's thesis,"[13] he recalls. And yet, Freeman continued to use the method after he left the company. Writing narratives is simply "one of the most powerful ways you can organize your thoughts to share with others."

COACHING DRILL

Write narratives before creating slides. Although PowerPoint is banned at Amazon senior-level meetings, Amazon executives use PowerPoint with customers, partners, and external audiences. But PowerPoint is not a storytelling tool, and bullet points are not stories. Build the story first by experimenting with written narratives. Narrative structure requires a theme, titles and subtitles, and fully formed sentences with nouns, verbs, and objects. Try writing the story you want to convey *before* you start building slides. PowerPoint slides don't tell the story; slides *complement* the story.

NARRATIVE IS TOO GOOD TO IGNORE

The Amazon six-pager is "the start of a fruitful conversation," says Whole Foods cofounder and CEO John Mackey. Amazon bought the natural foods grocery chain for $13 billion in 2017. Mackey told me that he "embraced" the six-pager when he first learned about it at Amazon and brought it to Whole Foods.

"It's part of why the merger has been such a positive one,"[14] Mackey says. "At Whole Foods, we tended to lead with our gut, and Amazon tends to lead with the data. I believe we've really benefited from the rigor of that process. Amazon hasn't dictated a different culture at Whole Foods, but rather we've benefited from using some of their processes to improve our business of delivering high-quality natural food. It's been a terrific marriage in that way."

Mackey isn't alone. Former Amazonians and leaders whose companies partner with Amazon have adopted the narrative process.

We've already heard from Adam Selipsky, who said, "One of the things I flagrantly ripped off from Amazon was the narrative."[15] Selipsky first joined Amazon in 2005, where, for the next eleven years, he participated in preparing six-pagers for S-Team meetings. One of those six-pagers launched Amazon's cloud division, AWS. In 2021, five years after Selipsky had left the company, he returned to run AWS, which brings in $50 billion a year and commands 47 percent of the cloud market.

Selipsky admitted that the narrative tool seemed "weird" at first, but its benefit was too great to ignore.

"Just try it," says former Amazon director Ronny Kohavi.

You probably don't know Kohavi, but his work knows you. The tools he's developed for Amazon, Microsoft, and Airbnb might even know your habits better than you know yourself.

Kohavi is among the most influential scholars in the field of artificial intelligence and machine learning. Out of 140,000 employees at Microsoft, Kohavi was one of only forty Technical Fellows, a designation informally known as the company's "big brains."

Before joining Microsoft, Kohavi led data mining and personalization at Amazon. His ideas turned into features worth hundreds of millions of dollars in annual revenue. Kohavi explained data mining to me as "the process of discovering novel patterns in data using tools like machine learning. By mining the data, we [data mining experts] help companies make better predictions and personalize the experience for each customer."[16]

When you visit the Amazon home page, you're greeted by name and offered recommendations on what to buy, what to watch, or what to do. That's personalization. When you're craving a pizza and type in your location into Google or Bing, it returns pizza joints near your location. That's personalization. When you log in to your Netflix account, it recommends movies for you. That's personalization. Suppose your friends or family members visit their profiles. In that case, Netflix will serve up different recommendations based on what *they've* watched in the past, what they've searched for, how long they've watched a program, and many other individual metrics. If you feel like the company really knows you, that's because it does. That's why the field has become known as 'one-to-one' personalization.

Think about it this way: When you walk into a brick-and-mortar retail store, the aisles don't arrange themselves based on your preferences and shopping history. Walk through the digital door of an online retailer, and the aisles rearrange themselves instantly. The website or mobile app predicts what you're looking for and invites you to learn about choices you've never considered.

Experts like Kohavi are behind every one of those personalized digital experiences. He just happens to be one of the best at it.

Kohavi had a secret code on his Washington license plate that communicated his status to other computer scientists. It read: DM P13N. It's a numeronym, a number-based word. DM stands for *data mining* and the numeral *13* represents the number of letters between *P* and *N* that spell *personalization.*

Kohavi was on the email string in 2004 that announced the ban on PowerPoint in S-Team meetings. It marked the first time Kohavi, who has a Ph.D. in machine learning, had been exposed to the narrative process. It didn't take him long to recognize its value as a "forcing function," challenging the writer to think clearly about expressing their idea. Kohavi didn't just like writing narratives; he became an evangelist, introducing it to teams in his next company, Microsoft.

"Try it. That's my key message," Kohavi says. "When I came to Microsoft, narrative documents had never been used. I started using it with my team. People from other groups who attended our meetings were surprised at the silence while everyone read the document, but once we explained the process, they not only participated in the process, they brought it to their groups."

Kohavi says introducing a new way of presenting ideas is a lot like introducing A/B testing to an organization. At Microsoft, Kohavi led a team of 110 data scientists and developers who started controlled experiments (A/B testing). Their research helped Microsoft transition from a shrink-wrapped software company to a cloud company.[17]

A/B testing is a data-driven method to test an idea's potential quickly. Today, companies from Amazon to Walmart and Microsoft to LinkedIn use A/B testing to identify revenue-generating features or to improve customer satisfaction (which, in turn, boosts 'customer lifetime revenue,' a critical metric for the success of a company).

Bezos touted the value of experimentation in his 2013 letter. "We have our own internal experimentation platform called Weblab that we use to evaluate improvements to our websites and products. In 2013, we ran 1,976 Weblabs worldwide, up from 546 in 2011,"[18] he wrote. "One recent success is our new feature called 'Ask an owner' . . . from a product page, customers can ask any question related to the product. *Is the product compatible with my TV/Stereo/PC? Is it easy to assemble? How long does the battery last?* We then route these questions to *owners* of the product. As is the case with reviews, customers are happy to share their knowledge to directly help other customers."

Kohavi says that seemingly minor changes can increase revenues by tens of millions of dollars. In one test Kohavi performed at Microsoft, the data showed improving a website's loading speed by one hundred milliseconds would result in an additional $18 million in incremental revenue. "Amazon's experiments, for instance, revealed that moving credit card offers from its home page to the shopping cart page boosted profits by tens of millions of dollars annually. Clearly, small investments can yield big returns."

Kohavi says that most companies did not recognize the value of such testing until they were introduced to the method. "Once teams are exposed to this scientific method of running A/B tests, they love it, and they bring it into other work," Kohavi says. "When I started at Microsoft, no A/B testing was going on. When I left Microsoft, we were starting one hundred new controlled experiments every day on my team's platform. The company went from zero to conducting twenty thousand experiments every year. It catches on and scales."

Narratives will catch on with your team once they recognize its value.

Kohavi offers the following advice to business professionals in any occupation, but especially to those in technical fields: "Storytelling is part of your job. Writing and presenting skills are critical. Math is important to learn, but many people miss the fact that in a real-world setting, in any organization, your job is to convince others to take action based upon some pattern that you discovered in the data. The ability to translate technical findings into a convincing narrative that is accessible to others who are not as technical is a super-critical skill."

Kohavi says that Bezos is a brilliant translator. "He can go technical, but he can step back and write an amazing and thoughtful piece. The ability to take an idea and make it into something memorable is one of those things that Jeff did amazingly well."

Former Amazonian Brad Porter, the distinguished engineer who spent thirteen years at the company, says narrative is a critical element of Amazon's success. "Amazon absolutely runs better, makes better decisions, and scales better because of this particular innovation,"[19] according to Porter. "Imagine for a moment that you could go into a meeting, and everyone in the meeting would have very deep context on the topic you're going to discuss. They would be well-versed in the critical data for your business. Imagine if everyone understood the core tenets you operate by and internalized how you're applying them to your decisions. This is what meetings are like at Amazon, and it is magical."

COACHING DRILL

Jeff Bezos wrote twenty-four years of annual Amazon shareholder letters. Many take the form of well-written narratives. Each letter has a theme, a clear and logical order, and supporting stories and data. Visit the website, AboutAmazon.com, and search "shareholder letters." The following letters are a good starting point: 1997, 2006, 2013, 2014, 2017, and 2020. These letters are well structured, have clear overarching themes, and use metaphorical language to explain complex ideas.

The magic doesn't end at six pages. The narrative memo is only one type of narrative document that leaders at Amazon use to make critical decisions. In the next chapter, you'll learn about another tool that will change the way you pitch ideas and elevate your influence in any organization. Get ready to move forward by working backwards.

10

WORKING BACKWARDS TO GET AHEAD

We have a whole process that starts with the customer and works backwards.

—Jeff Bezos

Bill Carr entered a meeting with Jeff Bezos armed with the tools he had sharpened since business school. Carr was a spreadsheet warrior; PowerPoint and Excel were his weapons of choice.

Carr feared he had been demoted just a few weeks earlier. After four years of rising through Amazon's leadership ranks, he was serving as a director for the company's massive U.S. books, music, and video unit—a division that made up 77 percent of Amazon's global revenue. That's why Carr could not wrap his head around his boss's decision to put him in charge of Amazon's smallest venture, a new "digital media" business. It didn't take long for Carr to accept the role. Once Carr learned that Bezos had given his personal blessing, he was sold. Bezos was the most extraordinary entrepreneur Carr had ever met, a visionary who could see around corners. He wanted to play a role in anything Bezos set his sights on.

Although Carr had a new title (vice president) and a new role, he relied on the same tools he had always used to build a business case: a SWOT analysis, financial forecasts, and detailed spreadsheets calculating operating margins and market size. "I was an MBA. That's what I did,"[1] Carr told me.

Bezos sat at the table and carefully studied Carr's projections. He didn't seem convinced. Finally, Bezos looked up and asked, "Where are the mock-ups?"

Mock-ups at Amazon were created to show the entire customer journey on a website—from how the page looks to how customers navigate the site. Mock-ups required time and capital. Carr didn't have any mock-ups. He simply wanted to get budget approval to assemble a digital media team.

Bezos did not approve Carr's budget request and sent him back to the drawing board. Carr returned a few weeks later and brought the mock-ups Bezos had requested.

Bezos posed tough questions:

- How would the music service be different from iTunes?
- How much would ebooks cost?
- Would readers prefer to read ebooks on a tablet, phone, or PC?
- How, exactly, would Amazon's digital offerings be better for customers than anything currently available?

Carr's answers failed to satisfy Bezos. "To Jeff, a half-baked mock-up was evidence of half-baked thinking," says Carr.

After several frustrating meetings, Bezos suggested a different approach. "Forget the spreadsheets and slides," he said. Instead, for the next meeting, all ten executives were required to write a narrative, a memo in which they described their best idea for the digital media business.

The next meeting was more productive and sparked creative ideas. One executive proposed an ebook reader with new screen technology. Others offered new versions of MP3 players. Bezos proposed an idea he called the "Amazon Puck," a device that sits on the counter and responds to voice command. Ten years later, Amazon introduced the Echo Dot, a hockey puck–shaped smart speaker. Putting their ideas in writing "freed executives from the quantitative demands of Excel and the visual seduction of PowerPoint."[2]

Bezos, seeing the success of the narrative process, took it one step further. "Let's write the press release first," he said.

When a company launches a product and service, it typically distributes a press release to announce the new offering. In most organizations, the press release is a function delegated to marketing and public relations. Bezos flipped the script, challenging his executives to work backwards from the customer's perspective and to ask themselves *why* their customers will love the product or service.

Pitching an idea by starting with the press release focuses the team's attention on developing features and services that will truly delight customers. It answers the question *So what?* When a customer hears about a product or service for the first time, they think, *So what? What does it mean to me?*

When Amazon began using the future press release system—another one of those Amazon "mechanisms"—it soon became apparent that another narrative process would be required to address internal challenges and technical issues that arose during the development process. The solution was to add several pages of frequently asked questions (FAQs). The FAQ gives developers and decision-makers a clear view of the hurdles they'll have to overcome to turn their ideas into reality.

The working-backwards document at Amazon became known as the *PR/FAQ*. Since there's no requirement to include an FAQ as part of the process, the remainder of this chapter will focus on the press release, a memo that anyone can write to pitch ideas, evaluate ideas, and align teams around a common vision for new products, services, and businesses.

The method of working backwards from the customer is so central to Amazon's model that Carr named the book he cowrote with former Amazonian Bill Bryar *Working Backwards*. Their combined twenty-seven years of experience at Amazon yields insights, leadership, and management strategies for anyone at any level in business.

My conversations with Carr and Bryar convinced me that the mock press release is one of the most powerful writing techniques you can adopt to launch a company or kick off the development of a new product or service. It works because it forces you and your team to put the customer at the center of the conversation.

The PR/FAQ turned ideas into products, services, and companies that touch your life every day, even if you don't buy products on Amazon. Here's a short list of ideas that started off as PR/FAQs:

- Amazon Prime
- Amazon Prime Video
- Amazon Studios
- Amazon Music
- Amazon Smile
- Amazon Marketplace

- Amazon Echo and Alexa
- Fulfillment by Amazon

Those are only some of the Amazon examples. Start-ups and companies in every major business category have adopted the PR/FAQ system that Amazon pioneered. I've talked to many start-up founders and career professionals who are taught to follow the mock press release system to draft new ideas or pitch new projects—and some of them aren't even aware that Bezos was behind it. They just know that once they tried it, they wished they had discovered it sooner.

Simply put, working backwards is the best way to build the future.

OPRAH'S FAVORITE "FAVORITE THING"

The PR/FAQ was born of frustration. Amazon's leadership team struggled to identify the type of products that customers would crave from the newly formed digital media division.

One of the first products that began its development journey as a PR/FAQ revolutionized the publishing industry and changed the reading habits of millions of people. The product was called the Kindle.

Amazon launched the Kindle e-reader on November 19, 2007. The first batch sold out in six hours. Sales exploded the following year when Oprah, queen of the book club, gave Kindle her stamp of approval. "It's absolutely my new favorite, favorite thing in the world,"[3] Oprah raved. "I'm really not a gadget person at all, but I have fallen in love with this little baby."

If the press release had not been the first step in Kindle's development, Oprah would have had a lot less to love. Oprah loved the product for one of its key features: She could think of a book and get it in sixty seconds.

Working backwards from the PR/FAQ gave Kindle developers the idea that customers would genuinely be delighted to download books from anywhere, with no need to connect to a PC or purchase a separate wireless contract. "If you're like me and a little computer challenged, do not be afraid of the Kindle—do not be afraid—because you don't even have to have a computer for it to work," added Oprah. "That's the brilliant thing about it."

Oprah is not a secondary character in the evolution of the Amazon

PR/FAQ. She's top of mind. Amazonians are trained to write mock press releases in "Oprah-speak." Imagine yourself sitting on the couch opposite Oprah. How would you describe the product to Oprah and millions of viewers representing a broad range of knowledge? *Geek-speak* is fine for internal conversations with peers, but *Oprah-speak* is the language of the masses.

Six elements make up the Amazon press release formula. Keep in mind that a "future" press release is a document that's written, debated, rewritten, and debated. The first drafts are messy and imperfect. The final document brings clarity, aligning the team around a common vision. Since the official Kindle press release closely resembled the team's original vision, I'll use it as a blueprint to explain the six parts of the Amazon press release.

1. HEADLINE

Introducing Amazon Kindle.[4]

The headline is a trumpet that heralds the product's arrival. In one or two lines, it clarifies *who* is making the announcement and *what* they're announcing. The header includes the name of the product when appropriate, but it's not reserved for product announcements. On February 2, 2021, Amazon's press department issued a release with the following headline: "Amazon.com Announces CEO Transition." It answers *who* is making the announcement and *what* they're announcing.

2. SUBHEADING

Revolutionary Portable Reader Lets Customers Wirelessly
Download Books in Less Than a Minute and Automatically
Receive Newspapers, Magazines and Blogs. No PC Required,
No Hunting for Wi-Fi Hot Spots.

The subheading is the first sentence under the title that describes a product's most compelling customer benefit or differentiator. The subheading is the hook that gives readers a reason to pay attention. It must be written in concise and everyday language, highlighting the most eye-catching benefit that will delight the customer.

The subheading is critical. It acts as the logline you learned about in chapter 4. You'll recall that a logline is a prerequisite for Hollywood pitch meetings. It answers the fundamental question, *What's the movie about?* An ideal logline should be no more than thirty words. The subheading in Kindle's press release is twenty-nine words.

3. SUMMARY PARAGRAPH

Seattle—November 19, 2007—Amazon.com today introduced Amazon Kindle, a revolutionary portable reader that wirelessly downloads books, blogs, magazines and newspapers to a crisp, high-resolution electronic paper display that looks and reads like real paper, even in bright sunlight. More than 90,000 books are now available in the Kindle Store, including 101 of 112 current New York Times Best Sellers and New Releases, which are $9.99, unless marked otherwise. Kindle is available starting today for $399.

The introductory first paragraph of a press release is known as a *summary paragraph*. It begins with a location and a date. It's important to add a date even in a "future" press release because it forces a discussion about the feasibility of the project. The introduction offers a concise summary of the product and its benefits. Put 80 percent of your creative energy into the title, subtitle, and summary paragraph because 80 percent of your readers will stop reading at this point.

4. PROBLEM PARAGRAPH

"We've been working on Kindle for more than three years. Our top design objective was for Kindle to disappear in your hands—to get out of the way—so you can enjoy your reading," said Jeff Bezos, Amazon.com Founder and CEO. "We also wanted to go beyond the physical book. Kindle is wireless, so whether you're lying in bed or riding a train, you can think of a book, and have it in less than 60 seconds. No computer is needed—you do your shopping directly from the device. We're excited to make Kindle available today."

The second paragraph explains the problem your product or service intends to solve. There's no requirement that quotes appear in the problem paragraph, but in the Kindle press release, they made the creative decision to let Bezos do the talking. The critical thing to remember about the second paragraph is that it must raise a problem the product solves—otherwise, there's no reason for the solution.

5. SOLUTION AND BENEFITS PARAGRAPHS (THREE TO SIX)

Downloads Content Wirelessly, No PC Required, No Hunting for Wi-Fi Hot Spots

The Kindle wireless delivery system, Amazon Whispernet, uses the same nationwide high-speed data network (EVDO) as advanced cell phones. Kindle customers can wirelessly shop the Kindle Store, download or receive new content—all without a PC, Wi-Fi hot spot, or syncing.

The third paragraph of a press release begins to take a deeper dive into the details of the product, service, or idea. Customer problems are resolved simply and delightfully. Solution paragraphs include an explanation of how the product or service works and how easy it is to get started. Keep these paragraphs short, no more than three or four sentences.

In the Kindle press release, bold subheads call out the benefits of the product. A few short details follow each bullet point. For example, "Download Content Wirelessly" was the chief benefit. Others included:

- No Monthly Wireless Bills or Commitments
- Reads Like Paper
- Books, Blogs, Magazines and Newspapers
- Holds Hundreds of Books in 10.3 Ounces
- Built-In Dictionary and Wikipedia
- Long Battery Life

Be selective about the benefits you highlight. The entire press release should fit on a page. If you've written one and a half pages, it's too long.

6. PARTNERSHIPS HIGHLIGHTS, EXECUTIVE QUOTES, OR CUSTOMER TESTIMONIALS

> *Kindle customers can select from the most recognized U.S.*
> *newspapers, as well as popular magazines and journals, such*
> *as* The New York Times, Wall Street Journal, Washington
> Post, Atlantic Monthly, TIME *and* Fortune. *The Kindle Store*
> *also includes top international newspapers from France,*
> *Germany, and Ireland, including* Le Monde, Frankfurter
> Allgemeine *and* The Irish Times.

Engaging quotes or testimonials from company spokespeople, part-ners, and customers make up the sixth element of an ideal press release. In this press release, a Bezos quote was offered earlier, so this paragraph highlights partnerships. Even if you're writing a future press release for a product that's nothing more than a sparkle in your eye, you should still go through the exercise of including quotes from hypothetical customers ex-pressing their joy or highlighting your ideal partners. This is your chance to clarify precisely why customers will love your idea.

"Before we write a line of code, we start with the press release," says Amazon CEO Andy Jassy. "The press release is designed to flush out all the benefits of the product to make sure that you're really solving the cus-tomer problem."[5]

THE BEZOS "RED PEN"

While Carr's team was working on the Kindle in 2004, Jassy was also experimenting with the press release technique to pitch his idea for a com-puting storage business, an idea that became Amazon Web Services.

"Contrary to how other companies think about development, Andy and the AWS team spent their first eighteen months just working with Jeff Bezos, writing and refining PR/FAQ documents,"[6] Carr recalls.

Engineers on that team complained to Jeff's technical assistant. They said, "Doesn't Jeff know that we're engineers who are paid to write code, not Word documents?" But Jeff and Andy were committed to the process. They spent a year and a half writing narratives and press releases before they started writing code for the business that became AWS, a division that became the fastest business in history to reach $10 billion in sales. The secret to success for AWS is that they spent all this time up front: planning, writing, and documenting what they should do before they started doing it.

"If I was the dean of a business school," Carr adds, "I would insist on formal training for writing a cogent business memo or document."[7]

In the first quarter of 2021, Amazon recorded its highest quarterly sales ever, $108 billion. The company credited a 36 percent increase in Amazon Prime and other subscription revenue for propelling its sales. Bezos announced that Amazon had topped two hundred million Prime members worldwide. Today, nearly 60 percent of American households have a Prime membership, which offers free shipping, fast delivery, and other perks in exchange for an annual fee.

Amazon announced the launch of Prime in February of 2005. Customers received an email about the new program in the form of a letter signed by Jeff Bezos. The letter began: "Dear Customers, I am very excited to announce Amazon Prime, our first ever membership program, which provides 'all-you-can-eat' express shipping."[8]

In just over two hundred words, Bezos described the service and its benefits in clear, straightforward language. He even highlighted the simplicity of the program.

"It's simple," he wrote. "For a flat annual membership fee, you get unlimited two-day shipping for free on over a million in-stock items." The idea worked and the number of items available to purchase directly from Amazon has exploded to more than twelve million today (not including the hundreds of millions of products sold through third-party sellers).

"Amazon Prime takes the effort out of ordering: no minimum purchase and no consolidating orders," Bezos continued. "Two-day shipping becomes an everyday experience rather than an occasional indulgence." The rest of the letter explained the fee and some other benefits that customers would find appealing. Bezos ended the letter with a call to action—a link to sign up as easy as "1-click."

What customers didn't know was that Bezos had drafted the letter a couple of months earlier during Prime's development process. The official launch letter closely resembled earlier versions of the release. The "all-you-can-eat" analogy was the result of a collaborative process while the name, Prime, was all Bezos.

Amazon Prime is now the internet's most successful membership program, creating a powerful recurring revenue engine for the company. The majority of American households are now Prime members, spending an average of $3,000 a year on Amazon. Prime Day, a popular forty-eight-hour event for members, generates more sales than all retailers *combined* on Black Friday, historically the biggest retail shopping day of the year in the U.S.

The "all-you-can-eat" analogy was unanimously supported by Amazon's senior leaders. As Bezos later joked, "What happens when you offer a free, all-you-can-eat buffet? Who shows up first? The heavy eaters! It's scary. It's like, 'Oh my God, did I really say you can have as many prawns as you can eat?' That's what happened. But we saw the trend lines and what kind of customers we were attracting."[9]

"Bezos takes a red pen to press releases, product descriptions, speeches, and shareholder letters, crossing out anything that does not speak simply and positively to customers,"[10] writes Brad Stone in *The Everything Store*. "Bezos didn't believe anyone could make a good decision about a feature or a product without knowing precisely how it would be communicated to the world—and what the hallowed customer would make of it."

Bezos maintains high standards during the narrative-writing process. According to Stone, it's not unusual for Bezos to suggest a punchier headline or to say, "I'm already bored," after he's read a few sentences of a memo. "He wanted people thinking deeply and taking the time to express their thoughts cogently."

Stone got the hint. When he requested direct access to Bezos for his book, he made his request in the form of a narrative, imagining what the book's press release would say upon publication.

WRITING THAT FORCES CLEAR AND PRECISE THINKING

Writing a mock press release is meant to be hard. It forces you to clarify your ideas with precision, more so than you could ever do with bullet points on a slide. It requires clear explanations to the following questions:

- How will customers interact with the product?
- How is it different from anything that exists today?
- What features will customers find most appealing?
- Why will customers love the product or service?

These questions were on Jennifer Cast's mind in 2015 when she wrote a PR/FAQ to win internal support for a new idea that, at first glance, seemed counterintuitive for a company that had made its fortune online. Cast had been tapped to lead Amazon's first move into physical locations.

As vice president of Amazon Books, Cast was excited about giving consumers another channel to find books they love. Cast was Amazon's twenty-fifth employee, living and breathing the mantra of customer obsession. Cast wasn't interested in creating another physical bookstore; she was obsessed with giving customers something entirely different. Cast's research uncovered a critical find: If the company that had opened the world's biggest bookstore wanted to reimagine the in-store customer experience, it would have to think smaller than traditional stores. By building smaller stores that fit in higher-trafficked areas and offering a smaller selection of books, Amazon could offer customers something different. Cast was excited to share her ideas, but first she had to put them in writing.

"The first thing to know is that writing a PR/FAQ is a big commitment that takes time and tenacity,"[11] Cast says. "Over the six weeks that I wrote the Amazon Books PR/FAQ, I spent at least 120 hours writing at least twelve drafts." Cast's work paid off. Her "working backwards" meeting lasted ninety minutes, concluding with Bezos and members of the S-Team giving the green light to the development of Amazon's first physical stores.

Table 10 shows the elements of Cast's mock press release that gave life to Amazon Books.

Table 10: Mock Press Release for Amazon Books[12]

Headline:	Amazon Opens Offline Bookstores with Online Features and Benefits
Subheading:	Stores Include Amazon's Full Line of Devices and Offer Customers Same Low Prices as Amazon.com.
First Paragraph:	In this paragraph, Cast announced that Amazon had opened its first physical store. She specified its location along with several customer benefits.
Second Paragraph:	Cast made a creative choice in this paragraph. She opted to avoid stating a "problem" since there wasn't really a problem with brick-and-mortar bookstores. Instead, she opted to write a hypothetical quote from Jeff Bezos highlighting some of the differences that would make Amazon Books a better experience for the company's customers.

Paragraphs Three to Six:	Cast provided details that would guide designers as they created the in-store experience.
Company Quotes / Customer Testimonials:	She included quotes from customers—again, hypothetical. The customers expressed their enthusiasm about seeing books faced out, reading Amazon ratings and reviews, comparing Amazon tablets, discovering new items like Fire TV Stick, and using the mobile app to place orders or find more information. Cast says customer testimonials are a key part of the press release process because they help decision-makers evaluate the strength of the idea. If the quotes are weak, then it's likely the idea fails to deliver substantial value to a large enough customer base to make the project worthwhile.

Amazon opened its first physical bookstore at Seattle's University Village mall on November 3, 2015. Jennifer Cast credits the PR/FAQ for providing a clear direction and keeping the team obsessed with the customer experience. She points out that Amazon's first Leadership Principle doesn't read customer "service" or customer "focus." It reads, "Customer Obsession: Leaders start with the customer and work backwards." The press release forces everyone on the team to put the customer at the center of the experience.

COACHING DRILL

Use the table below to draft a mock press release for your idea: a start-up, product, service, company, or plan.

Topic:	(Product, initiative, service, or company.)
Headline:	(It answers *who* is making the announcement and *what* they're announcing.)
Subheading:	(The subheading is the hook that gives the reader a reason to pay attention. It must be concise. Keep it under thirty words.)
First (Summary) Paragraph:	(This first paragraph is an introduction that offers a concise summary of the product, initiative, service, or company and its benefits.)
Second (Problem) Paragraph:	(The second paragraph explains the problem your product, initiative, service, or company intends to solve.)

Paragraphs Three to Six:	(The third to sixth paragraphs dive deeper into the details of your product, initiative, service, or company and how it solves the problem.)
Company Quotes / Customer Testimonials:	(Use engaging quotes from company spokespeople, partners, and customers, even if they don't exist yet.)

WORKING BACKWARDS FAST-TRACKS CAREERS

Anyone can use the press release template to guide product development, align teams, clarify proposals, or pitch ideas for new businesses, products, and services.

John, a division president for an international medical-device company, told me about his experience with the Amazon press release. John had flown to Seattle with some members of his team to discuss a potential partnership with Amazon. It was the first time John had been exposed to Amazon's press release writing assignment.

While John appreciated Amazon's commitment to the PR/FAQ, he doubted the value of the exercise for his company. John admits he only went along with it because Amazon had graciously invited his team to a brainstorming meeting. "Yes, we were skeptical. We'd honor their process but, frankly, we thought it would be a waste of time," John told me. But as he went through the exercise, John found that it forced him to explain his idea in a clear and simple way so anyone would immediately recognize its value. "By the time we left the meeting, we were sold," John said. "We loved it. We became evangelists for the press release. I'm not exaggerating. It changed the world for our team."

John's not exaggerating. Upon returning home, John and his team began preparing a pitch for the company's CEO. The team would ask for approval to partner with Amazon and the funding to complete the project. The team was given sixty minutes to make their case. The company has locations across 150 countries, and the CEO's time is precious. They were grateful for getting a full hour.

John then made a bold decision. He convinced the team to create a twenty-minute presentation, giving the CEO forty minutes of his time back. If the chief executive had more questions, they'd come armed with answers. But the pitch itself would last no more than twenty minutes.

John is a student of communication and recognized that long presentations are often convoluted, disjointed, overwhelming, and just plain boring. Short presentations are almost always more persuasive than long ones.

John's team went to work. They created a twenty-minute presentation to summarize the meeting they had with Amazon, define the potential partnership, paint a picture of how the idea would benefit patients, and persuade the CEO to approve a significant budget request.

John had not forgotten about the future press release model he learned at Amazon. But instead of writing a memo, he took the concept one step further. "If we're going to work backwards from the patient's perspective, let's start with the TV ad that would air after the product is released," John suggested. "The video will demonstrate how easy it is for a patient to order the therapy and to use it from the convenience of their home. The video will also show how we partner with Amazon cloud technology to send the test results to a patient's doctor quickly and easily."

John's team created a two-minute video with actors playing the role of future patients. They inserted the video into the presentation. John watched the CEO as the video played. "His eyes lit up," John recalls.

The video ended, and John returned to the slides. "Now that you've seen the vision, let me show you how we'll get there: We need an investment in people, talent, and resources."

The meeting, originally scheduled for one hour, lasted about thirty minutes. The CEO enthusiastically approved John's budget request. The therapy is expected to enter clinical trials in 2022, followed by submission for regulatory approval in 2023. It promises to leverage cutting-edge medical technology and Amazon's cloud-computing power to catch certain types of cancers very early, preventing millions of deaths.

Working backwards from the press release did, indeed, change John's life. John earned a promotion to lead the groundbreaking project. He's been named one of only twenty division presidents in a global company of more than one hundred thousand employees. "I wouldn't be in this position if it hadn't been for communication skills," John told me. "The ability to convey compelling ideas clearly and concisely is a critical skill. If you want to grow in a large company—or raise money for a start-up—you have to convince a boss, CEO, or investor. I'm an example of how presentation skills can make a career."

GETTING EVERYONE ON THE SAME PAGE

"Alignment" is a common theme that comes up in my conversations with business professionals who adopt the working-backwards system.

Zane, an ambitious product manager for a high-tech firm, told me that his company uses the PR/FAQ to keep stakeholders aligned around strategic initiatives. Zane's executive team imposes a strict one-page limit to the press release, which he writes at least once a quarter to propose new ideas.

"If you can't explain the problem your idea solves in a sentence or two, you probably don't understand the problem well enough," Zane says. "If you can't state the customer benefits in a few sentences, and show— with quotes—why they'll love the product, you don't know your customer well enough. If you can't explain—again in a sentence or two—how your product is different from the competition or how it will make your customer's life easier, it'll be nearly impossible to build the support you'll need internally."

Zane is a thirty-one-year-old manager who dreams big and hopes to be the CEO of a large company. During the COVID pandemic, Zane's company allowed all its employees to work remotely. Like many companies, Zane's firm discovered that managing a "distributed workforce" was not only possible, many employees preferred it.

"Now, with everyone on my team working remotely and in different time zones, writing is more important than ever," says Zane. "I need to distill my thoughts into a concise format that everyone will understand. I have to make sure my stakeholders across finance, sales, technology, and customer success are all aligned."

Product managers are known as "mini CEOs" because of their cross-functional role. "I'm dealing with four or five different audiences," says Zane. "I have to talk in engineering language to developers building the product. I have to talk numbers with the CFO and clearly explain the impact of our product on the company's bottom line. I have to convince our salespeople that customers will love the product and spend more money with us. Everything I communicate must be specific to the audience. If I'm not able to adapt my message for different audiences, I'll be inefficient and less successful."

Working backwards is a critical step for anyone proposing new ideas. Rocket scientist Ozan Varol says NASA has its own form of the Amazon press release they call *backcasting*. Varol and the team of scientists behind the Mars rover expeditions wrote future press releases to drive the project. "Instead of letting our resources drive our vision, backcasting lets our vision drive the resources."[13]

Varol says backcasting enables moon shot thinking, driving NASA to accomplish the impossible. For example, the rocket technology required to send humans to the moon and return them safely to Earth simply didn't exist in the early 1960s. "NASA began with the result of landing humans on the moon and worked backward to determine the steps necessary to get there,"[14] says Varol. "Get a rocket off the ground first, then put a person in orbit around Earth, then do a spacewalk, then rendezvous and dock with a target vehicle in Earth orbit, and then send a manned spacecraft to the moon to circle around it and come back. Only after these progressive steps in the road map were completed was a moon landing attempted."

"Communication, oral and written, is one of the most important skills that a scientist or a professional can develop,"[15] Varol told me. "Being able to distill what you've been working on—especially on a complicated subject—into language that anyone can understand is a rare but valuable skill. The people who have mastered that skill really tend to stand out."

Good writers stand out.

In the last chapter of this section, you'll learn how great speakers find creative ways to explain their ideas and why they never run out of stories. It's another underappreciated aspect of Amazon's growth—any company that puts a premium on writing also values the power of reading to become a better writer.

11

LEADERS ARE READERS

Good leaders must be good communicators, and the hard work of writing is best sharpened on the whetstone of reading.

—Admiral James Stavridis, U.S. Navy (ret.)

Three decades before launching Earth's biggest bookstore, Jeff Bezos discovered a small selection of novels that inspired him to dream big.

Bezos spent the summers of his formative years between the ages of four and sixteen living and working on his grandfather's cattle ranch in Cotulla, Texas. The ranchers who work the land in West Texas are proud to call Cotulla home, though they find it difficult to describe where it is. "It's halfway between San Antonio and Laredo," Bezos says.

When a local benefactor donated science-fiction books to the town's library, it stirred a passion in Bezos to pursue interstellar travel, a vision that would never leave him. Bezos, a precocious student, devoured the works of Jules Verne, Isaac Asimov, and Robert Heinlein. As a sixth grader, Bezos could articulate the values he learned from J. R. R. Tolkien's *The Hobbit*. The book's theme that uncommon heroes can rise from ordinary circumstances strongly resonated with the future adventure-seeker.

Books lit a competitive fire in young Bezos. At the age of twelve, he read a variety of books to earn a special reader's certificate. Revealing an early competitive instinct, he was determined not to be out-read by other students. Bezos even "compared himself unfavorably to another classmate who claimed, improbably, that she was reading a dozen books a week."

Bezos surrounds himself with books. Hundreds of volumes are on display in his lakefront Seattle home, including the works of futurist Arthur C. Clarke, whom Bezos quotes in his shareholder letters. According to biographer Brad Stone, "While others read these classics and only dreamed of alternate realities, Bezos seemed to consider the books blueprints for an exciting future."[1]

The Jules Verne classic *From the Earth to the Moon* resonated deeply with Bezos. His friend Danny Hillis once remarked that "Jeff sees himself and Blue Origin as part of a bigger story. It's the next step in what Jules Verne was writing about and what the Apollo missions accomplished."[2]

In the atrium of Blue Origin's headquarters about seventeen miles south of Seattle, visitors find a two-story model rocket inspired by Verne's classic novel. According to Stone, the model is "a full-scale steampunk model of a Victorian-era spaceship as it might have been described in the fiction of Jules Verne, complete with a cockpit, brass controls, and nineteenth-century furnishings. Visitors can venture inside, sit on the velvet-covered seats, and imagine themselves as intrepid explorers in the time of Captain Nemo and Phileas Fogg."[3]

Amazon wasn't the first entrepreneurial venture Bezos dreamed up. While attending Palmetto Senior High School, Bezos came up with an idea for a summer camp for middle school students—the DREAM Institute. Students would be required to read a selection of books Bezos curated himself: *David Copperfield, Stranger in a Strange Land, Gulliver's Travels, Black Beauty, The Once and Future King, Lord of the Rings, Treasure Island,* and *Watership Down.*

Although the venture failed to launch, Bezos never lost his passion for sharing books with those in his orbit.

Bezos believes that a leader's role is sharing the knowledge they acquire through books. Over the summer of 2013, Bezos held three all-day book clubs for Amazon's senior executives. "We read business books together and talked about the strategy, the vision, and the context,"[4] Bezos told a CNBC reporter. "Those books really just become frameworks that we can use to talk about the business. It gives us a chance to know each other better."

Bezos isn't the only billionaire to make reading books a top priority. From Richard Branson to Warren Buffett, Sara Blakely to Oprah Winfrey, Ray Dalio to Elon Musk, billionaires read far more books than average.

One comprehensive survey of Americans' reading habits found that about one-quarter of U.S. adults (27 percent) don't read any books. Only one out of every five people surveyed said they read twelve or more books a year.[5] To put that into perspective, if you simply read one book a month and get through half of another, you'll join an elite group of avid readers and super achievers.

Retired U.S. Navy admiral James Stavridis is a reading outlier. He reads at least one hundred books a year, nearly ten times the number of books the average American adult consumes per year. "I can tell you with direct knowledge that by the time someone has ascended to four-star rank as a full general or admiral, they are profoundly deep readers,"[6] Stavridis told me.

Stavridis doesn't expect other leaders to read two to three books a week or match his library of four thousand books. But he does urge aspiring leaders in any profession to read far more books—fiction and nonfiction—than others in their field.

FOUR REASONS TO READ MORE BOOKS THAN YOU DO NOW

1. Books are simulators for the mind.

"Reading is the sole means by which we slip, involuntarily, often helplessly into another's skin, another's voice, another's soul,"[7] says novelist Joyce Carol Oates.

By allowing you to slip into another person's soul, books act as simulators for the mind. According to neuroscientists, the human brain doesn't distinguish between reading about an experience and experiencing an event in real life. When you place yourself in the middle of circumstances the book's characters face, you can ask yourself, *What would I have done in that situation?*

A little over two decades ago, Stavridis prepared to command a navy destroyer by reading the classic sea novels of Patrick O'Brian, beginning with *Master and Commander*. He also found inspiration in Steven Pressfield's epic novel *Gates of Fire*, about the Spartans who make the ultimate commitment to fight and to die at the Battle of Thermopylae. "When reading that book, you can put yourself in their shoes, understand their motivations, and ask yourself, would I have had the courage, and the commitment, and the honor to undertake that mission?"[8]

2. Books offer perspective.

"Books provide the chance to experience an enormous variety of life experiences without leaving home or school,"[9] says Stavridis. "How else can a young aspiring leader learn how Ernest Shackleton managed to save his entire crew after his ship, *Endurance,* was crushed by ice and destroyed in Antarctica in 1915? As I think back on my lifetime of reading, many of the people I admire most deeply are known to me only through books—either by them or about them."

Entrepreneurs often find inspiration by reading first-person accounts of those who overcame overwhelming odds to turn their vision into reality. For example, in a 2009 *Newsweek* interview, Bezos said, "If you read *The Remains of the Day,* which is one of my favorite books, you can't help but come away and think, I just spent 10 hours living an alternate life, and I learned something about life and regret. You can't do that in a blog post."[10]

3. Books are a valuable form of condensed knowledge.

Even investors who clamor for a piece of the next hot start-up can't match the return on investment a good business book provides.

This book is just under eighty thousand words. If you read it at an average pace, you should be able to finish in a little over four hours. In return for that four-hour commitment, you get twenty-three years of insights from one of the world's richest people, an entrepreneur who turned an idea into a $1.7 trillion colossus. In addition, you're learning communication strategies from former Amazon executives and successful business leaders who have modeled the Bezos blueprint to start their own companies.

A book is the single most valuable tool to boost your leadership skills.

4. Readers are better speakers.

According to Admiral Stavridis, "The essence of leadership is the ability to communicate and inspire. And, to do that, you have to be a good speaker and a good writer. By reading good literature, both fiction and nonfiction, you can enhance your written and verbal skills."

In my own experience, nearly every chief executive who invites me to speak to their organization has read one or more of my books. And, although I read at least fifty books a year, these CEOs and entrepreneurs almost always teach me about books that have yet to cross my radar. Most of these leaders are above-average communicators who want their teams to elevate their speaking and writing skills, too. Leaders who value the written word also put a premium on reading to help them become better writers.

Simply put, voracious readers are better speakers. People who read an assortment of books in fiction and nonfiction categories have a broad, interesting variety of stories from which to pull. They have more arrows in the quiver: stories, insights, examples, and wisdom. They offer fresh, surprising, and unique ways of looking at the world and explaining what they see. Since humans are natural explorers who love to learn new things, we're attracted to readers because they act as culture keepers; they inform, illuminate, and inspire. Bezos once said that the secret to creating compelling content—books, movies, memos—is to be interesting. You have to be "riveting," he said.

One of the most riveting personalities in sports today is Golf Channel analyst Brandel Chamblee. I call Chamblee the da Vinci of sports commentators because he draws insights from the fields of math, science, physics, art, and literature. I spoke with Chamblee during the week of the 2021 U.S. Open. Our conversation covered writers and storytellers from Friedrich Nietzsche to Neil deGrasse Tyson, Aristotle to Aaron Sorkin, and William Shakespeare to Nora Ephron.

Chamblee told me that he always packs books for his frequent trips to cover golf tournaments. He picked up the reading habit during his fifteen-year PGA Tour career, enjoying the company of writers when he winded down from a day's round. Chamblee once asked a famous golf writer how he kept his articles fresh, always finding new and novel metaphors and analogies to engage his readers. "You don't sound like any other golf writer,"[11] Chamblee said. "That's because I don't read other golf writers," the columnist answered.

According to Chamblee, "If you just read subject matter that's only relevant to your game or sport, you will sound like everybody else. You have to read as broadly as possible."

Not all readers are riveting, but all riveting leaders are readers.

THREE WAYS TO READ WITH PURPOSE

1. Follow leaders in relevant categories.

We live in the golden age of reading. Millions of titles are available in a variety of formats, from hardcover to paperback and from audiobooks to ebooks. Condensed knowledge is at our fingertips But as you know, too many choices cause decision paralysis. Here's an astonishing statistic: Amazon adds one new book to its selection every five minutes. There are more than thirty million titles now available for shipping, downloading, or listening. How should you choose your next read?

Getting the most out of the books you read means reading the books you'll get the most out of.

Let's assume you're a lifelong learner and you decide to read one book a month from the time you graduate college at the age of twenty-three through the age of ninety. That's 804 books, which sounds like an enormous number until you consider that it represents only 0.002 percent of the titles currently available.

Successful leaders know they can't read everything, so they try to read everything other successful leaders do.

"To read one hundred meaningful books a year, you have to have a system,"[12] according to billionaire philanthropist David Rubenstein. Rubenstein cofounded Carlyle Group, one of the largest private equity firms with $230 billion under management. Rubenstein hosts a television show where he interviews the world's top business and political leaders. He reads books written by the leaders he interviews and also relies on book reviews and recommendations. You can make it a habit to ask other successful people what books they've found particularly valuable.

Although Rubenstein reads far more books than the average American, he knows it's inefficient to read books that he randomly stumbles upon. Yes, he leaves room for serendipitous discoveries when he visits a bookstore. Still, Rubenstein sticks largely to relevant categories: philanthropy, business, politics, leadership, and history (he donates hundreds of millions of dollars to preserve monuments and historical sites and paid $24 million for one of only four surviving originals of the eight-hundred-year-old Magna Carta).

"Leaders need to expand their knowledge every day—to exercise their most unique muscle; their brain,"[13] writes Rubenstein. "Failing to do so makes it difficult to keep up with a rapidly changing world. I have tried to continue to learn by somewhat obsessive reading. Nothing focuses the mind like a well-written book."

Although Rubenstein has amassed a net worth of more than $4 billion, he continues to improve his writing and speaking skills, which reinforces the important role that communication plays in our society. According to Rubenstein, "It is impossible to lead if no one is following. A leader can persuade others to follow through one of three basic means of communication: writing something that inspires readers; saying something that motivates listeners; or doing something that sets an example for others to follow."[14]

Rubenstein says great leaders share similar qualities in addition to excellent communication skills. The books they've written provide a wealth of knowledge and shortcuts to success. Step one is to identify the most relevant categories to your career, business, and interests. Step two is to identify leaders and entrepreneurs you admire. Step three is to read their books, blogs, interviews, and articles. Books likely opened up a new world for those leaders, and they're eager to share their recommendations. So take them up on it.

2. Take notes.

Be an active reader. Kindle and other mobile devices make it easy to highlight passages or write notes in books. If you're reading a hardcover, the margins are created for a purpose: to make room for your thumbs while you're holding it. The half-inch outside margin also provides space to take notes, unless, of course, you checked it out from the local library—in that case, a Post-it Note will do the trick.

When you take notes, you give your brain more channels to encode the information. In other words, you'll remember more of what you read.

3. Share and talk about your favorite books.

"When I was preparing to become a ship captain for the first time in my midthirties, I spent a great deal of time reading books about sea captains," Stavridis told me. "Reading those books was helpful, but the real payout was discussing them with more senior officers who had already been through the crucible of command."

In 2003, Jeff Bezos assigned his technical assistant, Colin Bryar, the task of selecting books for Amazon's senior leadership team. "They were smart businesspeople, but they needed more technical knowledge on how to build scalable and robust software,"[15] says Bryar. "One of Amazon's Leadership Principles is *Learn and Be Curious.* So although they had very demanding jobs, our S-Team embraced the idea of a book club. Jeff would assign a book, and he read it along with everyone else. Then, we'd get together as a group to discuss it. We did that every four to six weeks."

Bryar and Bezos selected Fred Brooks's *The Mythical Man-Month,* a book that inspired Amazon's now famous "two-pizza teams." The S-Team also read *Good to Great,* which inspired the flywheel strategy that propelled Amazon's growth. *Built to Last* and *Creation* inspired Amazon Web Services, *The Innovator's Dilemma* inspired the Kindle, and Sam Walton's *Made in America* inspired Amazon's sixteen Leadership Principles.

Another book, *Zingerman's Guide to Giving Great Service,* offered ideas on how to amaze and delight customers, while *The Goal* taught Amazon executives to manage bottlenecks, logistics, and other operational challenges in its fast-growing e-commerce business. And where did Bezos get the idea to attach the original 1997 shareholder letter to every letter he wrote over the next two decades? Alan Greenberg's *Memos from the Chairman.*

"Most of the world's knowledge is encoded in books, so if you're not a voracious reader, you are missing out on an opportunity,"[16] says Bryar. "Bezos is a very well-rounded person. He was aware of different topics and looked for knowledge he could bring into the organization."

As word spread about the S-Team book club, employees emailed Bryar to find out what executives were reading every month. Bezos began to share and review the books he was reading so everyone would be on the same page, literally.

Effective leaders read more books than others in the organization, and they share their newfound knowledge with everyone else. Pulitzer Prize–winning historian Barbara Tuchman once said, "Books are the carriers of civilization. Without books, history is silent, literature dumb, science crippled, thought and speculation at a standstill. Without books, the development of civilization would have been impossible. They are engines of change (as the poet said), windows on the world and lighthouses erected in the sea of time. They are companions, teachers, magicians, bankers of the treasures of the mind. Books are humanity in print."[17]

The single best way to learn to lead is through the power of reading. Here's the best part: Never in the history of the printed word has the average person had such easy access to the accumulated wisdom of those who built the world in which we live. Take those authors along your life's journey. They're great companions.

Part III

DELIVER THE PLAN

12

AMP YOUR PRESENTATIONS TO INSPIRE YOUR AUDIENCE

> Where you are going to spend your time and your energy is one of the most important decisions you get to make in life.
>
> —Jeff Bezos

My daughter had an extreme fear of spiders. She wouldn't go outside if she thought a spider was on the other side of the door. Over time, she learned to manage her anxiety thanks to a therapist who taught us a clever strategy. We posted several photographs of spiders around the house. After each week, we rotated the photos and suspended them in different locations. Over time, our daughter grew desensitized to the eight-legged creatures.

The therapist had provided us with a tool called *exposure therapy,* a popular treatment to help people confront their fears so they can maintain healthy functioning in their daily routines. Avoiding a fear in the moment brings instant relief and comfort. But over time, avoiding the things you fear gives power to those things, places, or events that trigger your anxiety. Eventually, you don't control your fear; your fear controls you.

As you probably know, public speaking is considered one of the top fears people experience. According to the National Institute of Mental Health, the fear of public speaking (a.k.a. glossophobia) affects about 73 percent of the population. Public-speaking anxiety is hardwired in our ancient brains, which is why it's so prevalent. We're conditioned to crave acceptance and tend to put too much weight on how we *perceive* others are judging us.

Unfortunately, avoiding public speaking is not an option for business professionals who want to advance their careers. According to survey results conducted by iCIMS, a talent acquisition software company, 65 percent of recruiters and hiring managers say they put more weight on strong writing and verbal skills than they do on a candidate's college major.[1] In another survey commissioned by Prezi, a cloud-based presentation platform, 70 percent of those surveyed said presentations are critical to their career success, yet 12 percent of women and 7 percent of men admit they've pretended to be sick to get out of making a presentation.[2]

The billionaire Warren Buffett once said that public speaking will raise your value in the workplace by 50 percent. Unfortunately, too many working professionals fail to leverage that value because they experience anxiety or full-blown panic attacks at just the thought of giving a presentation.

The good news: Great presenters are made, not born.

Anyone can be transformed from an anxious or awkward speaker to one who captivates the room. We've seen it happen over and over. Vanessa Gallo, my business partner, has a psychology background. She works with our clients—CEOs and senior executives—on their body language, verbal delivery, messaging skills, and executive presence. Together, Vanessa and I developed a system of turning average presenters into great ones. The Gallo AMP model is based on three variables that will strengthen every aspect of your public-speaking performance.

AMP YOUR PRESENTATIONS

When clients come to us to transform their speaking skills, we rely on a model that enables them to "AMP" their presentations. *Amp* is a transitive verb whose definition is "to excite and energize." We use it as an acronym to describe the three variables that will transform you into a dynamic speaker who excites and energizes your audiences.

First, take a look at table 12.1 (page 175). It shows the three variables all speakers need to improve: *A*bility, *M*essage, and *P*ractice. Second, I'll show you how to assess these variables to become the speaker you've always imagined.

Table 12.1: AMP: Ability, Message, Practice

Variable	Explanation
Ability (Constant) Your natural ability is largely constant. These are individual strengths and talents that you already have. These strengths are noticeable at every stage of your presentation skill development. They are foundational skills you will build upon.	Natural abilities include: • Comfortable speaking in front of others. • Deep content knowledge. • Creative with words, imagery, metaphors, or art. • A strong, resonating vocal tone. • Comfortable finding the humor in situations. • Good posture, perhaps from a background in sports or performing arts.
Message **(NOT Constant)** The content of your presentation: theme, clarity, word choice, stories, slides, and visuals.	Your message is a variable you can change and develop. A strong message includes: • Emotionally engaging content (stories, images, videos). • A short, clearly expressed theme. • Three supporting examples. • Short sentences written in the active voice. • Visually engaging slides. • Stories that grab attention. • Simple, understandable sequence.
Practice **(NOT Constant)** The time you spend rehearsing and internalizing the content is the second variable that you can control. The more time you commit to deliberate practice, the more confident you'll feel on performance day.	You can adjust the amount of time you devote to this variable. Rehearse your presentation until: • You've internalized the key messages on each slide and you can deliver those messages without looking at notes. • You can deliver the presentation in a conversational style, like you're having dinner with friends. • You're comfortable with demonstrations, knowing how they're going to work and how long it will require to complete the demo. • You've shortened the stories you tell so they're concise, relevant, and keep the action moving.

The first step to sharpening your speaking skills is to understand your *Ability.* A person with more natural strengths still needs to have a great *Message* and commit the *Practice* time to refine their delivery. A person who shows fewer natural strengths early in their public-speaking journey must still learn to craft a great *Message.* They'll also have to devote far

More Natural
Strengths

Less Natural
Strengths

20% Practice
(not constant)

PRACTICE

PRACTICE

50% Practice
(not constant)

30% Message
(not constant)

MESSAGE

EQUALLY
GREAT
PRESENTERS

MESSAGE

30% Message
(not constant)

50% Natural Ability
(constant)

NATURAL
ABILITY

NATURAL
ABILITY

20% Natural Ability
(constant)

Figure 12: How Two Different Individuals Develop into Great Presenters

more practice time than other speakers, but the practice will help them shine.

By first identifying your natural abilities, you can customize how much time you spend on crafting the message and perfecting your delivery. In figure 12, you'll see an example of how two people became equally strong public speakers though they took different paths to get there. The speaker on the left has more natural strengths, so she feels comfortable with less practice. But she still needs to spend 30 percent of her preparation time building a well-crafted message. The speaker on the right has fewer natural strengths and might be uncomfortable onstage. He still has to spend 30 percent of his time on messaging and must schedule more practice time to feel comfortable. The point is that both speakers are exceptional but have taken different paths and adjusted the AMP variables to reach the top.

With the Gallo AMP model, anyone can be a great speaker as long as they understand their natural strengths, build on those strengths, and make investments in the other variables. Everyone's "recipe" will vary, but the final outcome will be a treat to watch.

BEZOS TRANSFORMED HIMSELF INTO A GREAT COMMUNICATOR

Bezos once said, "We are our choices. Build yourself a great story." And that's exactly what he did in his own life. Bezos made the decision early in his career at Amazon to refine his public-speaking skills. How do I know? The speaker Bezos today is not the speaker Bezos was twenty-five years ago. He worked at sharpening his skills, and it shows.

In the following section, Vanessa examines three speeches and presentations spanning twenty years of public speaking. First, let's begin with an early speech Bezos delivered shortly after launching Amazon. It took place at Lake Forest College in 1998. Whenever we examine video samples of our clients, the first step is to identify natural abilities or strengths—attributes we can leverage as we develop our clients' speaking abilities. Based on this 1998 video sample, Bezos brings strengths to the table: creativity, a sense of humor, and substantial topic knowledge. Table 12.2 shows specific quotes from the Lake Forest speech that demonstrate these natural abilities. Once again, these are natural strengths the speaker will build on throughout his career.

Table 12.2: Bezos Presentation Strengths—Lake Forest University 1998[3]

Strengths	Quotes	Notes
Creativity	"If you were to print the Amazon.com catalog, it would be the size of more than forty New York City phone books."	It takes a creative mind to put statistics into context and to create a vivid image in people's minds.
	"It might be like taking a sip from a fire hose."	Bezos used this metaphor to describe what would happen to their orders if Yahoo! featured Amazon on a list of popular sites. Metaphors, as we've discussed, are creative tools to make concepts simple and memorable. He'll use a lot more of them throughout his career.
	"The owner of the house had installed a big potbellied stove right in the center of the garage."	Bezos is showing an early flair for storytelling by making note of small, descriptive details that bring stories to life.

Strengths	Quotes	Notes
Sense of Humor	"The human brain can immediately tell by reading somebody else's writing whether the person is smart or crazy within the first five words."	Bezos has a sense of humor. Here he's explaining why Amazon allows positive and negative reviews, and why customers will instinctively know which ones to consider.
	"They had packed up our stuff, and they wanted to know where to take it. So I told them, just head west and call us tomorrow and we'll tell you."	Bezos tells a funny story about the day he and his ex-wife, MacKenzie, drove from Texas and headed west to start the company. As noted earlier, in the language of the Hero's Journey, this would be an example of "crossing the threshold" from the ordinary world to the world of adventure.
	"We thought, *Wow, these packing tables are really good.*"	In Amazon's early days, Bezos and his employees packed hundreds of packages while sitting uncomfortably on the floor. He was so laser-focused on getting the packages out the door on time, he failed to realize packing tables would help. When someone raised the suggestion, Bezos laughed because it was such a simple solution. Bezos adds humorous anecdotes throughout his speech, a tactic he used for the next two decades.
Topic Knowledge	"In the spring of '94, web usage was growing at 2,300 percent a year . . . things don't grow this fast outside petri dishes."	Bezos has a natural skill for numbers. He makes data memorable by putting statistics into context.
	"The Amazon River is ten times the size of the Mississippi River in terms of volume of water that flows through it."	Bezos explains the metaphor behind the company name, Amazon. He also uses anecdotes and supporting research to reinforce his message.
	"These things that are important to our customer selection base: ease of use . . . convenience . . . price."	Here Bezos reflects the deep understanding he had about the customer—what they were looking for and how his company would satisfy their desires.

Creativity is a desirable skill for professionals in today's workplace, but it's not easy to teach. The fact that Bezos demonstrated creativity early in his speaking career would turn out to be a highly valuable skill.

Now let's take a deeper dive into the Lake Forest speech. While Bezos has natural strengths, he had room to improve on the other variables: message and practice. He could have taken more time to refine the story and practice his delivery. Bezos was long-winded during many parts of the presentation, he read from notes, and often stumbled or paused when he lost his place. Here are a few examples.

- "So let's see. [looks down at notes] I tried to actually pick the more interesting anecdotes." [scans notes for stories]
- "So, we, which was basically that way, May of, I guess, '96, it took them about a year from that point to launch a website."
- "Who was the contemporary of Jane Austen, who, uh, was jealous of her all the time? It's slipping my mind right now. ["Brontë!" Mackenzie shouts]. Yeah, it's Brontë. That's my wife in the audience, by the way, saving me yet once again."
- "Finally, it's a, it's a win for . . . I can't remember who I did already." [Bezos refers to notes and tells the audience he's trying to remember the examples he's already used.]

As you can probably tell, it's not the smoothest speech. But Bezos delivers the speech with a great sense of humor, which keeps the audience laughing, and he clearly has extensive topic knowledge. Bezos gave an informative speech that day in 1998, but his delivery, style, and message would continue to improve in the years ahead.

A speaker's natural strengths are important. They help create a baseline my coleader, Vanessa, and I use as a foundation. The Lake Forest speech would have been far more impactful had Bezos refined his message and practiced the speech. We find that rehearsing a speech or presentation at least ten times gives a speaker the confidence they'll need to own the room.

Let's turn to a second example, a presentation that Bezos delivered five years after his Lake Forest speech when he gave a TED Talk in 2003. His strengths are still there: creativity, humor, and topic knowledge (see table 12.3).

Table 12.3: Bezos 2003 TED Talk: Presentation Strengths[4]

Strengths	Quotes	Notes
Creativity	"The tempting analogy for the boom-bust that we just went through is the internet gold rush."	Bezos explains the power of analogies and why the gold rush should be replaced with a more accurate comparison.
	"This is a commercial that was played on the Super Bowl in the year 2000 (OurBeginning .com)."	Bezos creatively embeds a video in his presentation to illustrate one of his examples.
	"There are a lot of similarities between the internet and the electric industry."	Bezos transitions from the gold rush metaphor into his creative analysis of how the internet has more in common with the history of electricity than it had with the gold rush.
Sense of Humor	"By about 1852, they're thinking, 'Am I the stupidest person on Earth by not rushing to California?'"	Bezos sprinkles light observations throughout his speech. In this case, he has fun at the expense of East Coasters in the 1850s who heard about the riches in California and decide to leave everything they had to strike it rich in California.
	"This is the electric tie press, which never really did catch on. People, I guess, decided that they would not wrinkle their ties."	Bezos makes the audience laugh several times with his humorous take on past inventions.
Topic Knowledge	"This guy on the left, Dr. Richard Beverley Cole, he lived in Philadelphia, and he took the Panama route."	Bezos is growing as a storyteller. He tells true stories of people who gave up prominent livelihoods to search for gold.
	"The San Francisco harbor was clogged with six hundred ships at the peak because ships would get there, and the crews would abandon them to go search for gold."	The specific number of ships gives this story credibility and makes it more impactful.
	"The Edison Electric Company, which became Edison General Electric, which became General Electric, paid for all of this digging up of the streets."	A few details add credibility to a story and vividly recreate an event.

When we analyze the TED Talk that Bezos delivered in 2003, we can see that he still had the natural strengths he'd exhibited several years earlier. If anything, those strengths came into sharper focus. The variable that *did* change was his delivery. In the first sixty seconds of his Lake Forest speech, Bezos uses the filler words *uh* or *um* seven times. In the first sixty seconds of his TED Talk five years later, he said *uh* only once. Bezos also spent less time looking at notes, used fewer filler words, and spoke in tighter, shorter sentences.

Let's fast-forward to 2019 when Bezos delivered a keynote about space exploration and his company, Blue Origin. Sixteen years after the TED Talk where Bezos used electricity as a metaphor for the future of the internet, we see him relying on the same creative strengths to create a captivating multimedia presentation.

By 2019, Bezos has substantially improved his delivery. His sentences are sharp, precise, and concise. He appears comfortable and unhurried. He pauses after expressing big ideas to let the concepts sink in. Bezos crafted and practiced well-written lines:

- "Guess what the best planet is in the solar system? We've sent robotic probes to all the planets in our solar system. Earth is the best planet. It is not close. This one is really good. Don't even get me started on Venus."[5]
- "You don't choose your passions. Your passions choose you."
- "Look at Earth. Earth is incredible."
- "It will be a beautiful place to live. It will be a beautiful place to visit. It will be a beautiful place to go to school."
- "It's time to go back to the moon. This time to stay."
- "What I'm laying out here today is obviously a multigeneration vision. This is not going to get done by any one generation. One of the things that we have to do is inspire those future generations."
- "We're going to build a road to space, and then amazing things will happen."
- "I want to inspire those future space entrepreneurs. People are so creative once they're unleashed."
- "This vision sounds very big, and it is. None of this is easy. All of it is hard. But I want to inspire you. And so think about this: Big things start small."

The sentences that Bezos wrote are clear, concise, and well structured. Combined with his delivery and visually appealing slides, the presentation is far more impressive than the wordy, disjointed, fragmented speech Bezos gave in 1998.

True inspiration happens when you make the effort to build on your strengths, craft the best message possible, and practice delivering that message until you've built the confidence to command the stage.

Communicators at every level of their professional careers have room to improve, but only a few speakers actively put in the work to make it happen. Join the few who stand out.

COACHING DRILL

Video is a simple, valuable tool to help you assess your natural strengths and the areas where you need to improve. Grab a smartphone and record yourself practicing a presentation, sales pitch, job interview, and so on. Watch and rate the video yourself, but also solicit feedback from a trusted friend or peer. Among the things to look for:

- What natural strengths do you notice? (e.g., creative language, strong writing, well-designed slides, good posture, strong voice tone or vocal variation, creative stories to enhance the message). Embrace your strengths and play them up.
- Are you using too many words to get your point across? What sentences can you eliminate the next time you practice?
- Do you have too much text on your slides? Is the font too small? If you can't read the text, neither can the audience.
- Do you use filler words like *uh, um,* or *ah*? Do you end your sentences with annoying, extraneous phrases like *you know?* or *right?* We all use filler words in our natural conversations, but excessive fillers become a distraction. If you eliminate more filler words with each practice session, you'll sound polished and confident when it's time to deliver the real thing.
- Is your theme—the logline—clear? Do you deliver it consistently every time you say it?

Video is the single best tool that you have at your fingertips to improve your public-speaking skills. You'll be surprised at the problems you can catch on your own—and how much improvement you can make from one video to the next.

THE HARD WORK THAT TURNED STEVE JOBS INTO A "NATURAL" SPEAKER

Practice is not something you do because you're bad; practice is something you do because you are good. Great communicators instinctively know that practice matters, and they always make time for it.

Steve Jobs was one of the best business storytellers of our time. His famous presentations were a collaborative effort: Jobs and his trusted team worked on message development, slide creation, and extensive rehearsals. Like Bezos, Jobs showed natural abilities early in his career, but it took years before he became the charismatic speaker who was legendary for his keynote presentations. Jobs worked on the craft of public speaking. And he worked hard on it. Jobs only developed a dynamic speaking style after years of deliberate practice.

Let's examine a video sample of a young Steve Jobs preparing for his first TV interview in 1978. In the video, you can see the studio crew getting Jobs ready for a remote satellite interview. In just one minute and thirty-six seconds of video, we get a glimpse of how nervous Jobs must have felt. His behavior reflects extreme anxiety. For example, we see Jobs:

- Frequently dodging his eyes from the floor to the ceiling to those around him.
- Exhaling and saying the word *god* four times.
- Running his fingers through his hair.
- Clenching his jaw, smiling awkwardly and through gritted teeth, and squinting under the lights as he looks up.
- Swiveling side to side in his chair.
- Finally, asking for the location of a bathroom because he feels ill.

Jobs was so uncomfortable, the video is difficult to watch. And yet, despite his clear anxiety about speaking on television, a skilled communication coach can still identify some natural strengths in his performance.

If I had been there to coach Steve Jobs, my first step would be to help Jobs see his own strengths that he could build on. Those strengths did, indeed, turn Jobs into a magnificent storyteller. For example, although he was nervous, Jobs used assertive language and spoke in crisp, clear sentences. Instead of rambling, he cut to the chase. He found humor in the situation and had a strong vocal tone. Table 12.4 shows examples of Job's strengths in one of his earliest interviews.

Table 12.4: Steve Jobs Early Presentation Strengths[6]

Strengths	Quotes	Notes
Assertive Language	"What's that? [waits to hear question] No. No." "Am I really? Are you serious?" "You could bring me some water."	Although Jobs is fidgety and nervous before the camera starts filming, Jobs is seen communicating with his staff off camera. When he asks questions and talks to people directly, he avoids weasel words and makes specific, simple comments or statements.
Sense of Humor	"Look at that! Look, I'm on television!" Jobs says playfully with a smile. "You need to tell me where the restroom is, too, because I'm deathly ill and ready to get sick any minute. I'm not kidding!" he says with a slight smile.	When a person can find the humor in a stressful situation, it's a good sign they'll have a great sense of humor as they build their public-speaking skills. Yes, Jobs would later become known for presentations filled with humor, passion, and personality.
Dynamic Vocal Ability	"This is *not* the real thing, right?" "Well, I'm not gonna have to sit here until you're ready, *right*?" "I'm *not* joking!"	The italicized words highlight those parts of the video where Jobs raised the pitch and volume of his voice. Here we see his ability to vary his vocal delivery to emphasize key points or express emotion.
Concise Language	"Look at that!" "Look, I'm on television." "Are you serious?" "I'm not joking!"	It is easy to grab quotes from this video because Jobs uses succint sentences to ask a question or make a statement. It's clear where one sentence ends and another begins. You can already tell that this speaker, though exhibiting signs of stage fright, will develop into a writer who keeps his sentences simple and concise.

After years of delivering presentations and relentlessly rehearsing for each one, Jobs transformed himself into a public speaker widely admired on the global stage. If you watch his Apple keynotes recorded later in his career (1998–2007), it's hard to believe that Jobs is the same speaker who was once terrified of appearing on camera. He didn't fidget, tousle his hair, swivel nervously, or dodge his eyes. But Jobs maintained the natural strengths that were noticeable in his earliest videos: assertiveness, humor, vocal variation, and conciseness.

Steve Jobs unveiled the iPhone in 2007 and gave one of the most captivating and memorable business presentations of all time. Jobs and his presentation design team crafted a keynote that informed, captivated, and entertained the audience. The video on YouTube has been viewed more than eighty million times. In table 12.5, you can see how Jobs turned his natural strengths into presentation gold.

Table 12.5: Steve Jobs Presentation Strengths—2007 iPhone Presentation[7]

Strengths	Quotes	Notes
Assertive Language	"We didn't just change Apple. We changed the whole computer industry." "The problem is, they're not so smart, and they are not so easy to use." "We don't want to do either one of these." "We are going to get rid of all these buttons and just make a giant screen."	Jobs uses assertive language and the active voice: subject, verb, object. He rarely uses passive language and eliminates filler and weasel words that take up space but don't advance the story.
Sense of Humor	"Here it is." [shows image of a smartphone with an old-fashioned phone dial on it; audience laughs] "We're going to use a stylus. [pause] No! [sarcastic tone] Who wants a stylus? You have to get 'em . . . you lose 'em. Yuck!" "We have invented a new technology called multi-touch . . . and, boy, have we patented it!" [audience laughs]	Jobs doesn't tell traditional jokes, but he uses humorous observations and anecdotes to entertain the audience.

Strengths	Quotes	Notes
Dynamic Vocal Delivery	"Today [pause] we're introducing three revolutionary products of this class. The *first* one is a wide-screen iPod with touch controls. The *second* is a revolutionary mobile phone. And the *third* is a breakthrough internet communications device." "Three things [pause]: a wide-screen iPod with touch controls, a revolutionary mobile phone, and a breakthrough internet communications device. [pause] An iPod, a phone, and an internet communicator." [pace speeds up] "An iPod, a phone, are you getting it?! These are not three separate devices. [pause] This is one device. [pause] And we are calling it iPhone."	Jobs's vocal delivery in this portion of the presentation is pure genius. He knows exactly when to pause, speed up, and repeat lines because he had practiced the delivery for weeks ahead of the presentation. The result is suspenseful and pure magic. Jobs leaves his audience spellbound.
Concise Language	"Today, Apple is going to reinvent the phone." "This is what iPhone is." "It doesn't work because the buttons and controls can't change." "Software on mobile phones is like baby software. It's not so powerful."	Almost every line in the script is clean and concise. Most sentences are made up of simple one-to two-syllable words.

The 2007 iPhone presentation took place almost three decades after the 1978 television interview where we saw Jobs as a very uneasy and anxious speaker. Jobs made an incredible transformation. He brought some natural abilities to the table, but it was only after relentless, dedicated focus on message creation and rehearsal that he developed into the world's most astonishing corporate storyteller.

The key to becoming an authentic and charismatic speaker is not to change who you are. Embrace the attributes that make you unique. Celebrate your strengths and abilities. We all have them. They are qualities that won't change. Build on them. Save your efforts for the two qualities you can sharpen: message and practice. If you invest in these two things, you will become an amazing communicator. It will happen. Great communicators put in practice time because *time* is what makes communicators great. AMP your presentations and you'll be thrilled with the results.

13

MAKE THE MISSION
YOUR MANTRA

Missionaries love their product and love their customers.

—Jeff Bezos

A person's spoken and written words reveal what drives them. One word has driven Jeff Bezos for the past three decades, a word that appears five hundred times in his shareholder letters. The word is now coded into Amazon's DNA:

CUSTOMER

Jeff Bezos wasted no time in telling the world what he cared about the most. In his very first letter to Amazon shareholders in 1997, he cited the customer twenty-five times, setting the stage for what would become Amazon's secret sauce: "Amazon.com uses the Internet to create real value for its customers and, by doing so, hopes to create an enduring franchise, even in established and large markets."[1]

According to Bezos, customer obsession wasn't just a good strategy, it was an absolute requirement in 1997 when the majority of Americans had never been online, let alone purchased a product over the internet. Everything from how to use a modem to navigating a website had to be explained in "excruciating detail," Bezos said. Making the experience easy for customers fueled Amazon's rapid rise.

Obsessing over the customer evolved into a mission that would drive Amazon's business decisions then and now. But a mission doesn't just take hold and scale as a company gets bigger. A mission needs a repeater in chief who keeps everyone focused on the big picture. By 1998, Bezos had clarified the company's mission. Amazon, he said, "intends to become the world's most customer-centric company." For the next twenty-three years, Bezos became the chief evangelist for Amazon's mission and turned it into a mantra that everyone can recite.

OVERCOMMUNICATE BY A FACTOR OF TEN

Harvard business professor John Kotter found that most leaders *under-communicate* their vision by a factor of ten.

"Transformation is impossible unless hundreds or thousands of people are willing to help, often to the point of making short-term sacrifices,"[2] Kotter wrote in the *Harvard Business Review*. "Without credible communication, and a lot of it, the hearts and minds of the troops are never captured."

Jeff Bezos, on the other hand, is a leader who doesn't believe that it's possible to overcommunicate a mission. In his first known public speech in 1998, Bezos talked about the "customer" a full sixty-two times. And he was just getting started. Bezos put the customer center stage for the next two decades. Figure 13 shows the most common words that appear throughout all twenty-four years of Bezos letters. The customer clearly rules.

As I mentioned, customer obsession began to take shape as the company's official mission in 1998. In his letter to shareholders that year, Bezos explained how the mission should guide decision-making at every level of the company. "I constantly remind our employees to be afraid," he wrote. "To wake up every morning terrified, not of our competition, but our customers."[3]

Bezos continued to clarify the mission the following year. Customer ob-

Figure 13: Word Cloud of All Twenty-Four Bezos Letters

session, he said, meant that Amazonians should listen to customers, invent on their behalf, and personalize the service for each customer. You don't want to hire mercenaries at your company, you want to be surrounded with missionaries, Bezos would later say. Missionaries care about the mission. Years before "purpose-driven" companies became part of the business vernacular, Bezos was telling his senior leaders to keep Amazon's purpose top of mind and to hire those people who believed in its mission. People crave meaning in their lives, and they want to work for an organization whose mission they admire.

The customer-focused mission serves as a defining element of the company culture and unites Amazonians across teams and locations. Employees work in thirty-four job categories, such as marketing, engineering, operations, warehouse, business development, human resources, product management, and software development. Regardless of which position people apply for, Amazon reminds them the company's intense focus on the customer is the reason it's one of the world's most admired brands. It's hard to forget the mission when it's the first Leadership Principle that every job candidate and every Amazonian is expected to know: customer obsession. Its definition is inspired by those early Bezos letters. The principle reads, "Leaders start with the customer and work backwards. They work vigorously to earn and keep customer trust. Although leaders pay attention to competitors, they obsess over customers."

The mission is everything, and Bezos never let anyone forget it.

Just as DNA is the blueprint of life, containing the instructions that make us who we are, a company's mission is its blueprint as it grows from a start-up to an enterprise. A shared mission aligns everyone to a common purpose, regardless of what they do or where they live.

What better way to remember a mission than to turn it into a mantra? A mantra is a statement or slogan that builds in strength as it's repeated. Overcommunication fuels its impact.

Cognitive psychologists say the "mere-exposure effect" is a phenomenon that simply means the more you hear something, the more you like it. When it comes to a company's mission statement, the more you hear it, the more you like it. If you like the message and internalize it, you'll be more likely to act on it. A mantra takes a mental highlighter to the mission. You can't miss it.

Jeff Bezos doesn't under-communicate his mission by a factor of ten; he *amplifies* the mission by a factor of ten.

Bezos repeated the mantra of customer obsession relentlessly in nearly every interview, memo, speech, shareholder letter, and media interview. He did so day after day, year after year, decade after decade.

In a 1999 interview for CNBC, Bezos made twenty-one references to the company's mission. Since the interview lasted just seven minutes, that means Bezos talked about the customer every twenty-four seconds. Although Amazon's market cap had surpassed $30 billion for the first time, Bezos warned that it was too early to predict which internet companies would come out on top. He didn't have a crystal ball, but his uncompromising belief in the mission fueled his faith in Amazon's future.

"There are no guarantees, but I believe if you can focus obsessively enough on customer experience—selection, ease of use, low prices, more information—plus great customer service, then I think you have a good chance."[4]

"Are you a pure internet play?" the CNBC reporter asked.

"Internet, schminternet. That doesn't matter. You should be investing in a company that obsesses over customer experience."

Bezos then used a powerful rhetorical device to reinforce his key message. He set the message apart. He began a concluding sentence as follows:

If there's one thing to know about Amazon, it's that it pays "obsessive attention to the customer, end to end."

COACHING DRILL

When you start a sentence with "If there's one thing to know, it's this . . . ," whatever comes next is what your audience will remember. They'll write it down and share the message with others because it's like taking a mental highlighter to your main point. Here are some other phrases you can substitute to highlight your key message.

- "The most important thing you need to know is . . ."
- "If there's one thing you can take away from this presentation, it's this . . ."
- "What I can tell you is this . . ."

Your audience is looking for road maps. Guide them in the direction you want to take them.

Unlike most leaders who under-communicate their company's mission, Bezos continued to repeat his mantra until everyone internalized it. His purpose-driven outlook inspired him to partner with others who also shared his passion for mission. One of those partners was an entrepreneur whose company became famous for its founder's vision to deliver happiness to every customer: Zappos.

OBSESSIVE, COMPULSIVE FOCUS ON THE CUSTOMER

"I get all weak-kneed when I see a customer-obsessed company,"[5] Bezos said about Zappos, the online shoe retailer Amazon had purchased for $1.2 billion.

Zappos CEO and culture guru Tony Hsieh had rejected one of Bezos's offers a few years earlier. Hsieh had built a legendary culture that came to define exceptional customer service—online or offline. Hsieh didn't consider his role at Zappos a job; it was a calling.

In April of 2009, Hsieh flew to Seattle for an hour-long meeting with Bezos. According to Hsieh, "I gave him my standard presentation on Zappos, which is mostly about our culture. Toward the end of the presentation, I started talking about the science of happiness—and how we try to use it to serve our customers and employees better."[6]

Bezos interrupted and said, "Did you know that people are very bad at predicting what will make them happy?"

Yes, they are, Hsieh agreed. "But apparently, you're very good at predicting PowerPoint slides."

Bezos's observation matched the exact words on Tony's next slide.

"After that moment, things got comfortable," Tony said. "It seemed clear that Amazon had come to appreciate our company culture as well as our strong sales."

Bezos had recorded an internal video to announce the Zappos purchase. In it, he didn't use PowerPoint or fancy graphics. Instead, he pointed to a simple flip chart.

"We've made mistakes and we've learned some things,"[7] he said. "But here's what I know: You need to obsess over customers. We have been doing this since the very beginning. It's the only reason why Amazon.com exists today in any form. When given the choice of obsessing over competitors or obsessing over customers, we always obsess over customers. We like to start with customers and work backwards."

Hsieh continued to work as CEO of Zappos for a reduced salary of $36,000 a year. He stayed in the role for the next eleven years. It's easy to leave a job; it's hard to leave a calling.

Hsieh died tragically in a house fire in November 2020.

"The world lost you way too soon," Jeff Bezos wrote upon hearing about Hsieh's death. "Your curiosity, vision, and relentless focus on customers leave an indelible mark."

"The number one thing that has made us successful by far is obsessive, compulsive focus on the customer, as opposed to obsession over the competitor," Bezos told David Rubenstein in a 2018 interview for Bloomberg Television. "It is a huge advantage to any company if you can stay focused on the customer instead of your competitor."[8] The company that started with eleven people in a Seattle garage has topped 1.6 million employees worldwide and is intimately entwined in the U.S. economy. While a lot has changed for Amazon since its founding in 1994, one thing has remained consistent from Day One—a relentless focus on one overarching mission, a mission driven by its founder and his successor.

When the news broke that former AWS chief Andy Jassy had been named only the second CEO in Amazon's history, reporters turned to early investor John Doerr for comment. "Is Amazon about to lose its edge?" they asked. Doerr replied that, in his opinion, Amazon would continue to thrive under Jassy because the new leadership had internalized the company's mission and mantra. Doerr remained confident about Amazon's future because "customer obsession" is simply too ingrained in its culture. And it's been that way since Day One.

Mission matters. Business leaders often face the difficult task of getting everyone aligned around a common goal. A remote workforce makes it even harder to keep everyone on track. Your message will get diluted or ignored as it's passed from person to person and from department to department. The solution is to clarify your mission and repeat it so often you get tired of hearing yourself say it. But once people on your team use your words and act on the message, you'll know they've internalized the mission. You've created missionaries who will run through walls for you.

In the next section, you'll learn how to identify a mission that should drive the decisions you make in business and the choices you make in life.

I'll also offer you specific tips and techniques to turn your mission into a mantra that aligns everyone toward one big, dreamy, irresistible goal.

THE CORE OF APPLE

Amazon's breakneck speed positioned it nicely for an IPO in 1997. At the same time, eight hundred miles south of Seattle, another company led by a visionary entrepreneur stood on the brink of bankruptcy.

After a twelve-year absence from the company he started, Steve Jobs returned to Apple to find a company in financial ruin. Jobs discovered that Apple's leadership had done serious damage to the company, which was "hemorrhaging money." While Amazon was adding jobs, Apple was eliminating them. More than one-third of Apple's workforce—four thousand employees—had been eliminated.

Jobs diagnosed the problem. Apple, he said, had betrayed its core mission to create beautifully designed computing products that delighted its customers. Jobs said 30 percent of Apple's products were excellent, real "gems." But 70 percent were lousy and diverted resources from the fewer, high-quality products.

In a CNBC interview on October 2, 1997, Jobs said, "If you do the right things on the top line, the bottom line will follow."[9] Jobs believed that if a company has the right strategy, the right people, and the right culture, sales will follow. As a leader, Jobs said his focus would remain fixed on product *and* communication strategy. Apple employees had to rally around a joint mission, he said, and recommit to its values. His job was to clear "the bramble and the brush" so employees and customers could see the path.

Apple's employees needed more than a pep talk. They needed to know that their work meant something larger than themselves and that their day-to-day tasks supported that mission. They craved meaning.

Jobs addressed Apple employees in a confidential internal meeting on September 23, a few days before appearing on CNBC. Jobs had returned to Apple just eight weeks earlier and knew what he had to do—inspire the team with a mission and a mantra.

"We're going to get back to basics with great products and great marketing," Jobs began.

First, Jobs reminded his audience that Apple had brand value: "Right up there with Nike, Disney, Coke, Sony."[10] But even a great brand needs investment and caring "if it's going to retain its relevance and vitality."

Jobs said the company would have to stop talking about "speeds and feeds, MIPS and megahertz" to bring the brand back to greatness. Customers didn't care about all that. They cared about their goals, hopes, and dreams.

Jobs then asked a series of rhetorical questions: *Who is Apple? What do we stand for? Where do we fit in the world? What do we want customers to know about us?*

Apple wasn't in the business of "making boxes for people to get their jobs done," he said. "Our core value is we believe that people with passion can change the world for the better, and those are the people we're making tools for."

Success was far from guaranteed at the time of Jobs's speech. Earlier that summer, Jobs expressed his anxiety to the executive team at Pixar, the animation studio he had purchased ten years earlier. Jobs told them that he might not be able to save Apple, but he had to try. Jobs truly believed that the world would be a better place with Apple in it. The company's mission fueled Jobs's desire to reinvigorate the brand, and if he could rally everyone behind that mission, Jobs said, it would have a better chance of surviving.

Amazon is one of the greatest success stories in corporate history, but Apple is the greatest *comeback* story in corporate history. Twenty-three years after Jobs gave his speech to employees, Apple became the first U.S. company to hit $2 trillion in market value. Mission matters.

WHY STEVE JOBS USED 190-POINT FONT

Guy Kawasaki's former boss, Steve Jobs, taught him a lot about simplifying a message. Kawasaki learned that a captivating mission can be expressed in a few words. How short should a mission statement be? Short enough to fit on a slide typed in 190-point font.

The 190-font rule comes from a tip Kawasaki learned from Steve Jobs. Most people cram too many words on a slide with tiny text. Presentation design experts, including Kawasaki, says that no slide should contain text smaller than 30-point font. Steve Jobs went even bigger. Much bigger. Why? According to Kawasaki, "Bigger text is easier to read. Duh!"[11]

Yes, it's easier to read. If people can't see your mission, it won't matter how well crafted it is. Steve Jobs also had a strategic reason to use a larger font. It forces the speaker to use fewer words to get their point across. As you learned in chapter 3, removing extraneous words lends power to the text that is left.

When Steve Jobs revealed the company's core purpose to his employees in 1997, he said, "People who are crazy enough to change the world are the ones that do." The only words on Steve's slide read: "Here's to the Crazy Ones."

PURPOSE CHAMPIONS

"Effective public speaking and communication skills have always been important for leaders,"[12] says Whole Foods cofounder John Mackey. "Purpose is foundational. Connecting people to purpose is the first and foremost job of a conscious leader."

An organization's purpose is more than a slogan, although it can often become a company's mantra. "The key to discovering an organization's higher purpose, if it isn't already clear, entails discerning the intrinsic good that is at the heart of its value proposition," Mackey writes.

In other words, purpose is not necessarily the product or service that you sell. Purpose is how your work will make the community a better place and elevate the lives of your customers.

From the day Mackey cofounded Whole Foods in 1980, its purpose has been "to nourish people and the planet." That mission continued to permeate the brand's messages and Mackey's interviews after Amazon purchased Whole Foods in 2017 for $13.7 billion.

Mackey says that corporate mergers are like a marriage. For Whole Foods and Amazon, it was love at first sight, followed by a whirlwind romance. When I caught up with Mackey three years after the merger, the marriage was still healthy.

Mackey says he admired Jeff Bezos from the day they met. The two entrepreneurs shared a lot in common, and that included building mission-driven brands.

Like its marriage partner, Whole Foods was purpose-driven from Day One. Its mission was to make the world a better place by inspiring people to eat natural, healthy foods.

Mackey announced his retirement from the company he nourished over forty-four years, but he still calls himself the Whole Foods "purpose champion," a moniker he believes every leader should adopt. According to Mackey, "Every company needs individuals who keep alive the higher purpose of the company . . . nothing motivates people or transforms organizations like the possibility of discovering a higher purpose embedded in the essential work of the enterprise itself."[13]

There's data to back up Mackey's advice.

"Purpose-oriented companies have higher productivity and growth rates,"[14] according to a report by Deloitte Consulting. "Purpose-oriented organizations also report 30 percent higher levels of innovation and 40 percent greater workforce retention than their competitors." Deloitte's research found that leaders and organizations who fail to articulate the company's purpose to customers, employees, partners, and investors "run the risk of falling behind or failing entirely. This trend will only strengthen as younger consumers who grew up with a deeper sense of purpose than previous generations seek out brands that share their values."

COACHING DRILL

A successful strategy starts with a clear and compelling—and repeatable—mission. The words matter. Words define your actions, and your actions define your outcome. Use precise words and conversational language that you feel comfortable repeating over and over. Condense the mission until you can say it in five seconds (twelve words or less). Amazon is America's biggest company, whose mission is expressed in four words: Earth's most customer-centric company.

Many of the world's most successful brands are driven by leaders who articulate the company's overarching purpose clearly, consistently, and frequently. For example:

Nike: To bring inspiration and innovation to every athlete in the world.
Unilever: To make sustainable living commonplace.
Tesla: To accelerate the world's transition to sustainable transport.
TED Talks: To spread ideas.
Twilio: To fuel the future of communications. (Twilio founder Jeff Lawson learned the power of mission as an executive at Amazon Web Services.)

Make your mission short, make every word count, and repeat it until you're tired of hearing it. Then repeat it again.

As the COVID-19 pandemic reminded us, the only thing certain about the future is that it's uncertain. As leaders grapple with unprecedented changes in the workplace, they should recommit to articulating their company's purpose and communicating it as vividly and frequently as possible. "A higher purpose is like a living thing: it must be nurtured,"[15] Mackey reminds us. "At every step of the journey, it is the leader's role to seek, refine, and champion that purpose."

Hubert Joly agrees with Mackey that a company's "noble purpose" delights customers, engages employees, and rewards shareholders. But a purpose needs an advocate to champion it. Joly surprised the business world by striking an unlikely partnership with Amazon. As CEO of retailer Best Buy, he had heard the stories about how Amazon would shift consumers' habits, effectively ending the need for the big-box electronic store. But rather than seeing Amazon as an existential threat, Joly decided to showcase Amazon's products to create a mutually beneficial relationship. Joly shares the details of Best Buy's turnaround in his book, *The Heart of Business*.

According to Joly, "Best Buy's noble purpose of enriching lives through technology unleashed significant innovation and growth."[16] Employees will rally around a noble purpose, and customers profoundly relate to it, says Joly, only if there's a leader who acts as its chief storyteller, a purpose champion. "Our brains are wired to connect through storytelling," Joly writes. "Telling everyday stories—stories of employees, customers, communities, and how they impact each other's lives—fosters a sense of purpose and connection with where we work and whom we work with."

Your employees want to know why they matter and why their work matters. It's up to you to model the purpose in everything you do, write, and say. Because once people buy into the purpose of the mission, they'll be inspired to execute it.

THE POWER OUTAGE THAT SPARKED A $150 BILLION IDEA

Halloween started early on October 31, 1957. At 9:00 A.M., a blown transformer sparked a power outage in parts of Minnesota and Wisconsin. Power was restored to most homes by the end of the day. By nightfall, porch lights were on, and children went trick-or-treating like they do every Halloween. Others weren't as lucky.

Some patients recovering from open-heart surgery in hospitals were connected to pacemakers to regulate their heartbeats. At the time, pacemakers were large and bulky boxes plugged into electrical outlets. Newspaper clippings from the era show patients walking away from their beds only as far as the electrical cord could reach.

Today, pacemakers are implanted directly in the heart. Unfortunately, in 1957, some heart surgery patients died when the power failed—including a child.

The event traumatized a medical-device repairman working in his Minneapolis garage. Earl Bakken retreated to his workspace and worked feverishly for four weeks. He emerged from his garage having built the first battery-powered pacemaker. "We're not going to lose another child to a power failure,"[17] he said.

Bakken and his company, Medtronic, invented the first implantable pacemaker one year later. Today, Medtronic's products impact the lives of two patients every second.

How did Bakken turn a one-person repair shop that made $8 in its first month into a $150 billion medical-device company?

As Bakken himself revealed, it all starts with a compelling mission. "Our mission guides our day-to-day work and reminds us that we're transforming the lives of millions of people each year,"[18] he said.

As a teenager, Bakken had decided that his life's mission would be to use science to help people. It was a vague dream, but aspirational, and drove Bakken's curiosity as an inventor. He was already a believer in mission statements when he needed one the most.

In 1960, Bakken's company faced financial hardship. The company's revenue didn't support the number of employees that he needed to make medical equipment. Bakken turned to banks for loans. Most banks turned him down.

One bank approved the loan as long as they could put someone on the board to help oversee the company's finances. The board member recommended that Bakken sit down, put pen to paper, and write a statement about what he wanted the company to stand for.

The board rejected Bakken's early drafts of the Medtronic mission statement. He continued to modify it with the board's input for the next two years.

In 1962, Bakken and his board members accepted a mission that guides the company's decisions to this day.

In full, Medtronic's mission is:

> To contribute to human welfare by application of biomedical engineering in the research, design, manufacture, and sale of instruments or appliances that alleviate pain, restore health, and extend life.

The short version, which Medtronic's employees know by heart, is:

> To alleviate pain, restore health, and extend life.

Shortly before Bakken passed away at the age of ninety-four, he recorded a video for employees. He recited the mission and made one request: "I ask you to live by it every day."[19]

Today, Medtronic is the world's largest medical-device maker. More than ninety thousand employees develop products and therapies to treat seventy health conditions. Although they're separated by geography across 150 countries, they all work for one company bound by one mission.

According to Bakken, when employees can see a direct line from their work to a real benefit for millions of patients, "it makes people feel positive about their efforts."

The accolades show it. *The Wall Street Journal* named Medtronic one of the best-run companies in the world, *Fortune* named Medtronic one of the most admired companies, while *Forbes* named Medtronic one of the best companies for new grads.

It's easy for Medtronic's employees to remember the company's mission when they're handed the statement in the form of a medallion. Since 1974, Medtronic holds "medallion ceremonies" at facilities around the world. The ceremony is a celebration of purpose. New employees are handed medallions emblazoned with the company's purpose that serve as a constant reminder that their work matters. The medallion transforms the mission into a physical symbol that brings people together to achieve a common purpose. In the next chapter, you'll learn more about symbols and how they can be used as a vivid reminder of your company's mission.

OBSESSIONS WILL FIND YOU

Michael Moritz invests in crazy ideas that others overlook, including those two guys in a garage who created Apple. Moritz also invested in Google, Airbnb, PayPal, and WhatsApp through his legendary venture capital firm, Sequoia Capital.

"The people who do remarkable things tend to be obsessed by what they are working on,"[20] Moritz once told me in an interview for *Forbes*. Moritz defined an "obsession" as being so captivated by an idea that you simply have no choice but to pursue. It's an idea that stalks you at night and walks by your side in the daylight. It doesn't let you go. Jeff Bezos once said an obsession is an idea that you passionately believe in. You don't chase passions, he added. They come looking for you.

We now know the obsession that came looking for Bezos. We learned how the founders of Apple, Whole Foods, and Medtronic started with little more than ideas and, fueled by a purpose bigger than their products, revolutionized the world.

Your mission will be different from theirs. It is distinctly and uniquely yours and yours alone. Once you identify your mission, share it. Proclaim it. Shout it. Announce it. Publish it on social media. Declare it. Live it. Above all, keep it alive in the hearts and minds of everyone who crosses your path. You might inspire them to join your quest. Since nothing worth building is accomplished alone, you'll need to attract the best and the brightest. Make your journey irresistible, an adventure that people will be delighted to join.

14

SYMBOLS CONVEY BIG IDEAS

Symbols can be very powerful.

—Jeff Bezos

Jeff Bezos is building a clock that you can't buy on Amazon. The five-hundred-foot-tall clock will sit inside a West Texas mountain. At the cost of more than $40 million (so far), it'll tell time for ten thousand years. Engineers are designing the enormously complicated mechanical timepiece to tick once per year and chime once every thousand years.

Before you write off the project as an eccentric Howard Hughes–esque whim, listen to what Bezos has to say about the ten-thousand-year clock:

> The clock is a symbol for long-term thinking. The symbol is important for a couple of reasons. One, if we think long term, we can accomplish things that we couldn't otherwise accomplish. If I said to you, I want you to solve world hunger in five years, you would rightly decline the challenge. But if I said, I want you to solve world hunger in a hundred years, that's more interesting. You would first create the conditions under which such change could occur. We didn't change the challenge. We changed the time horizon. Time horizons matter. They matter a lot. The other thing I would point out is that we humans are getting awfully sophisticated in technological ways and have a lot of potential to be very dangerous to ourselves. It seems to me that we, as a species, have to start thinking longer term. So, this is a symbol. I think symbols can be very powerful.[1]

Bezos created a website to keep the public updated on the clock's progress, but visiting the clock will take a commitment. The nearest airport is several hours away by car, and you will have to climb a rugged trail two thousand feet above the valley floor to reach the site. And don't get too excited about seeing the timepiece anytime soon. According to Bezos, the clock will not be finished for "many years into the future."[2]

Bezos says thinking over longer time periods than their competitors was one of the pillars that fueled Amazon's innovation engine. The monumental clock is a symbol, a physical icon to that philosophy.

SYMBOLISM IS HARDWIRED IN THE ANCIENT BRAIN

According to former Amazon executive Bill Carr, who cowrote *Working Backwards*, the secret sauce that creates Amazon's culture is made of four ingredients: customer obsession, long-term thinking, eagerness to invent, and taking pride in operational excellence. "Amazon has never wavered in its commitment to these four core principles,"[3] Carr says. "And they are in large part the reason that in 2015 Amazon became the company that reached $100 billion in annual sales faster than any other in the world."

Carr says that Amazon Prime Video, which has more than one hundred million viewers, resulted from a decade of research, development, and content acquisition. "Having that long time horizon is critical if you want to build something big and enduring. Many companies will give up on an idea if it doesn't produce returns in a quarter or a year. Amazon will stick with an initiative for five, six, seven years—all the while keeping the investment manageable, constantly learning and improving—until it gains momentum and acceptance."

While Bezos served as Amazon's CEO, he consistently reminded employees of Amazon's core values through written and spoken words, as we've already covered. But he also used a third potent communication tactic: symbols.

Jeff Bezos is big on big symbols like the ten-thousand-year clock. He's also big on small symbols that have a big impact. In the hands of a skilled communicator, for example, an empty chair is imbued with meaning.

"In the early days at Amazon, Jeff Bezos left a single chair empty around the boardroom table,"[4] says John Rossman. "It informed all attendees that they should consider that seat occupied by their customer, the most important person in the room." Rossman worked closely with Bezos and played a crucial role in launching Amazon Marketplace, now responsible for 50 percent of all units sold at Amazon.com. The chair resonated deeply with Rossman who never forgot the symbol or its message.

The chair served to align every discussion around the question, "What's best for our customers?" According to Rossman, the chair was one of many calculated, highly-symbolic gestures that served to repeat core messages to reinforce Amazon's leadership principles. In this case, every decision in one way or another had to consider the customer's perspective.

Inspiring leaders communicate with passion, purpose, and vision. They use metaphors and analogies, stories, and anecdotes to convey their ideas. Symbols are also part of the rhetorical tool kit because they evoke a powerful sensory experience. Since our senses evolved to work together—vision influences hearing, smell influences taste—we learn best when several senses are stimulated at once.

A symbol is a thing (image, object, or place) that stands for an idea: a clock represents long-range thinking, or an empty chair stands for the voice of the customer. Symbols predate language, which is why symbolism is hardwired in the ancient brain. The most ordinary artifacts can express profound ideas. For example, when is a door not a door? When it's turned into a desk.

In the summer of 1998, two months after Reed Hastings and Marc Randolph launched Netflix, the two entrepreneurs were invited to Seattle to meet with Bezos. Although Amazon was strictly in the book business, Bezos had the vision to build the Everything Store. Selling music and videos would be the logical next step.

Randolph recalls being surprised at seeing the sparse workplace. Although it was a young start-up, Amazon had already grown to six hundred employees. But instead of office desks that you'd expect to see in an elegant corporate office, employees worked on desks made of recycled doors. The holes where doorknobs used to be were patched up with circular plugs of wood.

"Okay, Jeff,"[5] Marc said, grinning. "What's with all the doors?"

"It's a deliberate message," Bezos explained. "Everyone in the company has them. It's a way of saying that we spend money on things that affect our customers, not on things that don't."

At the time, Bezos offered $15 million for Netflix. Marc, a serial entrepreneur, thought the offer would make for a nice payday. Reed Hastings, Netflix's CEO today, talked him out of it. They weren't ready to hand over the keys to their young start-up. They decided to decline the offer and let Amazon down "lightly—and politely."

Although the Netflix cofounders were not ready to sell, Bezos left an impression on them. Marc recalls that Bezos had a vision that inspired loyalty. Bezos conveyed his vision through the words he spoke, the words he wrote, and the symbols that brought those words to life.

Powerful symbols come in many forms.

SYMBOLS ARE POWERFUL DEVICES IN YOUR RHETORICAL TOOL KIT

Visual symbols are images or objects that people can see and touch. Coins and flags are visual, as are empty chairs and door desks.

Auditory symbols are what you hear. Stirring music or a group cheer are auditory symbols. In Amazon's early days, a ringing bell signified a sale. It was motivating at first when the company had half a dozen orders per day. As the company's sales soared, the bell went from inspiring to annoying. The symbol had a short life.

Spatial symbols are places and space that carry special meaning. Buildings and spaces tell a story. At Amazon, Bezos worked in a building named "Day 1." When he moved buildings, he took the name with him. The simple phrase captures the emotional vitality of a start-up and serves as a reminder to have a beginner's mind, no matter how large the organization grows.

Communication comes in different languages, and symbolism is an important language. Yes, money motivates. But researchers are finding that meaning is a powerful motivator as well. In his book *Conscious Leadership*, Whole Foods cofounder John Mackey writes, "In order to successfully use a higher purpose to guide and motivate an organization, the purpose must be kept at the forefront of people's awareness. A great example of this comes from Jeff Bezos, who, in the early days of Amazon's growth, famously communicated the company's stated purpose of being 'Earth's most customer-centric company' by leaving an empty chair open in his meetings to represent the customer. Physical symbols such as this create a powerful reminder that infuses the mission of the company into everyone's decision-making."[6]

Motivating a group of people to do the impossible is possible, but it'll require every device in your communication tool belt to pull it off. So keep symbols on the table, even if the table is really a door.

15

HUMANIZE DATA

Humans aren't good at understanding exponential growth.

—Jeff Bezos

Twenty-three hundred percent. This number might not mean a lot to you, but it impressed Jeff Bezos. He ran with it and built a company that touches nearly every aspect of your life—from the way you shop to how you consume entertainment to how you interact digitally with millions of governments, universities, and businesses worldwide.

In the spring of 1994, Bezos was working for D. E. Shaw, a Wall Street investment firm. One day, his boss handed Bezos an assignment: study the commercial potential of the internet. As Bezos sifted through the mountain of research papers, a nugget caught his eye: Web usage was growing by 2,300 percent. He later called it a wake-up call because "things just don't grow that fast. It's highly unusual."[1]

Bezos came across the statistic in *Matrix News,* a monthly publication about networking computer systems. While others had seen the same number, Bezos immediately grasped its implication. "Human beings are not good at understanding exponential growth," he said later.

Bezos is right. Through the magic of compounding, numbers that look small at first can add up to enormous sums. Albert Einstein called compounding the "eighth wonder of the world." Compounding is the process that explains how investing just $25 a month at a 7 percent rate of return will add up to $65,000 forty years later, even though you only contributed $12,000. The same phenomenon explains why virologists sounded the alarm when only a few cases of the coronavirus had been reported in cities and countries. If one sick person infects two others, then two infect four, four infect eight, and so on. Exponential growth explains why the U.S. went from one confirmed case of COVID-19 on January 21, 2020, to a raging pandemic five weeks later.

Exponential growth is different from linear growth. Most people are familiar with linear growth rates: if the tomato plant in your yard grows three tomatoes a day, you'll have three today, six tomorrow, and nine the next day. In two weeks, you can proudly say that your plant has produced a total of forty-two tomatoes.

Exponential growth is harder to wrap our heads around. Let's travel to a hypothetical magical garden where you've discovered a secret fertilizer formula that accelerates the growth of your tomato garden: Each tomato produces another three tomatoes, each of those tomatoes produces three others, and so on and so on. After two weeks of exponential growth, you'll need a bigger garden to hold 1,594,323 tomatoes.

This type of acceleration is so misunderstood, psychologists have a name for it: *exponential growth bias.* It's a simple mathematical mistake that has real-world consequences when it's underestimated, and massive opportunities when it's appreciated. Bezos understood exponential growth, recognized its implications, and took advantage of the data's underlying story.

Data only leads to action if people understand the story the numbers tell.

ANCIENT BRAINS IN A HIGH-TECH WORLD

While the human brain allows us to perform extraordinary feats of imagination and information processing, it has limitations. It simply wasn't made to process large numbers.

IDC estimates that the sum of the world's data, compounding at an annual rate of 60 percent, will grow from 33 zettabytes in 2018 to 175 zettabytes by 2025. With no context, there's no way to get your mind around such a number. Put it this way: 175 zettabytes is the equivalent of a trillion gigabytes. Still confused? Let's try it another way: If you could store 175 zettabytes on DVDs, the stack of disks would circle the Earth 222 times.[2]

The people you're trying to persuade are bombarded by greater and greater amounts of data—much more information than their brains are

built to handle. Our brains evolved to deal with very small numbers ranging from one to seven, not the mind-boggling numbers thrown at us every
day. But that data, or information, contains valuable insights that promise
to transform every field, every business, and every life. Data will drive
waves of innovation and drive breakthroughs in everything from health
care, manufacturing, sustainability, and every other part of our world—
that is, if people can figure out what the data means.

When it comes to numbers, the secret to grabbing a person's attention
and convincing them to take action on your ideas is not to overwhelm them
with even more numbers, statistics, and data points. The secret is to hold
your fire. Then choose your target carefully—identify the most important
number your audience needs to know. The next step is to make the data
relatable.

You'll recall from chapter 6 that the human brain is an analogy machine, constantly comparing the new and abstract to the old and familiar.
Your new idea is more likely to stick when you compare it to something
the audience knows. The same approach applies to communicating data.
Cognitive scientists say, "People have difficulty reasoning about magnitudes outside of human perception."[3] Numbers that are too small, like
nanoseconds, or too large, like the number of stars in the universe, are
beyond what we can perceive in our mind's eye. Fortunately, there are
simple ways to rescale numbers that will make them easier to comprehend. The most common comparisons are made to size, distance, and
time.

SIZE

Size and weight comparisons are common because they work. Bezos is
fond of such comparisons and began using them early and often in his
shareholder letters and public presentations:

- "If you were to print the Amazon.com catalog, it would be the size of
  more than forty New York City phone books."[4]
- "We set out to offer customers something they simply could not get
  any other way and began serving them with books. We brought them
  much more selection than was possible in a physical store (our store
  would now occupy 6 football fields)."[5]

- "We now have more than 45,000 items in our electronics store (about 7 times the selection you're likely to find at a big-box electronics store)."[6]

Bezos founded Blue Origin to create the building blocks that will allow people to move to space to benefit Earth as the population grows. As you might imagine, it's a bold vision whose outcome is far removed from our lifetimes. Making a case for Blue Origin requires that Bezos use all the rhetorical tools he's sharpened over the past three decades. Not surprisingly, Bezos turns to data comparisons to make the case that Earth's resources are finite:

> The historic rate of compounding of global energy usage is three percent a year. Three percent a year doesn't sound like very much, but over many years the power of compounding is so extreme. A three percent annual compounding is the equivalent of doubling human energy use every 25 years. If you take global energy use today, you can power everything by covering Nevada in solar cells. It seems challenging. It also seems possible. But in just a couple of hundred years, we'll have to cover the entire surface of the Earth in solar cells. That's a very impractical solution.[7]

The solution, says Bezos, is to build colonies—not on the surface of planets—but in space.

Steve Jobs loved using size and weight to explain data. In *The Presentation Secrets of Steve Jobs,* I feature many examples of Jobs putting data into context, but few presentations were as memorable as the introduction of the iPod. In 2001, Jobs revolutionized the music industry with the introduction of Apple's first iPod. Jobs knew that few people would understand or care that the device stored 5 gigabytes of data (music). But wait! he exclaimed. The iPod was much more than 5 gigabytes of data. It's "1,000 songs in your pocket." And with a magician's flourish, Jobs pulled an iPod from the pocket of his blue jeans as the audience gasped and cheered.

While I was writing this book, a group of scientists invited me to visit a highly-secure government lab where they're working on technology that might produce clean, reliable, abundant energy for future generations. They showed me the world's largest laser which is actually made up of 192 beams housed in a building the size of "three football fields" and aimed at a target the size of a "pencil eraser." The search for fusion power (the process that powers the sun), is a considered a scientific Grand Challenge. But part of the challenge is translating the complex science into everyday language to attract funding, partnerships, and media attention. Everyone involved in my tour—from the lab's director to scientists performing experiments—used the same size comparisons to explain their work. They were all trained to bring big numbers down to Earth.

Make data tangible by using size and weight comparisons we all understand.

DISTANCE

Using distance measures is another way to make data relatable. One executive I worked with at AWS gave a presentation about the company's Snowball service—appliances that customers use to transport massive data files securely to the cloud. "AWS Snowball appliances to transport data from on-premise to AWS facilities have traveled a distance equal to circling the world 250 times."

The Sagan Planet Walk in Ithaca, New York, was built to put the mind-bending distances of space into context the average person could understand. Stone obelisks represent the sun and planets—the space between them has been reduced in size by a factor of five billion. Visitors walk about nine yards to get from the Earth to the sun but must hike fifteen minutes to reach Pluto. The exhibit expanded considerably with the addition of a stone representing Alpha Centauri, the nearest star to our sun, which shines 4.3 light-years away. The star's obelisk, reduced to scale, sits five thousand miles away at the 'Imiloa Astronomy Center in Hawaii.

The Planet Walk doesn't just translate big numbers into language everyday people can read. Distances are put into context that people can *feel* as they walk.

TIME

Bezos also loves making time comparisons, especially when he can relate data to how much time the consumer saves.

"Consumers complete 28% of purchases on Amazon in three minutes or less,"[8] Bezos wrote in the 2020 shareholder letter. Left alone, those two numbers—twenty-eight and three—don't mean much. That's why Bezos adds the following explanation:

> Compare that to the typical shopping trip to a physical store—driving, parking, searching store aisles, waiting in the check-out line, finding your car, and driving home. Research suggests the typical physical store trip takes about an hour. If you assume a typical Amazon purchase takes 15 minutes and that it saves you a couple of trips to a physical store a week, that's more than 75 hours a year saved. That's important. We're all busy.

To add impact to the comparison, Bezos continued:

> So that we can get a dollar figure, let's value the time savings at $10 per hour, which is conservative. Seventy-five hours multiplied by $10 an hour . . . gives you value creation for each Prime member of about $630. We have 200 million Prime members, for a total in 2020 of $126 billion of value creation.

COACHING DRILL

Practice taking the following data point and put it into context: A Grande Mocha Frappuccino contains about 55 grams of sugar.

Is 55 grams a lot or a little? Without context, it's only a number. But let's pretend you are a nutritionist trying to convince your client to cut down on flavored coffee drinks—how would you describe just how much sugar they're consuming in 55 grams? Perhaps you can compare it to how many teaspoons of sugar make up 55 grams (answer: 12 teaspoons). You might compare it to M&M's. A Grande Mocha Frappuccino has the equivalent of not one, not two, but three fun-size packages of M&M's. Now do you think the client might reconsider consuming too many Frappuccinos?

CREATE VALUE

Influential speakers avoid adding to the deluge of data overwhelming their listeners. Instead, they choose a few key statistics and build stories around those data points, using concrete examples that nonexperts can easily comprehend and remember. According to Google chief economist Dr. Hal

Varian, "The ability to take data—to be able to understand it, to process it, to extract value from it, to visualize it, to communicate it—is going to be a hugely important skill in the next decades."[9]

By making data relevant to your readers or listeners, you're helping them see numbers in a new way. Developing this persuasive communication skill also gives you the ability to reframe events as opportunities instead of setbacks, a key ingredient to persuade others to act on your idea.

I've often said that if you don't tell your story, someone else will. And you might not like their version. For example, the richest person in the world always has a target on their back. Activists, regulators, and the media know that the public pays the most attention to the people or companies at the top of a list. In a 2018 interview, Bezos was asked how he felt about being named the world's richest individual. "I never sought that title. It was fine being the second wealthiest person in the world,"[10] he said. The audience laughed because they knew exactly what he meant.

During that interview, Bezos introduced a metric he revisited a couple of years later in his 2020 shareholder letter. First, Bezos acknowledged that Amazon had created $1.6 trillion of wealth for shareholders. And he's one of them. "More than seven-eighths of the shares, representing $1.4 trillion of wealth creation, are owned by others."[11] Who? "Pension funds, universities, and 401(k)s." Then, Bezos personalizes the wealth even further by showing a letter he received from Mary and Larry, a couple who surprised their twelve-year-old son, Ryan, a voracious reader, with two shares of Amazon in 1997. The stock split several times over their holding period, leaving them with twenty-four shares. In 2021, Amazon's stock was trading at well over $3,000 per share. Ryan sold some of it to help buy a house. "Those two shares have had a wonderful influence on our family," they wrote. "We all enjoyed watching Amazon value grow year after year, and it's a story we love to tell others."

Bezos used the story and the supporting data to offer this advice: "If you want to be successful in business (in life, actually), you have to create more than you consume. Your goal should be to create value for everyone you interact with. Any business that doesn't create value for those it touches, even if it appears successful on the surface, isn't long for this world. It's on the way out." Remember that we think in story. By wrapping data in story, you make it far easier for your listener or reader to understand your message.

By making data relevant for your listeners you demonstrate the value you're creating. Show the value your start-up will offer investors (how much your company will make, when you'll hit your goals, and when they will start seeing a return on their money). Show the value you'll add to a new company once you're hired (if you increased sales by 25 percent at your last company, tell them how you did it and how you can do the same for them). Show the value your business brings to customers and employees (saving them time and money, or helping them generate more sales). Bezos offers a valuable lesson when he says create value for everyone. But sometimes, you need to show your work.

16

THE GALLO METHOD: SELL YOUR IDEA IN FIFTEEN SECONDS

> If you can't communicate and talk to other people and get
> across your ideas, you're giving up your potential.
>
> —Warren Buffett

Pulitzer Prize–winning historian Doris Kearns Goodwin has studied leadership for more than fifty years. The essence of leadership, she says, is "the ability to use one's talent, skills, and emotional intelligence to mobilize people to a common purpose."[1]

Goodwin, whose book *Team of Rivals* served as the inspiration for the Steven Spielberg film *Lincoln,* says that great leaders communicate through stories that make people feel like they're part of the journey toward a common purpose.

Great leaders build successful companies because they have a vision of who the company serves, the problem the company solves, and how the company enriches the lives of everyone it touches. Communication is the key to rallying people around that vision and persuading them to become travelers on your epic journey.

At Gallo Communications Group, we've created a template that displays your story on one page. We refer to it as the Gallo Method: a tool to craft a clear, concise, and compelling message. It's intended to persuade people to take action on your ideas by taking them on a journey. The template acts as a guide to take your travelers from where they are today to your desired destination.

The Gallo Method is flexible, simple, and scalable. Use it to create a fifteen-second pitch or a fifteen-minute presentation. It brings together the concepts you've learned in this book: writing, creating loglines, telling stories, making data meaningful and memorable, and crafting analogies and metaphors. In addition to the communication tools we've already discussed, there is one more element critical to building a successful message map—the rule of three.

THE MOST POWERFUL NUMBER IN COMMUNICATION

The rule of three is a communication thread that runs through the fabric of cultures and literature, both ancient and contemporary. It simply states that the human brain cannot *easily* hold more than three things in short-term memory. Even when we try to memorize a series of digits longer than three numbers—like a phone number—we chunk the numbers in groups of three or four.

Quantum physicist Dominic Walliman says if you understand the rule of three, you can communicate anything to anyone. Walliman's specialty is writing children's books and making YouTube videos that simplify dense, complex subjects such as physics, nanotechnology, and rocket science. Walliman suggests that when you attempt to explain a subject to people who are not as familiar with the topic as you are, don't go too far down the rabbit hole. People can only consume a certain amount of information at any one time. "It's better to explain, say, three things that someone will understand rather than barrage them with a whole load of information that kind of undoes all of your good work to begin with,"[2] Walliman says.

Georgetown University researchers found that three charms but four alarms. The study intended to find out why consumers found some product messages more appealing than others. It turns out that consumers find three product claims to be persuasive. Consumers lose interest and become *less impressed* once product claims beginning climbing to four, five, or more. According to the research, if you're selling a product or pitching an idea, backing your argument with just one message isn't convincing.[3] Two supporting statements are better than one. But three is the magic number.

One remarkable study found that the rule of three pervades the world of start-ups and venture capital investing. DocSend, a cloud-based document-sharing company, conducted a data-driven survey and found that investors spend an average of three minutes reviewing a pitch deck. Investors put more money into start-ups with three founders. And investors spend most of their time reviewing three slides in a pitch deck: solution, product, and team. In other words, out of a twenty-slide pitch deck, three are more important than the others.[4]

Effective communicators like Jeff Bezos speak in threes:

- "We've had three big ideas at Amazon that we've stuck with for 18 years, and they're the reason we're successful: Put the customer first. Invent. And be patient."
- "The keys to success are patience, persistence, and obsessive attention to detail."
- "Amazon's success is built on three pillars: selection, convenience, and low prices."
- "In this turbulent global economy, our fundamental approach remains the same: stay heads down, focused on the long term, and obsessed with customers."
- "We ask people to consider three questions before making a hiring decision: Will you admire this person? Will this person raise the effectiveness of the group? On what dimension will this person be a superstar?"
- "Work hard, have fun, make history."

THE GALLO METHOD MESSAGE MAP TEMPLATE

The Gallo Method Message Map template leverages the rule of three to power your story. It works like this:

First, draft a logline. Ask yourself, *What is the one most important thing I want my audience to know?* The logline should be specific, clear, and concise. It should be no more than thirty words (ten words is even better). If your logline can't fit in a Twitter post of 140 characters, it's way too long. Recall what Bezos repeatedly said about Amazon: "Our mission is to be Earth's most customer-centric company." Nine words, fifty-nine characters. Keep your vision bold—and short.

Second, craft three messages to reinforce the logline. None of the messages are important enough to *replace* your big idea—they *support* the big picture.

Third, bring those messages to life with stories, data, or analogies. These figures of speech will enhance your message and make it more persuasive.

Let's turn to a straightforward product—shirts—to make sense of the Message Map:

UNTUCKit is a New York–based retailer that started the untucked shirts trend. Founder Chris Riccobono is a student of effective communication. "If you can't say in one sentence what makes you different from the competition, then you're wasting your time,"[5] Riccobono says. UNTUCKit's logline in one sentence reads: "Shirts designed to be worn untucked." Six words tell you almost everything you need to know about the company and what it sells. Those six words are consistent across the company's platforms: website, retail stores, social media, and public presentations.

The conversation doesn't stop there. The company communicates three supporting messages: perfect length, fits for every shape and size, and contoured hemlines that make the shirts look good untucked.

All of these messages are easily contained in the Gallo Method Message Map template. The message is so concise it's displayed on the walls of more than eighty of the store's physical locations in North America and the UK. Figure 16.1 shows you the UNTUCKit Message Map.

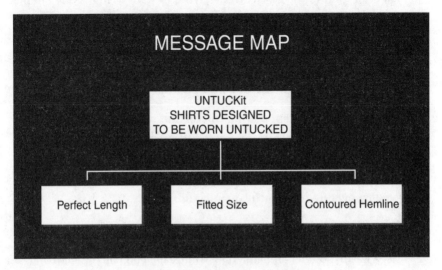

Figure 16.1: UNTUCKit Message Map

UNTUCKit is a simple product example. But you can use the Gallo Method to prepare for any type of communication: launching a company, selling a product, pitching an idea, or interviewing for a job.

For example, during the week I was working on this chapter, I met with the CEO of an influential, publicly traded tech company with a $100 billion market capitalization. The investment community was anticipating its quarterly results as a sign of where its industry was heading.

When I met the CEO in a large conference room attached to his office, he had just left the quarterly financial call where he spent an hour wading in the deep weeds with stock analysts who cover the company. They know more about the company than the average CNBC viewer, so part of my job was to pull the CEO out of the weeds, where he could see the sky. We created a Message Map with a logline and three supporting messages.

First came the logline. "What is the one thing you want investors to know about your company?" I asked.

The CEO responded with a long, convoluted answer. He said, "Due to our strong technological leadership and disciplined financial management, our company is well-positioned to capitalize on market trends affecting the underlying business."

"So, you're telling me that your company's balance sheet is strong, and you're optimistic about your product mix?" I responded.

"Very much. We've never been in a better position. Ever."

"Then let's cut to the chase. Your investors want to know one simple thing: Your company is healthier and stronger than ever. Tell them clearly and concisely."

Our logline for the interview began to take shape. It read:

Our company is healthier and stronger than ever.

Next, we worked on supporting the logline with three messages that would tell investors what they wanted to know, what they needed to know, and what they should know but perhaps didn't know.

The CEO, with input from his financial team and me, decided to focus on the following three supporting messages:

1. The company hit record revenue across all its product categories.
2. Prices for its products remained so strong, the company was raising its revenue and profit estimates for the next quarter.

3. Future demand trends were strong in data centers, 5G phones, and electric vehicles, three of the categories fueling the company's growth.

The morning after the CEO's interview, CNBC called the quarter a "blowout" for the company and used the CEO's statements for the headline to its story. Television reporters found the story easy to follow because we *made* the story easy to follow.

COACHING DRILL

Follow the Gallo Method to structure the content for your next pitch or presentation. The Message Map template shown in figure 16.2 gives you a place to draft your logline and three supporting points. The first step is to start writing. You can cut words, edit, and wordsmith later. Collaborate with others. Get their input. When you finish the message map, you will have a simple, easy-to-follow story displayed on one page. Memorize it for a pitch, conversation, or interview. Use it as an outline for a slide presentation. Share it with your team to get everyone on the same page. Send it to your website developer or anyone who creates written marketing material for your company. The message map is your story on one page.

Figure 16.2: The Message Map Template

An executive in one of my Harvard classes implemented the message map concept to make his team's virtual meetings more effective and efficient. Colin works for the second-largest financial services firm in Europe and heads an asset management group with sixty people. The team invests money for wealthy clients.

"The message map was unbelievable," Colin told me after the class. "It led to a 50 percent reduction in the time it takes our team to prepare a client presentation."

Colin's team prepares and delivers at least two presentations a week: pitches to attract new clients and presentations to update existing clients. The Gallo Method made it easy for a smaller subset of the team to craft unique messages for each conversation tailored to their audience. The rest of the team could easily see the flow of the discussion on one page.

The Message Map also reduced the size of presentations from thirty slides to ten. The logline appeared on one slide, followed by two or three slides to reinforce each of the three key supporting messages. Figure 16.3 shows a visual of a fourteen-slide layout using content taken directly from a Message Map structure.

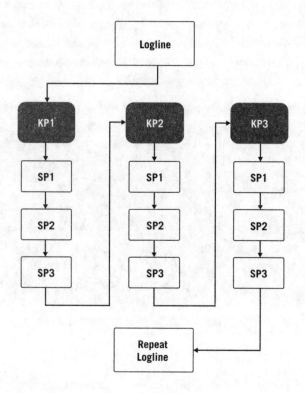

KP = key point; SP = supporting point

Figure 16.3: Fourteen-Slide Layout Created from a Message Map Structure

The Gallo Method also saved time. Instead of three thirty-minute meetings to prepare for each presentation, the Message Map was so simple, the team only needed one thirty-minute meeting to get aligned on their story—the template cut the meeting time to prepare presentations by two-thirds.

Clients loved it. Instead of sitting through a forty-five-minute update, they got the information they needed in twenty minutes, leaving another twenty minutes to engage with the team. But in many cases, the clients found the presentations so simple and straightforward, they were delighted with the outcome and happy to get time back in their busy lives.

"After twenty-five years in the financial field, I've never come across a simpler communication tool to create alignment among the team and create clear and concise presentations," Colin told me.

The poet Henry David Thoreau was born nearly two hundred years before the invention of PowerPoint, but he could have been speaking to today's communicators when he wrote, "Simplicity, simplicity, simplicity! I say, let your affairs be as two or three, and not a hundred or a thousand."

Great leaders have a bold vision and successfully rally people around a common goal. But make no mistake, they've crafted their words ahead of time, and those words are cleverly packaged in a simple structure. They know where they're going and choose a clear and simple road map to convince others to join them on the journey.

CONCLUSION

Invent and Wander

You don't choose your passions. Your passions choose you.

—Jeff Bezos

Creativity is an essential ingredient of innovation, leadership, and communication. But to be your creative best, you must establish the conditions for creativity to flourish.

Breakthrough ideas don't appear on demand. Creative ideas rarely occur when you're staring at a blank page on a computer screen. Instead, epiphanies happen when five conditions are met.

First, get enough sleep.

"I am very focused on getting eight hours of sleep,"[1] Bezos says. "I think better. I have more energy." Once Bezos wakes up, he doesn't jump into work. In fact, he sets aside time every morning to "putter." He reads the paper, has coffee, enjoys breakfast with the kids. Bezos sets his first important meeting for 10:00 A.M. when his energy is at its highest. According to Bezos, leaders get paid to make a small number of high-quality decisions a day. If you can make three such decisions, you're above average, says Bezos. Getting enough sleep will give you the energy to make quality decisions and come up with new ideas.

Second, stay active.

Steve Jobs preferred to have serious conversations during long walks. Apple and Pixar employees recall these "brainstorming walks" as far more productive than conference room meetings: Walks are where Jobs came up with his most novel ideas.

According to a Stanford study, walking boosts our creative output by

60 percent.[2] The participants were given "divergent thinking" tests, which measure novel or innovative ideas. The researchers measured subjects while they walked and while they sat. The majority of participants were far more creative when they were active.

The act of walking sparks novel ideas because brains evolved from ancestors who walked up to twelve miles a day. It's unnatural to sit in a classroom for hours on end, or conduct Zoom calls all day, or to expect a spark of creativity as you gaze into a digital screen. Get sleep, stay active, and putter around—creative ideas can't be forced. They have to be allowed to flourish in the right conditions.

Third, let your passions choose you.

"Ever since I was five years old, when Neil Armstrong stepped on the surface of the moon, I've been passionate about space, rockets, rocket engines, and space travel,"[3] Bezos said to explain why he was stepping aside from Amazon to focus on his space company, Blue Origin. "I think we all have passions. And you don't get to choose them. They pick you. But you have to be alert to them. You have to be looking for them."

Fourth, be a learn-it-all.

One of Amazon's Leadership Principles is *Learn and Be Curious*. Leaders are never done learning and always seek to improve themselves. There are two types of people: learn-it-alls and know-it-alls. In a rapidly changing global landscape, only those who are constantly learning will develop novel ideas that move the world forward.

Author Walter Isaacson says Jeff Bezos reminds him of Leonardo da Vinci: "In his delight-filled notebooks, we see his mind dancing across all fields of nature with a curiosity that is exuberant and playful . . . Jeff Bezos embodies these traits. He has never outgrown his wonder years. He retains an insatiable, childlike, and joyful curiosity about almost everything."[4]

Fifth and finally, cultivate a limitless mindset.

Entrepreneurs who change the world actively fight the status quo bias in almost everything they do or pitch. The status quo bias simply means that we prefer the way things are today rather than trying new things. Bezos overcame the bias when he pitched the idea for an online bookstore. He overcame the bias when he pursued "crazy" ideas such as e-commerce, streaming entertainment, cloud computing, same-day delivery, and space exploration. Nothing seemed too far-fetched.

Bezos does not impose limits on his ideas. "The idea of going to the moon was so impossible that people actually used it as a metaphor for impossibility,"[5] Bezos says. "What I hope you take away from that is that anything you set your mind to, you can do."

When you set the conditions for success and creativity, you'll stand out. Differentiation is the key to survival at a time when others want you to be typical. In his last shareholder letter as CEO, Bezos wrote that it takes work to be distinctive when the world attempts to make you normal. It's easier and takes less energy to be like everyone else.

"We all know that distinctiveness—originality—is valuable,"[6] Bezos writes. "But the world wants you to be typical—in a thousand ways, it pulls at you. Don't let it happen."

It takes continuous effort, lifelong learning, abundant energy, and relentless passion to be original. "Never, never, never let the universe smooth you into your surroundings," Bezos said.

"It remains Day 1."

COACHING DRILLS AT A GLANCE

DRILL 1:

During Bezos's tenure as Amazon CEO, he helped to create sixteen Leadership Principles Amazonians use every day to discuss new projects, pitch ideas, or determine the best approach to solve a particular problem. Above all, the principles reinforce the company's ethos that keeps customers at the center of every decision.

The way the principles are written is one of the primary reasons they are thoroughly integrated and understood by people throughout every level of the organization. The entire document consists of just seven hundred words written in eighth-grade language. Each principle is simple and clear and includes a few short sentences that translate the principle into desirable behaviors.

For example, the first and most important guiding principle is:

CUSTOMER OBSESSION

According to Amazon, customer obsession means that "Leaders start with the customer and work backwards. They work vigorously to earn and keep customer trust. Although leaders pay attention to competitors, they obsess over customers."

Key principles that are also relevant to this book include: Ownership, Invent and Simplify, Learn and Be Curious, Think Big, Earn Trust, and Insist on the Highest Standards. You can see the principles clearly displayed on the Amazon website because the company wants every job candidate to know them, every new hire to learn them, and every leader to internalize and share them.

You can see the principles clearly displayed on the Amazon website because the company wants every job candidate to know them, every new hire to learn them, and every leader to internalize and share them.

Author Brad Stone who chronicled Amazon's rise in *The Everything Store*, wrote that the clear articulation of these principles is a calculated leadership strategy. While employees in many organizations muddle through their jobs because their company's goals are confusing or complicated, the Amazon principles are simple, clear, and consistent.

The principles or values that make up your company culture are intended to be acted upon. But it's impossible to act on a principle no one can remember or understand. Make your principles simple to read, remember, and follow.

DRILL 2:

If you're working on a complex topic, take a page from Warren Buffett's approach to writing his famous financial letters. Get to know your audience before you write by asking yourself three questions.

Who is your target audience? Buffett thinks about writing for his sisters, Doris and Bertie.
What do they need to know? Avoid telling them everything *you* know. What do they need to know that they don't know already?
Why should they care? Nobody cares about your ideas. They care about how your idea will help them lead a better life.

DRILL 3:

Put your message to the test. Select a sample of text from one of your presentation scripts. How many words or phrases are fancy, Latin-based? You can use an online etymology dictionary to identify the origin of words. Look for simpler, shorter words to replace the formal ones. You'll find that favoring short words will cut most of the jargon from your speech, words that confuse your audience. As a result, your sentences will be tight, clear, and strong. Replace long words with short ones and you'll be far more persuasive.

DRILL 4:

Use the Flesch-Kincaid test to simplify your writing. Several writing platforms offer the service, including Grammarly and Microsoft Word, which has added readability scores to its popular software. Under Word's options, you'll find a spelling and grammar tab. Check the box that says "Show readability statistics" and it will display the readability and reading level of the document. Amazon teaches its employees to aim for a "readability" level of 50 or higher and a grade level of 8. This chapter has a readability score of 59 and a Flesch-Kincaid grade level of 8, which means it's simple enough for a broad range of readers to clearly understand its content.

DRILL 5:

In this chapter, I've offered you simple writing strategies that will put you far ahead of your peers. But there's always more to learn from brilliant writing instructors whose books have a permanent place on my bookshelf. Here are a few titles that will elevate your writing skills.

Writing Tools: 55 Essential Strategies for Every Writer
by Roy Peter Clark
Writing to Persuade by Trish Hall
On Writing Well by William Zinsser
100 Ways to Improve Your Writing by Gary Provost
On Writing by Stephen King

DRILL 6:

Apply the *So what?* test to one of your presentations. Start with the topic of your conversation and answer the question, "So what?" Ask the question two more times until you craft a clear logline for your pitch or presentation.

Topic _____

So what? _____

_____

So what? _____

_____

So what? _____

_____

DRILL 7:

Search for comparisons outside your subject expertise, or "domain." See how many metaphors you can spot in books, articles, speeches, and presentations. Challenge yourself. Categorize the metaphors into motion, physical, or spatial comparisons. Being aware of the metaphors you see, hear, and read will spark creative ideas to help you write and deliver persuasive presentations.

DRILL 8:

Metaphors act as shortcuts to understanding. They help your audience comprehend complex or abstract ideas. They are so effective, we use metaphors constantly in everyday conversation. But try to avoid worn-out clichés in your business presentations. Metaphors that are too familiar lose their impact. Here are some common figures of speech to avoid.

- The ball is in your court
- Bring to the table
- Think outside the box
- A drop in the bucket
- A perfect storm
- A fly in the ointment

Avoid reaching for the easy metaphor. If you've heard a figure of speech a thousand times, so has your audience.

DRILL 9:

A simple metaphor format is "A is B" like "Time is money." The format works well to express complex ideas. Select a complex idea from your own subject area. Use the A is B format to explain it. Describe the comparison in conversational language.

Complex idea: _____ (A)

Familiar idea: _____ (B)

A is B format: _____ is _____

Example:

Complex idea: A good investment

Familiar idea: Castle with a moat

A is B format: A good investment is an economic castle with a deep moat around it to deter competitors.

DRILL 10:

The first step to leveraging the power of analogy in your writing and communication is to be aware of just how prevalent analogies are in our everyday language. Take note of how many analogies you encounter in conversations, books, articles, and videos. Pay extra attention to popular writers and speakers who cover complex topics. You'll find that they're more likely to use analogies to transfer their knowledge.

DRILL 11:

Consider your own presentation. Identify essential scenes or "beats" that you can incorporate into the narrative. These scenes keep the action moving and the audience engaged. Find events in your life or in your business that fall into one of these categories:

Catalyst: _____

Debate: _____

Fun and Games: _____

All Is Lost: _____

DRILL 12:

Build your origin story. Every start-up has one. Every company has one. What's yours? What person, thing, or event ignited your big idea? Tell the story in three acts: In act 1, tell us about your life before you embarked on your adventure. What was the problem or event that catalyzed your ideas? In act 2, talk about the challenges you faced. What obstacles got in the way of seeking the treasure you desired? Build the tension by reminding your audience how close you came to failure. In act 3, reveal the resolution. How did you overcome these hurdles, and how did you turn adversity into success? What lessons did you learn, and how did the experience transform you or your company for the better?

Your audience wants a neatly packaged origin story. And you have one to share.

DRILL 13:

Write narratives before creating slides. Although PowerPoint is banned at Amazon senior-level meetings, Amazon executives use PowerPoint with customers, partners, and external audiences. But PowerPoint is not a storytelling tool, and bullet points are not stories. Build the story first by experimenting with written narratives. Narrative structure requires a theme, titles and subtitles, and fully formed sentences with nouns, verbs, and objects. Try writing the story you want to convey *before* you start building slides. PowerPoint slides don't tell the story; slides *complement* the story.

DRILL 14:

Jeff Bezos wrote twenty-four years of annual Amazon shareholder letters. Many take the form of well-written narratives. Each letter has a theme, a clear and logical order, and supporting stories and data. Visit the website AboutAmazon.com and search "shareholder letters." The following letters are a good starting point: 1997, 2006, 2013, 2014, 2017, and 2020. These letters are well-structured, have clear overarching themes, and use metaphorical language to explain complex ideas.

DRILL 15:

Use the table below to draft a mock press release for your idea: a start-up, product, service, company, or plan.

Topic:	(Product, initiative, service, or company.)
Headline:	(It answers *who* is making the announcement and *what* they're announcing.)
Subheading:	(The subheading is the hook that gives the reader a reason to pay attention. It must be concise. Keep it under thirty words)
First (Summary) Paragraph:	(This first paragraph is an introduction that offers a concise summary of the product, initiative, service, or company and its benefits.)
Second (Problem) Paragraph:	(The second paragraph explains the problem your product, initiative, service, or company intends to solve.)
Paragraphs Three to Six:	(The third to sixth paragraphs dive deeper into the details of your product, initiative, service, or company and how it solves the problem.)
Company Quotes / Customer Testimonials:	(Use engaging quotes from company spokespeople, partners, and customers, even if they don't exist yet.)

DRILL 16:

Video is a simple, valuable tool to help you assess your natural strengths and the areas where you need to improve. Grab a smartphone and record yourself practicing a presentation, sales pitch, job interview, and so on. Watch and rate the video yourself, but also solicit feedback from a trusted friend or peer. Among the things to look for:

- What natural strengths do you notice? (e.g., creative language, strong writing, well-designed slides, good posture, strong voice tone or vocal variation, creative stories to enhance the message). Embrace your strengths and play them up.
- Are you using too many words to get your point across? What sentences can you eliminate the next time you practice?
- Do you have too much text on your slides? Is the font too small? If you can't read the text, neither can the audience.

- Do you use filler words like *uh, um,* or *ah?* Do you end your sentences with annoying, extraneous phrases like *you know?* or *right?* We all use filler words in our natural conversations, but excessive fillers become a distraction. If you eliminate more filler words with each practice session, you'll sound polished and confident when it's time to deliver the real thing.
- Is your theme—the logline—clear? Do you deliver it consistently every time you say it?

Video is the single best tool that you have at your fingertips to improve your public-speaking skills. You'll be surprised at the problems you can catch on your own—and how much improvement you can make from one video to the next.

DRILL 17:

When you start a sentence with "If there's one thing to know, it's this . . . ," whatever comes next is what your audience will remember. They'll write it down and share the message with others because it's like taking a mental highlighter to your main point. Here are some other phrases you can substitute to highlight your key message.

- "The most important thing you need to know is . . ."
- "If there's one thing you can take away from this presentation, it's this . . ."
- "What I can tell you is this . . ."

Your audience is looking for road maps. Guide them in the direction you want to take them.

DRILL 18:

A successful strategy starts with a clear and compelling—and repeatable—mission. The words matter. Words define your actions and your actions define your outcome. Use precise words and conversational language that you feel comfortable repeating over and over. Condense the mission until you can say it in five seconds (twelve words or less). Amazon is America's biggest company, whose mission is expressed in four words: Earth's most customer-centric company.

Many of the world's most successful brands are driven by leaders who articulate the company's overarching purpose clearly, consistently, and frequently. For example:

> **Nike:** To bring inspiration and innovation to every athlete in the world.
> **Unilever:** To make sustainable living commonplace.
> **Tesla:** To accelerate the world's transition to sustainable transport.
> **TED Talks:** To spread ideas.
> **Twilio:** To fuel the future of communications. (Twilio founder Jeff Lawson learned the power of mission as an executive at Amazon Web Services.)

Make your mission short, make every word count, and repeat it until you're tired of hearing it. Then repeat it again.

DRILL 19:

Practice taking the following data point and put it into context: A Grande Mocha Frappuccino contains about 55 grams of sugar.

Is 55 grams a lot or a little? Without context, it's only a number. But let's pretend you are a nutritionist trying to convince your client to cut down on flavored coffee drinks—how would you describe just how much sugar they're consuming in 55 grams? Perhaps you can compare it to how many teaspoons of sugar made up 55 grams (answer: 12 teaspoons). You might compare it to M&M's. A Grande Mocha Frappuccino has the equivalent of not one, not two, but three fun-size packages of M&M's. Now do you think the client might reconsider consuming too many Frappuccinos?

DRILL 20:

Follow the Gallo Method to structure the content for your next pitch or presentation. The Message Map template shown in figure 16.2 gives you a place to draft your logline and three supporting points. The first step is to start writing. You can cut words, edit, and wordsmith later. Collaborate with others. Get their input. When you finish the message map, you will have a simple, easy-to-follow story displayed on one page. Memorize it for a pitch, conversation, or interview. Use it as an outline for a slide presentation. Share it with your team to get everyone on the same page. Send it to your website developer or anyone who creates written marketing material for your company. The message map is your story on one page.

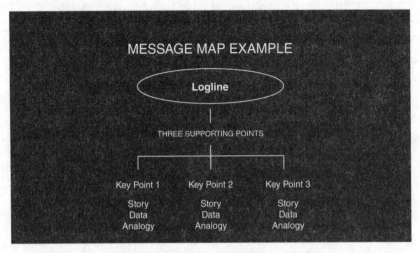

Figure 16.2: The Message Map Template

NOTES

Introduction

1. Dana Mattioli, "Amazon Has Become America's CEO Factory," *Wall Street Journal*, November 20, 2019, https://www.wsj.com/articles/amazon-is-americas-ceo-factory -11574263777, accessed December 15, 2021.
2. "Bloomberg Studio 1.0: AWA CEO Adam Seplipsky," Bloomberg, November 17, 2021, https://www.bloomberg.com/news/videos/2021–11–18/bloomberg-studio-1–0-aws-ceo -adam-selipsky, accessed December 15, 2021.
3. CNBC Television, "Early Amazon Investor John Doerr on the End of the Jeff Bezos Era," YouTube, July 2, 2021, https://www.youtube.com/watch?v=18JA3iD47B4, accessed December 15, 2021.
4. Ann Hiatt, *Bet on Yourself: Recognize, Own, and Implement Breakthrough Opportunities* (New York: HarperCollins, 2021), 30.
5. Marilyn Haigh, "Amazon's First-Known Job Listing: Jeff Bezos Sought Candidates to Work Faster Than 'Most Competent People Think Possible,'" CNBC, August 23, 2018, https://www.cnbc.com/2018/08/23/jeff-bezos-posted-the-first-job-ad-for-amazon-in -1994.html, accessed June 25, 2021.
6. Jeff Weiner, "LinkedIn CEO on the 'Soft' Skills Gap," CNBC, April 19, 2018, https:// www.cnbc.com/video/2018/04/19/linkedin-ceo-on-the-soft-skills-gap.html, accessed June 25, 2021.
7. Diane Brady, Chris Gagnon, and Elizabeth Myatt, "How to Future-Proof Your Organization," *The McKinsey Podcast*, June 17, 2021, https://www.mckinsey.com/business -functions/organization/our-insights/how-to-future-proof-your-organization, accessed October 8, 2021.
8. Walter Isaacson, *Invent and Wander: The Collected Writings of Jeff Bezos, with an Introduction* (Boston: Harvard Business Review Press, 2020), 1.
9. Ibid., 4.
10. Bill Birchard, "The Science of Strong Business Writing," *Harvard Business Review*, July–August 2021, https://hbr.org/2021/07/the-science-of-strong-business-writing, accessed October 8, 2021.

11. Jeff Bezos, "Letter to Shareholders," Amazon, 2016, https://s2.q4cdn.com/299287126 /files/doc_financials/annual/2016-Annual-Report.pdf, accessed June 25, 2021.

Chapter 1: Simple Is the New Superpower

1. CNBC, "Jeff Bezos at the Economic Club of Washington (9/13/18)," YouTube, https:// www.youtube.com/watch?v=xv_vkA0jsyo, accessed April 29, 2021.
2. "The Best Commencement Speeches, Ever," NPR, May 30, 2010, https://apps.npr.org /commencement/speech/jeff-bezos-princeton-university-2010/, accessed April 29, 2021.
3. Geek Wire, "Jeff Bezos Shares His Management Style and Philosophy," YouTube, October 28, 2016, https://www.youtube.com/watch?v=F7JMMy-yHSU&t=2s, accessed June 20, 2021.
4. Jeff Bezos, "Letter to Shareholders," Amazon, 2020, https://www.aboutamazon.com/news /company-news/2020-letter-to-shareholders, accessed April 29, 2021.
5. "Leadership Principles," Amazon, https://www.amazon.jobs/en/principles, accessed October 8, 2021.
6. Lisa Feldman Barrett, *Seven and a Half Lessons About the Brain* (New York: Houghton Mifflin Harcourt, 2020), 10.
7. Daniel Kahneman, *Thinking, Fast and Slow* (New York: Farrar, Straus and Giroux, 2011), 63.
8. Jay Elliot, former Apple executive, in conversation with the author, January 13, 2020.
9. Emma Martin, "Warren Buffett Writes His Annual Letter as If He's Talking to His Sisters Here's Why," CNBC, February 25, 2019, https://www.cnbc.com/2019/02/25/why-warren -buffett-writes-his-annual-letter-like-it-is-for-his-sisters.html, accessed April 29, 2021.
10. Warren Buffett, shareholder letter, Berkshire Hathaway, February 23, 2019, https:// berkshirehathaway.com/letters/2018ltr.pdf, accessed June 20, 2021.
11. "Email from Jeff Bezos to Employees," Amazon, February 2, 2021, https://www .aboutamazon.com/news/company-news/email-from-jeff-bezos-to-employees, accessed June 20, 2021.
12. Ibid.
13. Stephen Moret, CEO at Virginia Economic Development Partnership, in discussion with the author, April 23, 2021.
14. Florencia Iriondo, "The Greatest Minds in Business and Entertainment Share Their Career Success," LinkedIn, December 20, 2016, https://www.linkedin.com/pulse/greatest-minds -business-entertainment-share-career-advice-iriondo/?published=t, accessed June 13, 2021.

Chapter 2: A Modern Spin on Ancient Words

1. Jeff Bezos, "Letter to Shareholders," Amazon, 2007, https://s2.q4cdn.com/299287126 /files/doc_financials/annual/2007letter.pdf, accessed April 3, 2021.
2. Erik Larson, bestselling author of *Dead Wake* and *The Splendid and the Vile*, in discussion with the author, March 23, 2020.
3. "Emergency Executive Order NO. 100," City of New York Office of the Mayor, March 16, 2020, https://www1.nyc.gov/assets/home/downloads/pdf/executive-orders/2020/eeo-100 .pdf, accessed December 15, 2021.
4. Shawn Burton, "The Case for Plain-Language Contracts," *Harvard Business Review*, January–February 2018, https://hbr.org/2018/01/the-case-for-plain-language-contracts, accessed December 15, 2021.
5. Ibid.
6. Ibid.

7. Doris Kearns Goodwin, *Leadership in Turbulent Times* (New York: Simon & Schuster, 2018), 108.

8. "Form S-1 Registration Statement Under the Securities Act of 1933," United States Securities and Exchange Commission, February 12, 2021, https://www.sec.gov/Archives/edgar/data/1834584/000162828021001984/coupang-sx1.htm, accessed December 15, 2021.

9. Nassim Nicholas Taleb, *The Bed of Procrustes: Philosophical and Practical Aphorisms (Incerto)* (New York: Random House, 2010), 108.

10. Eric Meisfjord, "The Untold Truth of Bill Withers' Most Popular Songs," Grunge, April 7, 2020, https://www.grunge.com/199643/the-untold-truth-of-bill-withers-most-popular-songs/, accessed December 12, 2021.

11. Laura Coburn, Hana Karar, and Alexa Valiente, "Country Music Breakout Star Luke Combs on Songwriting, His Fans and Remembering the Las Vegas Shooting," ABC News, August 13, 2018, https://abcnews.go.com/Entertainment/country-music-breakout-star-luke-combs-songwriting-fans/story?id=57155998.

12. BarackObamadotcom, "Barack Obama: Yes We Can," YouTube, https://www.youtube.com/watch?v=Fe751kMBwms, accessed December 15, 2021.

Chapter 3: Writing That Dazzles, Shines, and Sparkles

1. Tim Ferriss, "Jerry Seinfeld—A Comedy Legend's Systems, Routines, and Methods for Success (#485)," *Tim Ferriss Show*, December 8, 2020, https://tim.blog/2020/12/08/jerry-seinfeld/?utm_source=convertkit&utm_medium=convertkit&utm_campaign=weekly-roundup-seinfeld, accessed December 12, 2021.

2. Ibid.

3. Roy Peter Clark, *Writing Tools (10th Anniversary Edition): 55 Essential Strategies for Every Writer* (New York: Little, Brown, 2006), 85.

4. Jeff Bezos, "Letter to Shareholders," Amazon, 1999, https://s2.q4cdn.com/299287126/files/doc_financials/annual/Shareholderletter99.pdf, accessed February 15, 2021.

5. Jeff Bezos, "Letter to Shareholders," Amazon, 2010, https://s2.q4cdn.com/299287126/files/doc_financials/annual/117006_ltr_ltr2.pdf, accessed April 3, 2021.

6. Jeff Bezos, "Letter to Shareholders," Amazon, 2012, https://s2.q4cdn.com/299287126/files/doc_financials/annual/2012-Shareholder-Letter.pdf, accessed April 3, 2021.

7. Clark, *Writing Tools*, 122.

8. Jeff Bezos, "Letter to Shareholders," Amazon, 1998, https://s2.q4cdn.com/299287126/files/doc_financials/annual/Shareholderletter98.pdf, accessed February 15, 2021.

9. Clark, *Writing Tools*, 19.

10. William Zinsser, *On Writing Well: The Classic Guide to Writing Nonfiction* (New York: HarperCollins, 2006), 67.

11. William Strunk Jr., *The Elements of Style*, 4th ed. (New York: Macmillan, 2000), 28.

12. Robin Madell, "How to Get into Harvard Business School, According to the Managing Director of Admissions, Grads, and Consultants, Business Insider, December 7, 2020," *Business Insider*, https://www.businessinsider.com/how-to-get-into-harvard-business-school-according-to-admissions-2019–7, accessed December 15, 2021.

13. Clark, *Writing Tools*, 249.

14. Gary Provost, *100 Ways to Improve Your Writing (Updated): Proven Professional Techniques for Writing with Style and Power* (New York: Penguin Random House, 2019), 73.

15. Ibid., 74.

16. Bezos, "Letter to Shareholders," 1999.

17. Jeff Bezos, "Letter to Shareholders," Amazon, 2002, https://s2.q4cdn.com/299287126/files/doc_financials/annual/2002_shareholderLetter.pdf, accessed April 3, 2021.

18. Jeff Bezos, "Letter to Shareholders," Amazon, 2009, https://s2.q4cdn.com/299287126 /files/doc_financials/annual/AMZN_Shareholder-Letter-2009-(final).pdf, accessed April 3, 2021.

19. Jeff Bezos, "Letter to Shareholders," Amazon, 2013, https://s2.q4cdn.com/299287126 /files/doc_financials/annual/2013-Letter-to-Shareholders.pdf, accessed April 3, 2021.

20. Jeff Bezos, "Letter to Shareholders," Amazon, 2016, https://s2.q4cdn.com/299287126 /files/doc_financials/annual/2016-Letter-to-Shareholders.pdf, accessed February 27, 2021.

21. 60 Minutes, "60 Minutes Archives: Le Carré," YouTube, December 14, 2020, https:// www.youtube.com/watch?v=bOfmgFT4KuU, accessed December 15, 2021.

22. Clark, *Writing Tools*, 88.

23. Bezos, "Letter to Shareholders," 2010.

24. Bezos, "Letter to Shareholders," 1998.

25. Jeff Bezos, "Letter to Shareholders," Amazon, 2014, https://s2.q4cdn.com/299287126/files /doc_financials/annual/AMAZON-2014-Shareholder-Letter.pdf, accessed April 3, 2021.

26. Jeff Bezos, "Letter to Shareholders," Amazon, 2000, https://s2.q4cdn.com/299287126 /files/doc_financials/annual/00ar_letter.pdf, accessed April 3, 2021.

27. Bezos, "Letter to Shareholders," 2009.

28. Jeff Bezos, "Letter to Shareholders," Amazon, 1997, https://s2.q4cdn.com/299287126 /files/doc_financials/annual/Shareholderletter97.pdf, accessed February 15, 2021.

Chapter 4: The Logline: Your Big Idea

1. Jeff Bezos, "Letter to Shareholders," Amazon, 2000, https://s2.q4cdn.com/299287126 /files/doc_financials/annual/00ar_letter.pdf, accessed April 3, 2021.

2. "James Patterson Teaches Writing," MasterClass, https://www.masterclass.com/classes /james-patterson-teaches-writing, accessed December 15, 2021.

3. Clayton M. Christensen, "How Will You Measure Your Life?: Don't Reserve Your Best Business Thinking for Your Career," *Harvard Business Review*, July–August 2010, https:// hbr.org/2010/07/how-will-you-measure-your-life?utm_medium=email&utm_source =newsletter_weekly &utm_campaign=insider_activesubs&utm_content=signinnudge& referral=03551&deliveryName=DM65685, accessed June 20, 2021.

4. "Shonda Rhimes Teaches Writing for Television," MasterClass, https://www.masterclass .com/classes/shonda-rhimes-teaches-writing-for-television, accessed December 15, 2021.

5. Derral Eves, *The YouTube Formula: How Anyone Can Unlock the Algorithm to Drive Views, Build an Audience and Grow Revenue* (Hoboken, NJ: John Wiley & Sons, 2021), 163.

6. Jeff Bezos, "Letter to Shareholders," Amazon, 2018, https://www.aboutamazon.com/news /companynews/2018-letter-to-shareholders, accessed June 20, 2021.

7. Jeff Bezos, "Letter to Shareholders," Amazon, 2007, https://s2.q4cdn.com/299287126 /files/doc_financials/annual/2007letter.pdf, accessed April 3, 2021.

8. Jeff Bezos, "Letter to Shareholders," Amazon, 2005, https://s2.q4cdn.com/299287126 /files/doc_financials/annual/shareholderletter2005.pdf, accessed June 21, 2021.

9. Jeff Bezos, "Email from Jeff Bezos to Employees," Amazon, https://www.aboutamazon .com/news/company-news/email-from-jeff-bezos-to-employees, accessed December 15, 2021.

Chapter 5: Metaphors That Stick

1. Jeff Bezos, "Letter to Shareholders," Amazon, 1997, https://s2.q4cdn.com/299287126 /files/doc_financials/annual/Shareholderletter97.pdf, accessed February 15, 2021.

2. Jeff Bezos, "Letter to Shareholders," Amazon, 2016, https://s2.q4cdn.com/299287126 /files/doc_financials/annual/2016-Letter-to-Shareholders.pdf, accessed February 27, 2021.

3. Ward Farnsworth, *Farnsworth's Classical English Metaphor* (Jaffrey, NH: David R. Godine, 2016), viii.

4. George Lakoff, *Metaphors We Live By* (Chicago: University of Chicago Press, 1980), 3.

5. Ibid., 4.

6. Nelson Goodman, "Metaphor as Moonlighting," Critical Inquiry, Vol. 6, No. 1, Autumn, 1979, 125–30, https://www.jstor.org/stable/1343090, accessed March 8, 2022.

7. Jason Del Rey, "Watch Jeff Bezos Lay Out His Grand Vision for Amazon's Future Dominance in This 1999 Video," Vox, November 22, 2015, https://www.vox.com/2015/11 /22/11620874/watch-jeff-bezos-lay-out-his-grand-vision-for-amazons-future, accessed December 15, 2021.

8. Jeff Hodgkinson, "Communications Is the Key to Project Success," International Project Management Association, https://www.ipma-usa.org/articles/CommunicationKey.pdf, accessed February 27, 2021.

9. Brad Stone, *The Everything Store: Jeff Bezos and the Age of Amazon* (New York: Hachette, 2014).

10. Colin Bryar and Bill Carr, *Working Backwards: Insights, Stories, and Secrets from Inside Amazon* (New York: St. Martin's, 2021).

11. Frederic Lalonde, founder and CEO of Hopper, in discussion with the author, March 12, 2021.

12. Jeff Lawson, CEO of Twilio, in discussion with the author, January 12, 2021.

13. Jim Collins, *Good to Great: Why Some Companies Make the Leap and Others Don't* (New York: HarperCollins, 2001), 165.

14. Brad Stone, *Amazon Unbound: Jeff Bezos and the Invention of a Global Empire* (New York: Simon & Schuster, 2021), 163.

15. 2015 Amazon Shareholder Letter, https://s2.q4cdn.com/299287126/files/doc_financials /annual/2015-Letter-to-Shareholders.pdf, accessed February 27, 2021.

16. "Chris Hadfield Teaches Space Exploration," MasterClass, https://www.masterclass.com /classes/chris-hadfield-teaches-space-exploration, accessed December 15, 2021.

17. "Morning Session-1995 Meeting," Warren Buffett Archive, November 28, 2018, https:// buffett.cnbc.com/video/1995/05/01/morning-session—1995-berkshire-hathaway -annual-meeting.html?&start=6714.55, accessed December 15, 2021.

18. Diane Swonk, chief economist at Grant Thornton, LLP, in discussion with the author, February 2, 2021.

Chapter 6: A Communicator's "Most Formidable" Weapon

1. Bill Carr, author of *Working Backwards*, in discussion with the author, February 3, 2021.

2. Ibid.

3. Ibid.

4. Ibid.

5. Diane Halpern, *Thought and Knowledge: An Introduction to Critical Thinking* (New York: Psychology Press, 2014), 125.

6. Ibid.

7. 2017 Amazon Shareholder Letter, https://s2.q4cdn.com/299287126/files/doc_financials /annual/Amazon_Shareholder_Letter.pdf, accessed February 28, 2021.

8. Ibid.

9. Jeff Bezos, "The Electricity Metaphor for the Web's Future," TED.com, February 2003, accessed February 28, 2021.

10. Ibid.
11. Amazon Staff, "The Deceptively Simple Origins of AWS," Amazon, March 17, 2021, https://www.aboutamazon.com/news/aws/the-deceptively-simple-origins-of-aws, accessed December 15, 2021.

Chapter 7: Epic Storytelling in Three Acts

1. Daniel Perez, "1997: Cheater Bella Can't Escape Stigma of '88 Jailbreak," *El Paso Times,* November 18, 2011, https://www.elpasotimes.com/story/news/history/blogs/tales-from-the-morgue/2011/11/18/1997-cheater-bella-cant-escape-stigma-of-88-jailbreak/31478655/, accessed December 15, 2021.
2. Walter Isaacson, *Invent and Wander: The Collected Writings of Jeff Bezos, with an Introduction* (Boston: Harvard Business Review Press, 2020), 4.
3. Syd Field, *Screenplay: The Foundations of Screenwriting (Newly Revised and Updated)* (New York: Random House, 1984), 246.
4. Amazon Staff, "Statement by Jeff Bezos to the U.S. House Committee on the Judiciary," Amazon, July 28, 2020, https://www.aboutamazon.com/news/policy-news-views/statement-by-jeff-bezos-to-the-u-s-house-committee-on-the-judiciary, accessed June 29, 2021.
5. Ibid.
6. Jeff Bezos, "The Economic Club of Washington D.C.," Economic Club's Milestone Celebration Event, September 13, 2018, https://www.economicclub.org/sites/default/files/transcripts/Jeff_Bezos_Edited_Transcript.pdf, accessed December 15, 2021.
7. Ibid.
8. Brad Stone, *Amazon Unbound: Jeff Bezos and the Invention of a Global Empire* (New York: Simon & Schuster, 2021), 152.
9. Ibid.
10. Josh Wigler, "'Jack Ryan' Season 2 Will Focus on the Decline of Democracy," *Hollywood Reporter,* September 4, 2018, https://www.hollywoodreporter.com/tv/tv-news/jack-ryan-season-one-explained-1139572/, accessed June 25, 2021.

Chapter 8: Origin Stories

1. Yuval Noah Harari, *Sapiens: A Brief History of Humankind* (New York: HarperCollins, 2015), 25.
2. Marc Randolph, cofounder of Netflix, in discussion with the author, November 22, 2019.
3. Ibid.
4. Melanie Perkins, cofounder and CEO of Canva, in discussion with the author, May 23, 2019.
5. Alli McKee, "Your Company in 100 Words: How Warby Parker Uses a New Pair of Sunglasses," Medium, November 1, 2017, https://medium.com/show-and-sell/your-company-in-100-words-e7558b0b1077, accessed December 16, 2021.
6. Ibid.

Chapter 9: The Narrative Information Multiplier

1. Stevie Smith, "The Cognitive Style of PowerPoint," University of Edinburgh, https://www.inf.ed.ac.uk/teaching/courses/pi/ 2016_2017/phil/tufte-powerpoint.pdf, accessed December 16, 2021.
2. Madeline Stone, "A 2004 Email from Jeff Bezos Explains Why PowerPoint Presentations Aren't Allowed at Amazon," Yahoo Finance, July 28, 2015, https://www.businessinsider.com/jeff-bezos-email-against-powerpoint-presentations-2015-7, accessed December 16, 2021.

3. "All-Hands Meeting," Amazon, February 2008, https://aws.amazon.com/blogs/startups/how-to-mechanize-prospecting-founder-sales-series-part-6/, accessed December 16, 2021.

4. Colin Bryar and Bill Carr, *Working Backwards: Insights, Stories, and Secrets from Inside Amazon* (New York: St. Martin's, 2021), 88.

5. Rob Adams McKean and Emil L. Hanzevack, "The Heart of the Matter: The Engineer's Essential One-Page Memo," ChE Classroom, University of South Carolina, Columbia, SC.

6. "P&G Good Every Day: Turning Everyday Actions into Acts of Good for the World," P&G, May 20, 2020, https://us.pg.com/blogs/pg-everyday-turning-everyday-actions-into-acts-of-good-for-the-world/, accessed June 25, 2021.

7. Caltech, "Bill Gates Remembers Richard Feynman-Bill Gates," YouTube, May 11, 2018, https://www.youtube.com/watch?v=HotLmqYFKKg, accessed June 25, 2021.

8. Richard Phillips Feynman, *What Do You Care What Other People Think: Further Adventures of a Curious Character* (New York: W. W. Norton, 2001), 127.

9. Ibid., 146.

10. 2017 Amazon Shareholder Letter, https://s2.q4cdn.com/299287126/files/doc_financials/annual/Amazon-Shareholder-Letter.pdf, accessed February 28, 2021.

11. Brad Porter, former Amazon robotics engineer, in discussion with the author, April 26, 2021.

12. Colin Bryar, former VP of Amazon and coauthor of *Working Backwards*, in discussion with the author, February 5, 2021.

13. Jesse Freeman, "The Anatomy of an Amazon 6-Pager," Writing Cooperative, July 16, 2020, https://writingcooperative.com/the-anatomy-of-an-amazon-6-pager-fc79f31a41c9, accessed December 16, 2021.

14. John Mackey, cofounder of Whole Foods, in discussion with the author, November 6, 2020.

15. Dana Mattioli, "Amazon Has Become America's CEO Factory," *Wall Street Journal*, November 20, 2019, https://www.wsj.com/articles/amazon-is-americas-ceo-factory-11574263777, accessed December 15, 2021.

16. Ronny Kohavi, former Amazon director of data mining and personalization, in discussion with author, April 8, 2021.

17. Ron Kohavi and Stefan Thomke, "The Surprising Power of Online Experiments: Getting the Most Out of A/B and Other Controlled Tests," *Harvard Business Review*, September–October 2017, https://hbr.org/2017/09/the-surprising-power-of-online-experiments, accessed June 25, 2021.

18. 2013 Amazon Shareholder Letter, https://s2.q4cdn.com/299287126/files/doc_financials/annual/2013-Letter-to-Shareholders.pdf, accessed April 3, 2021.

19. Brad Porter, in discussion with the author, April 26, 2021.

Chapter 10: Working Backwards to Get Ahead

1. Bill Carr, author of *Working Backwards*, in discussion with the author, February 3, 2021.

2. Colin Bryar and Bill Carr, *Working Backwards: Insights, Stories, and Secrets from Inside Amazon* (New York: St. Martin's, 2021), 104.

3. Oprah Winfrey, "Oprah's Favorite New Gadget," Oprah.com, https://www.oprah.com/oprahshow/oprahs-favorite-new-gadget/all#ixzz6tdLiW8Qd, accessed June 25, 2021.

4. Press Center, "Press Release: Introducing Amazon Kindle," Amazon, November 19, 2007, https://press.aboutamazon.com/news-releases/news-release-details/introducing-amazon-kindle, accessed December 16, 2021.

5. Montgomery Summit, "Andy Jassy, Amazon Web Services, at the 2015 Montgomery Summit," YouTube, July 14, 2015, https://www.youtube.com/watch?v=sfNdigibjlg, accessed June 25, 2021.

6. Bill Carr, in discussion with the author, February 3, 2021.

7. Ibid.

8. Jason Del Rey, "The Making of Amazon Prime, the Internet's Most Successful and Devastating Membership Program," Vox, May 3, 2019, https://www.vox.com/recode/2019/5/3/18511544/amazon-prime-oral-history-jeff-bezos-one-day-shipping, accessed December 16, 2021.

9. CNBC, "Jeff Bezos at the Economic Club of Washington," YouTube, September 13, 2018, https://www.youtube.com/watch?v=xv_vkA0jsyo, accessed June 25, 2021.

10. Brad Stone, *The Everything Store: Jeff Bezos and the Age of Amazon* (New York: Hachette, 2014); University of Washington Foster School of Business, "Working Backwards from the Customer," YouTube, December 8, 2020, https://www.youtube.com/watch?v=SiKyMxmfiss&t=1s, accessed December 16, 2021.

11. Ibid.

12. Ozan Varol, *Think Like a Rocket Scientist: Simple Strategies You Can Use to Make Giant Leaps in Work and Life* (New York: Hachette), 129.

13. Ibid.

14. Ozan Varol, rocket scientist and author of *Think Like a Rocket Scientist*, in discussion with author, November 24, 2020.

15. Ibid.

Chapter 11: Leaders Are Readers

1. Brad Stone, *Amazon Unbound: Jeff Bezos and the Invention of a Global Empire* (New York: Simon & Schuster, 2021), 23.

2. Brad Stone, *The Everything Store: Jeff Bezos and the Age of Amazon* (New York: Hachette, 2014).

3. Ibid.

4. "Amazon's Bezos: Control the Ecosystem," CNBC, https://www.cnbc.com/video/2013/09/25/amazons-bezos-control-the-ecosystem.html?play=1, accessed June 25, 2021.

5. Andrew Perrin, "Who Doesn't Read Books in America?," Pew Research Center, September 26, 2019, https://www.pewresearch.org/fact-tank/2019/09/26/who-doesnt-read-books-in-america/, accessed June 25, 2021.

6. James Stavridis, admiral, U.S. Navy (ret), and vice chair of the Carlyle Group, in discussion with author, May 18, 2021.

7. "Joyce Carol Oates Teaches the Art of the Short Story," MasterClass, https://www.masterclass.com/classes/joyce-carol-oates-teaches-the-art-of-the-short-story, accessed December 16, 2021.

8. James Stavridis, in discussion with author, May 18, 2021.

9. Ibid.

10. Daniel Lyons, "Why Bezos Was Surprised by the Kindle's Success," *Newsweek*, December 20, 2009, https://www.newsweek.com/why-bezos-was-surprised-kindles-success-75509, accessed June 25, 2021.

11. Brandel Chamblee, Golf Channel analyst, in discussion with the author, June 12, 2021.

12. Tim Ferriss, "David Rubenstein, Co-founder of the Carlyle Group, on Lessons Learned, Jeff Bezos, Raising Billions of Dollars, Advising Presidents, and Sprinting to the End (#495)," *Tim Ferriss Show*, https://tim.blog/2021/01/27/david-rubenstein/, accessed December 16, 2021.

13. David Rubenstein, *How to Lead: Wisdom from the World's Greatest CEOs, Founders, and Game Changers* (New York: Simon & Schuster, 2020), xx.

14. Ibid., xix.

15. Colin Bryar, former VP of Amazon and coauthor of *Working Backwards,* in discussion with the author, February 5, 2021.

16. Ibid.

17. JSTOR, *Bulletin of the American Academy of Arts and Sciences* 34, no. 2 (November 1980), https://www.jstor.org/journal/bullameracadarts?refreqid=fastly-default%3A9f38b 484f7773b99901d4e36f711a5d4, accessed December 16, 2021.

Chapter 12: AMP Your Presentations to Inspire Your Audience

1. Carmine Gallo, "College Seniors: 65% of Recruiters Say This One Skill Is More Important Than Your Major," *Forbes,* April 30, 2017, https://www.forbes.com/sites/carminegallo /2017/04/30/college-seniors-65-percent-of-recruiters-say-this-one-skill-is-more -important-than-your-major/?sh=7d5d119c757c, accessed April 11, 2021.

2. Don Tennant featuring Carmine Gallo, "Presentation Skills Linked to Career Success, Survey Finds—IT Business Edge," Carmine Gallo, https://www.carminegallo.com/presentation -skills-linked-to-career-success-survey-finds-it-business-edge/, accessed April 11, 2021.

3. Jeff Bezos, "Jeff Bezos—March 1998, Earliest Long Speech," YouTube, https://www .youtube.com/watch?v=PnSjKTW28qE&t=6s, accessed April 11, 2021.

4. Jeff Bezos, "The Electricity Metaphor for the Web's Future," TED, 2003, https://www .ted.com/talks/jeff_bezos_the_electricity_metaphor_for_the_web_s_future/transcript ?language=en#t-1013417/, accessed April 11, 2021.

5. Jeff Bezos, "Going to Space to Benefit Earth (Full Event Replay)," YouTube, May 9, 2019, https://www.youtube.com/watch?v=GQ98hGUe6FM, accessed April 11, 2021.

6. Steve Jobs, "Steve Jobs Early TV Appearance.mov," YouTube, February 5, 2011, https:// www.youtube.com/watch?v=FzDBiUemCSY, accessed April 13, 2021.

7. Steve Jobs, "Steve Jobs iPhone 2007 Presentation (HD)," YouTube, May 13, 2013, https://www.youtube.com/watch?v=vN4U5FqrOdQ, accessed April 13, 2021.

Chapter 13: Make the Mission Your Mantra

1. 1997 Amazon Shareholder Letter, https://s2.q4cdn.com/299287126/files/doc_financials / annual/Shareholderletter97.pdf, accessed February 15, 2021.

2. John P. Kotter, "Leading Change: Why Transformation Efforts Fail," *Harvard Business Review,* May–June 1995, https://hbr.org/1995/05/leading-change-why-transformation -efforts-fail-2, accessed December 16, 2021.

3. 1998 Amazon Shareholder Letter, https://s2.q4cdn.com/299287126/files/doc_financials /annual/Shareholderletter98.pdf, accessed February 15, 2021.

4. CNBC, "Jeff Bezos in 1999 on Amazon's Plans Before the Dotcom Crash," YouTube, February 8, 2019, https://www.youtube.com/watch?v=GltlJO56S1g, accessed December 16, 2021.

5. "Video from Jeff Bezos About Amazon and Zappos," YouTube, July 22, 2009, https:// www.youtube.com/watch?v=-hxX_Q5CnaA, accessed December 16, 2021.

6. "Inc.: Why I Sold Zappos," Delivering Happiness, https://blog.deliveringhappiness.com /blog/inc-why-i-sold-zappos, accessed December 16, 2021.

7. "Video from Jeff Bezos About Amazon and Zappos," YouTube.

8. David Rubenstein, "Amazon CEO Jeff Bezos on the David Rubenstein Show," YouTube, September 19, 2018, https://www.youtube.com/watch?v=f3NBQcAqyu4, accessed December 16, 2021.

9. CNBC, "Steve Jobs 1997 Interview: Defending His Commitment to Apple/CNBC," YouTube, April 27, 2018, https://www.youtube.com/watch?v=xchYT9wz5hk, accessed December 16, 2021.

10. Jose E. Puente, "Steve Jobs Holding a Small Staff Meeting in Sept 23, 1997," YouTube, https://www.youtube.com/watch?v=8-Fs0pD2Hsk, accessed December 16, 2021.

11. Guy Kawasaki, chief evangelist of Canva and creator of *Guy Kawasaki's Remarkable People* podcast, in discussion with the author, February 15, 2019.

12. John Mackey, cofounder of Whole Foods, in discussion with the author, November 6, 2020.

13. John Mackey, Steve McIntosh, and Carter Phipps, *Elevating Humanity Through Business: Conscious Leadership* (New York: Penguin Random House, 2020), 17.

14. "Leverage the Power of Purpose," *Wall Street Journal*, https://deloitte.wsj.com/articles/leverage-the-power-of-purpose-01575060972, accessed December 16, 2021.

15. John Mackey et al., *Elevating Humanity*, 17.

16. Hubert Joly with Caroline Lambert, *The Heart of Business: Leadership Principles for the Next Era of Capitalism* (Boston: Harvard Business Review Press, 2021), 270.

17. "Medtronic Mission Statement," Medtronic, https://www.medtronic.com/me-en/about/mission.html, accessed December 16, 2021.

18. Ibid.

19. Ibid.

20. Michael Moritz, partner at Sequoia Capital, in discussion with the author, October 23, 2015.

Chapter 14: Symbols Convey Big Ideas

1. Amazon Web Services, "2012 re:Invent Day 2: Fireside Chat with Jeff Bezos & Werner Vogels," YouTube, November 29, 2012, https://www.youtube.com/watch?v=O4MtQGRIIuA, accessed July 1, 2021.

2. 10,000 Year Clock, http://www.10000yearclock.net/learnmore.html, accessed July 1, 2021.

3. Bill Carr, author of *Working Backwards*, in discussion with the author, February 3, 2021; "Amazon Empire: The Rise and Reign of Jeff Bezos," PBS, https://www.pbs.org/wgbh/frontline/film/amazon-empire/transcript/, accessed December 16, 2021.

4. John Rossman, *Think Like Amazon: 50 and a Half Ways to Become a Digital Leader* (New York: McGraw Hill, 2019), 66.

5. Marc Randolph, *That Will Never Work: The Birth of Netflix and the Amazing Life of an Idea* (New York: Little, Brown, 2019), 150.

6. John Mackey, Steve McIntosh, and Carter Phipps, *Elevating Humanity Through Business: Conscious Leadership* (New York: Penguin Random House, 2020), 20.

Chapter 15: Humanize Data

1. Academy of Achievement, "Jeff Bezos, Academy Class of 2001, Full Interview," YouTube, July 12, 2016, https://www.youtube.com/watch?v=s7ZvBy1SROE, accessed June 27, 2021.

2. Andrew Cave, "What Will We Do When the World's Data Hits 163 Zettabytes in 2025?," *Forbes*, April 13, 2017, https://www.forbes.com/sites/andrewcave/2017/04/13/what-will-we-do-when-the-worlds-data-hits-163-zettabytes-in-2025/?sh=39ee1511349a, accessed December 16, 2021.

3. Ilyse Resnick, Nora S. Newcombe, and Thomas F. Shipley, "Dealing with Big Numbers: Representation and Understanding of Magnitudes Outside of Human Experience," *Cognitive Science* 41, no. 4 (2017): 1020–2041, accessed June 27, 2021, https://onlinelibrary.wiley.com/doi/full/10.1111/cogs.12388.

4. Jeff Bezos, "Jeff Bezos—March 1998, Earliest Long Speech," YouTube, https://www.youtube.com/watch?v=PnSjKTW28qE&t=6s, accessed April 11, 2021.

5. Jeff Bezos, "Letter to Shareholders," Amazon, 1997, https://s2.q4cdn.com/299287126/files/doc_financials/annual/Shareholderletter97.pdf, accessed February 15, 2021.

6. Jeff Bezos, "Letter to Shareholders," Amazon, 2001, https://s2.q4cdn.com/299287126 /files/doc_financials/annual/2001_shareholderLetter.pdf, accessed June 27, 2021.

7. Blue Origin, "Going to Space to Benefit Earth (Full Event Replay)," YouTube, May 9, 2019, https://www.youtube.com/watch?v=GQ98hGUe6FM, accessed December 16, 2021.

8. Jeff Bezos, "Letter to Shareholders," Amazon, 2020, https://www.aboutamazon.com/news /company-news/2020-letter-to-shareholders, accessed April 29, 2021.

9. Brent Dykes, "Data Storytelling: The Essential Data Science Skill Everyone Needs," *Forbes*, March 31, 2016, https://www.forbes.com/sites/brentdykes/2016/03/31/data -storytelling-the-essential-data-science-skill-everyone-needs/?sh=2381f06052ad, accessed December 16, 2021.

10. CNBC, "Jeff Bezos at the Economic Club of Washington (9/13/18)," YouTube, https:// www.youtube.com/watch?v=xv_vkA0jsyo, accessed December 16, 2021.

11. Ibid.

Chapter 16: The Gallo Method: Sell Your Idea in 15 Seconds

1. "Doris Kearns Goodwin Teaches U.S. Presidential History and Leadership," MasterClass, https://www.masterclass.com/classes/doris-kearns-goodwin-teaches-us-presidential -history-and-leadership, accessed December 16, 2021.

2. TEDx Talks, "Quantum Physics for 7 Year Olds, Dominic Walliman, TEDxEastVan," YouTube, May 24, 2016, https://www.youtube.com/watch?v=ARWBdfWpDyc, accessed December 16, 2021.

3. Kurt A. Carlson and Suzanne B. Shu, "When Three Charms but Four Alarms: Identify- ing the Optimal Number of Claims in Persuasion Settings," https://journals.sagepub.com /doi/10.1509/jm.11.0504, accessed December 16, 2021.

4. Dominick Reuter and Megan Hernbroth, "How Founders Can Use the 'Rule of 3' to Prepare Your Pitch and Quickly Raise Vital Funding to Launch Your Startup," *Business Insider*, August 11, 2020, https://www.businessinsider.com/how-to-pitch-startup-rule-of -3-founders-raise-most-seed-pitches, accessed December 16, 2021.

5. Dan Michel, "The Entrepreneur-Turned-Clothier Shares His Biggest Obstacles—Behind Creating UNTUCKit," UNTUCKit, https://www.untuckit.com/blogs/style/off-the-cuff -chris-riccobono, accessed December 16, 2021.

Conclusion

1. CNBC, "Jeff Bezos at the Economic Club of Washington (9/13/18)," YouTube, https:// www.youtube.com/watch?v=xv_vkA0jsyo, accessed December 16, 2021.

2. Shane O'Mara, "Why Walking Matters—Now More Than Ever," *Wall Street Journal*, April 18, 2020, https://www.wsj.com/articles/why-walking-mattersnow-more-than-ever -11587182460?mod=searchresults&page=1&pos=1, accessed December 16, 2021.

3. Charlie Rose, "A Conversation with Amazon's Founder and Chief Executive Officer, Jeff Bezos," Power of Questions, October 27, 1016, https://charlierose.com/videos/29412, accessed December 16, 2021.

4. Walter Isaacson, *Invent and Wander: The Collected Writings of Jeff Bezos, with an Intro- duction* (Boston: Harvard Business Review Press, 2020), 4.

5. Catherine Clifford, "Jeff Bezos: You Can't Pick Your Passions," CNBC, February 7, 2019, https://www.cnbc.com/2019/02/07/amazon-and-blue-origins-jeff-bezos-on-identifying -your-passion.html, accessed December 16, 2021.

6. 2020 Amazon Shareholder Letter, https://s2.q4cdn.com/299287126/files/doc_financials /2021/ar/Amazon-2020-Shareholder-Letter-and-1997-Shareholder-Letter.pdf, accessed December 16, 2021.

INDEX